INDIA
BRIEFING

Society

INDIA
BRIEFING

Quickening the Pace
of Change

Alyssa Ayres and Philip Oldenburg
Editors

Published in Cooperation with the Asia Society

An East Gate Book

M.E. Sharpe
Armonk, New York
London, England

An East Gate Book

Library of Congress Cataloging-in-Publication Data

Library of Congress ISSN: 0894-5136
ISBN 0-7656-0812-X (hardcover)
ISBN 0-7656-0813-8 (paperback)

Printed in the United States of America

The paper used in this publication meets the minimum requirements of
American National Standard for Information Sciences
Permanence of Paper for Printed Library Materials,
ANSI Z 39.48-1984.

BM (c) 10 9 8 7 6 5 4 3 2 1
BM (p) 10 9 8 7 6 5 4 3 2 1

Contents

Preface

This edition marks the ninth in our ongoing *India Briefing* series, one of the several Country Briefing series published by our Policy and Business Programs area. We are very pleased with this volume's range of issues, and especially with the fine essays written with care by our contributing authors.

Producing briefing volumes like this one requires a mysterious blend of regional knowledge, administrative tenacity, business sense, and ability to work well under pressure. Asia Society has been fortunate to find such a blend in the editorial partnership of Philip Oldenburg and Alyssa Ayres. Their efforts over the course of the last fourteen months—working late nights and during vacations, and on top of a whole host of other projects—brought this volume out in a timely fashion. But they could not have done anything without the commitment and good spirit of the chapter authors—John Echeverri-Gent, Joydeep Mukherji, Sadanand Dhume, Christophe Jaffrelot, Mark Nichter, David Van Sickle, Alok Rai, and Bandita Sijapati—who cheerfully tolerated Asia Society's rather involved editorial style and produced such high-caliber chapters under tight deadlines.

Asia Society would also like to thank Lisa J. Hacken, whose watchful eyes and steady hands steered the volume from manuscript through production, and Patricia Farr and Chris Reeves, who carefully copyedited the entire volume. Thanks go also to Sanjeev M. Sherchan of Asia Society, who provided support throughout the year of this volume's production.

This is Asia Society's fourth *India Briefing* published in collaboration with M.E. Sharpe's East Gate Books imprint, and we are again pleased with our partnership with Douglas Merwin, Patricia Loo, and Angela Piliouras.

No part of this volume would have been possible without the GE Fund's generous contribution. This is the second *India Briefing* that has benefited from the GE Fund's support, and we are most grateful to R. Michael Gadbaw and Scott Bayman of the General Electric Company for encouraging us to continue with this edition of *India Briefing* and to Evelyn Taylor of the GE Fund for providing the means for us to educate Americans about the important and fundamental changes taking place in India—changes that affect the United States as well. Educating Americans about Asia is, after all, the core mission of Asia Society, and we hope that this volume does its small part toward fulfilling that goal.

Finally, this edition of *India Briefing* coincides with the departure of Marshall M. Bouton, former executive vice president of Asia Society and the founding editor of the *India Briefing* series as well as Asia Society's resident South Asia expert for over twenty years. Dr. Bouton assumed the presidency of the Chicago Council on Foreign Relations in August 2001. We are sure he will do much to enrich that institution, as he has done at Asia Society.

We welcome reader comments and suggestions via e-mail: policy@asiasoc.org.

Nicholas Platt
President
Asia Society

Robert W. Radtke
Vice President, Policy and
    Business Programs
Asia Society

Editors' Note

This edition of *India Briefing* was already into production prior to the events of September 11, 2001. We are acutely aware that some of its contents may appear dated in light of the tragedy and its aftermath, but we believe that no major argument in any chapter requires revision.

The latter section of the Introduction to this volume focuses on the development of closer U.S.-India relations over the course of 1998–2001. At the time of this writing, Indian public opinion was beginning to turn against the United States' partnership with Pakistan in the military campaign in Afghanistan. From the Indian perspective, the global goals motivating U.S. policy, this time a "war on terrorism," threatened to overshadow a nascent U.S. sensitivity to Indian concerns.

It will not be easy for the United States to resume a quasi-alliance with Pakistan while simultaneously improving relations with India. If the "war on terrorism" can, through quiet diplomacy, bring about a decline in cross-border violence in Kashmir, then the United States. stands a better chance of being seen by India as holding a principled stance against terrorism wherever it occurs. There is no reason to believe that trade concessions for Pakistan will take place at India's expense; the opportunities for broadening the U.S.-India economic relationship are still plentiful. Yet the specter of "tilts" haunts this moment. The economic support package negotiated for Pakistan is being viewed in India as a "reward" rather than necessary assistance from the United States to help Pakistan achieve goals impossible without further economic aid. Should Indian policymakers continue to view these actions as rewarding Pakistan and by extension, punishing India, the U.S.-India relationship will suffer—regardless of U.S. intentions to forge relationships with India and Pakistan on their own merits, and outside a zero-sum game framework.

Even if there is another downturn in U.S.-India relations because of this crisis, we believe that an upturn will resume fairly quickly. The mutual recognition of the immense benefits of closer relations that had emerged just before September 11th will make it happen.

   We welcome all comments from readers: IndiaBriefing@asiasoc.org.

Alyssa Ayres and Philip Oldenburg
New York, November 2, 2001

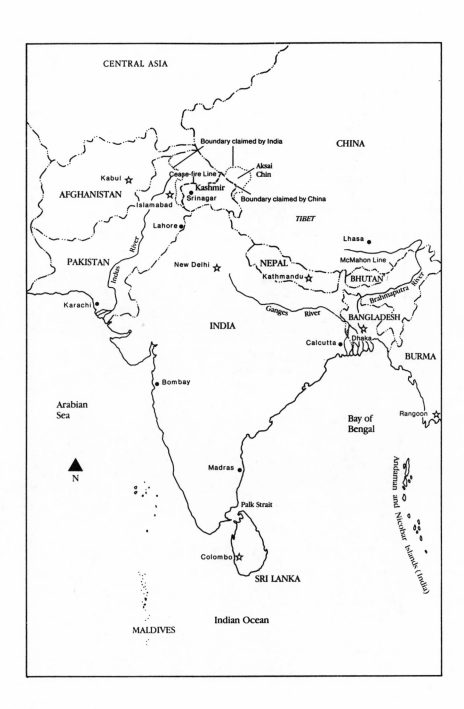

South Asia

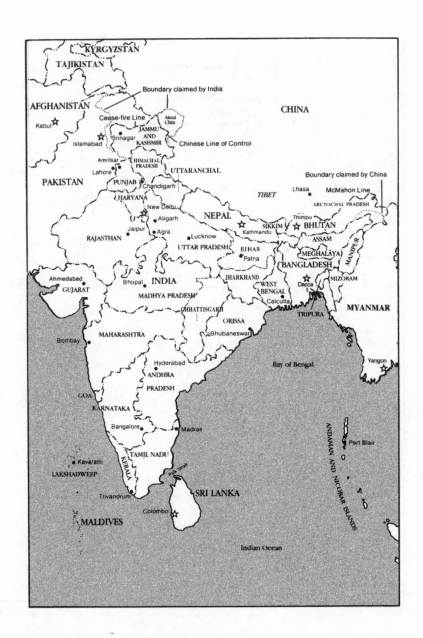

India

INDIA BRIEFING

Introduction

Alyssa Ayres

Quickening the Pace of Change

The previous volume in this series, *India Briefing: A Transformative Fifty Years*, took a broad overview of events in India from 1947 through 1997. In this volume, we return to focusing on recent changes and events—and there have been many. India has held two national elections, carried out nuclear tests, boomed as an information technology powerhouse, administered the world's largest mass immunization program, pushed forward on economic reforms, turned around its relationship with the U.S. government, and fought an undeclared war with Pakistan high in the Himalayas.

The *idea* of India has also changed in the past few years. "India" has become less distant, more understood, more *visible* to Americans than it was a few years ago. New writing on the Indian experience crowds best-seller lists and wins literary acclaim; businesspeople of Indian origin have risen to prominence in the United States; Indian cuisine has emerged in major U.S. cities as a new trend; the U.S. government in two successive administrations has reached out to India, a nation now viewed by the Bush administration as important to U.S. foreign policy.[1] Gone are the days when India evoked only exotic stereotypes of saints and beggars.

What has brought about these real and perceived changes, and what do they mean? The chapters in this volume answer these questions and pose many of their own. Our authors—from disciplines as disparate as economics, medical anthropology, English literature, and political science—began with a brief to cover developments in India since 1998 in their fields. They all found that India was changing in profound ways, and faster than before. The economy, the polity, society, health care,

---

1. President George W. Bush, press statement announcing intent to nominate Robert Blackwill as U.S. ambassador to India, February 2001.

and the India of fiction all are being rapidly transformed. In many cases these changes can be traced to globalization—a web of economic, travel, technological, and cultural links.

It is impossible to locate a point of origin, a sector in which we might say this process of globalization first took root. Striking, however, are the many arenas in which global trends are being mirrored or are even originating in India. Decentralization, for example, is both a political and an economic process taking place throughout the world. Is India's decentralization an aspect of the global trend, or a response to it? New industries rooted in new technologies are being created in India's Silicon Plateau, driving or perhaps being driven by the increasing flows of peoples and ideas they create—creating ever faster links among more places, connecting more people than ever before. Indian writing has emerged onto the world stage, both critically and commercially. This is also linked to flows of people, as the Indian diaspora writes prolifically of its imagined India, outlining its contours for a worldwide readership increasingly familiar with the Indian experience on the printed page.

Enabled by technological breakthroughs in communications, markets move faster than ever. India's markets, and its economy, are increasingly becoming part of the global flow of finances and mobile capital. These flows are changing the way in which the world views India, bringing focus to the economically vibrant southern and western states. These states have raced ahead of the rest of India by establishing themselves as destinations for global capital in their own right. India's economic opening up has also affected its health care systems in unanticipated ways, one example being the reduction or elimination of high tariffs that now permits private medical clinics to import their own diagnostic equipment. The state's monopoly on health care is over, and higher-priced private clinics have mushroomed—but those who are unable to afford the excellent private care available must either endure the overburdened state care system or suffer with sickness. A converse phenomenon, however, is taking place in the North as India's political arena opens up to the historically disadvantaged. Economic inequality is no longer synonymous with political disempowerment in India: subordinate caste groups in the North have politically mobilized (lagging some thirty years behind the South), with caste-based parties winning elections and making demands of the state—again, a decentralization process that mirrors global decentralization, in which groups traditionally outside the power structure (NGOs and new parties throughout the world) are creating change.

Thus these broader forces we loosely call "globalization" have made themselves felt in many dimensions of economic, political, and social life in India. In this sense, each chapter in this volume is part of a larger story of dynamism. The interrelationship between chapters is most evident in our first two, the traditional anchoring chapters covering economic and political developments in India. In this volume, John Echeverri-Gent and Joydeep Mukherji both chronicle competing pulls in the economic and political spheres that have resulted in the increasing decentralization of decision making, affecting economic and political realities in India.

John Echeverri-Gent's "Politics in India's Decentered Polity" explores the ways the impetus of decentralization has led to a dramatic shift in India's political center of gravity from a central nexus (New Delhi and the Congress Party) to a variety of regional parties and disaggregated institutions. Whether through the rise of local "single-state parties" without national reach or through the changing economic policy framework that is moving India from a planned to a privatized, though regulated, economy, decisions are being taken in more places and at more levels than ever before. This has produced a political calculus of coalition building—a calculus that the Bharatiya Janata Party (BJP) has employed with great success. But the power gained through forming such alliances is not absolute, and Echeverri-Gent shows us how the necessity of building coalitions has brought about the BJP's moderation on several issues once central to its political platform.

Joydeep Mukherji's "The Indian Economy: Pushing Ahead and Pulling Apart" focuses on the many and varied trends in the Indian economy over the past three years that illustrate divergence among states. As his title suggests, India has been pushing forward, albeit at a slower pace than many would like, in the process of liberalizing its economy. At the same time, individual states *within* India are acting increasingly autonomously in their own pursuit of liberalization to the extent that the southern and western states now independently seek foreign direct investment and multilateral assistance packages. What this has meant is a concentrated increase in economic, social, and human development in some parts of India while other parts—Bihar, for one—have fallen dramatically behind. How these two Indias—one of technologically advanced and cosmopolitan urbanity, the other of bleak limitations—will resolve their disparities remains the big question.

On the subject of migrations and flows of people, Sadanand Dhume describes a phenomenon of increasing *connectedness* in "From Bangalore to Silicon Valley and Back: How the Indian Diaspora in the United

States Is Changing India." The Indian diaspora in and of itself is not new, and it is not limited to the United States. As Dhume shows, however, the particular links that have arisen over the past fifteen years, specifically in the world of technology, as a result of Indian entrepreneurs working in the United States are having far-reaching effects on India itself. Corporate horizons have widened, some Indian companies have been listed on U.S. stock exchanges, and the resultant emphasis on good corporate governance and standard accounting practices is beginning to influence Indian firms. Financial flows—remittances, political contributions, and new kinds of philanthropy—also figure in his taxonomy of the ways this diaspora now has a greater effect on many kinds of developments in India. The potential economic and intellectual benefits of an involved diaspora have captured the attention of the Government of India, so much so that it has recently created financial and political institutions to cater to and include the advice of "non-resident Indians" and "persons of Indian origin."

Christophe Jaffrelot writes on an important development affecting India politically, socially, legally, and economically: the growing empowerment of subordinate caste groups. In "The Subordinate Caste Revolution," Jaffrelot first contextualizes this development historically, by noting that the first wave of political empowerment took place in the South with the Dravidian movement. The rise of subordinate caste parties such as the Bahujan Samaj Party and the Samajwadi Party is now taking place in the more populous and more economically troubled North. Unlike the United States, where social justice involves a discourse of historically underprivileged minorities, India's historically subordinate groups collectively form a numerical *majority*. The ways in which the political leadership now seeks to redress systemic discrimination thus has enormous transformative potential.

In "The Challenges of India's Health and Health Care Transitions," Mark Nichter and David Van Sickle comprehensively outline the demographic changes over the past several decades to create a profile of health and health care needs in India. They then go on to illustrate some of the critical successes in public health planning (notably immunizations) as well as some of the health concerns presenting a less sanguine picture. Nichter and Van Sickle then turn to analyzing the health *care* transition—a transition linked with economic reforms and India's move toward a privatized economy—which has produced mixed results. The authors also highlight the biggest challenges facing India: tuberculosis, sexually transmitted diseases, and HIV/AIDS; environmentally linked health problems such as pollution-precipitated asthma; and lifestyle-linked health problems resulting from tobacco use and anxiety-related mental health concerns. With more than a billion people in India, the sheer scale of needs is enormous—and of relevance not solely to those living within India's borders. The increasing movements of people characteristic of the contemporary world—such as tourism, migration, and temporary workers—mean that the challenges of health transcend national boundaries. The solutions India manages to craft for its citizens will have repercussions far beyond its borders.

In our final chapter, "Representing India: Indian Literature on the World Stage," Alok Rai writes of the recent literary phenomenon as he ponders the questions, Why are so many Indian novels appearing on best-seller lists and receiving critical attention these days? Why this emergence of Indian writing on the world stage? As Rai shows, the question itself is an ambiguous one, for it requires reflection upon the nature of the world stage, the notion of discovery, language and representation, and whether the concept of "Indian writing" is even a feasible one. A crucial part of his argument lies in recognizing that many of these authors are diasporic and are writing in English—two conditions that raise their own questions about representation and being representative of the billion resident citizens and speakers of a panoply of other languages.

India and the United States

India's foreign relations have often been the subject of separate chapters in previous editions of *India Briefing*. In our last volume, Howard Schaffer thoroughly covered India's foreign relations, including the nuclear tests and their aftermath. The basic lineaments of India's relations with Pakistan and the ceaseless Kashmir conflict continue to remain the same. What has changed significantly in the time frame covered in this edition is India's relationship with the United States. We felt that specific developments in U.S.-India relations warranted some focus, particularly in keeping with Asia Society's central mission of creating bridges between Asia and America. The bridge between India and the United States was built anew in the last three years. We thus devote a few words to our interpretation of what brought about this change.[2]

---

2. The section that follows bears the mark of Asia Society's longtime India expert, Dr. Marshall M. Bouton, to whom I am much indebted for his clarity of thinking on the U.S.-India bilateral relationship.

In the years from 1998 through 2001, U.S.-India relations ranged from a real low to a new and unprecedented high. Following India's nuclear tests of May 1998, the United States levied congressionally mandated sanctions on India. Then–U.S. secretary of state Madeleine Albright and Indian minister of external affairs Jaswant Singh exchanged acrimonious barbs in the press. U.S. foreign direct investment (FDI) in India actually *decreased* from 1997 to 1998, owing to sanctions as well as lost confidence. But by December 2000 the two countries had exchanged state visits, signed a series of agreements, and begun dialogue on a range of issues including nuclear matters, trade, science, counterterrorism, and commerce. By April 2001, India and the United States appeared poised for even greater cooperation, with India's issuing of the first public statement of support for the Bush administration's call to review the Anti-Ballistic Missile Treaty, launch a defense-shield program, and reduce nuclear arms. During the summer of 2001, a series of opinion pieces began to appear in the U.S. press that spoke of India as the new "ally" and the new "card" in the United States' "cold war" with China. As this volume went to press, it appeared nearly certain that most of the sanctions still in place against India would be removed. The contrast between 1998 and 2001 could not be starker.

What does it mean that India and the United States have swung so rapidly from being foes to becoming friends? More important, does this rapid shift represent a change in the fundamentals driving the relationship, or does it merely track something more ephemeral, a temporary and opportunistic coming together of interests that may again diverge? Could this current convergence of interests be an epiphenomenon of larger forces, indicating that India and the United States will only grow closer as the two elaborate a new relationship?

In the last decade, major changes in the global political economy, the rise of global processes of increasingly rapid capital, trade, migratory, and information flows,[3] and a technological revolution giving rise to new industries worldwide all produced an environment in which U.S.-India relations were finally able to move forward from their state of inertia and estrangement. In this sense, the story of U.S.-India relations is a story emblematic of its time, of globalization and its private sector forces,

---

3. I do not believe that global flows of capital, goods, and peoples are themselves a new phenomenon; the era of empire was in many ways a phase of greater interconnectedness than we see currently. However, there is something new about the speed and ease of these exchanges that marks today's globalization as somehow "different" from the old.

and of the ways these forces reverberate on official (government-to-government) relationships. Domestic politics has played a huge role on both sides, since the end of the Cold War gave political parties in both India and the United States a new set of choices.

Changing Political Ideologies

U.S.-India relations over the last two decades were first overdetermined by the politics of the Cold War and then circumscribed by the United States' nuclear nonproliferation concerns, which dominated the bilateral relationship after the Cold War. An absence of strong private sector ties meant that the relationship was fully dependent upon governmental sentiment. With state relations in the Cold War era predicated on security interests, India and the United States were effectively in oppositional blocs. While the two countries were not outright antagonists, India perceived the United States as imperialist, and the United States believed that India's vision of nonaligned socialism was, more or less, a Soviet alignment.

The United States' policies toward South Asia and India in particular were designed primarily to achieve its global goals, focused wholly elsewhere, so U.S.-India interactions took place as an afterthought. When the United States began a thaw in its relationship with China—a thaw calculated to counter the Soviet Union—India saw hypocrisy in its overtures toward authoritarian, communist China and hence viewed U.S. intentions with distrust. When greater Cold War rivalries following the Soviet invasion of Afghanistan resulted in a close U.S. military relationship with Pakistan, India saw the development as undermining its natural predominance in South Asia, and even as directed against it. American willingness to cooperate with Pakistan's then military ruler, General Zia ul-Haq, was viewed in India as hypocritical in the face of the United States' stated commitment to democratic values.

With the end of the Cold War, old structures crumbled, opening up new choices—strategic, economic, and ideological—for both countries. The India-Russia and U.S.-Pakistan dyads no longer presented theoretical constraints to broadening U.S.-India relations. Yet from 1991 to 1998, old habits and responses were not easily forgotten on either side, and the relationship saw no thaw. A long-standing U.S. propensity to view the subcontinent as a region qua region—implicitly "equating" India with Pakistan, or more specifically, not recognizing what India viewed as its natural role of leadership among smaller, less powerful nations—rankled Indian leadership.

India's numerous changes of government at the center also prevented consensus on what kind of relationship India wanted from the United States. But most important, nonproliferation replaced the Cold War as the monocle through which the United States peered at India. Congressional restrictions and mandated sanctions along with early Clinton administration policies narrowed the official relationship almost entirely to the nonproliferation issue. When the Indian nuclear tests of May 1998 forced the United States to confront the failure of its nonproliferation policy, it had to seek a better understanding of Indian viewpoints and concerns.

To be sure, the 1991–98 phase was not entirely without progress in the U.S.-India bilateral relationship. Following the beginning of the Indian economic reforms under Manmohan Singh in 1991, India experienced a surge of U.S. business interest. Yet the slow pace of bureaucratic change in India hampered U.S. investors from functioning in the way they had hoped to. The U.S. business community, traditionally a key constituency for advocating stronger official bilateral relationships between the United States and other nations, never built up enough momentum to view India as an investment destination worthy of heavy advocacy in the face of a fraught official relationship.

But the United States now sees India as relevant to many of its interests in a transnational system. Both countries want constructive relations with a China that is making its economic presence felt worldwide as well as in the Asian region. India and the United States now see eye to eye on counterterrorism. And the two now agree that both can benefit from cooperation on these and other matters of global concern.

Turning the Corner

India's economic reforms, though incomplete, have begun to bring the huge Indian economy into the international system. The years from 1998 through 2000 witnessed a critical change in economic interactions between the United States and India—not a change all for the good, but one in which India emerged for the United States as a destination of choice for information technology (IT). New private sector ventures, particularly in the IT and IT-enabled sectors, have been the biggest success story in expanding economic links. The enthusiasm in the U.S. and Indian press for the IT sector as a savior of the Indian economy is perhaps premature, particularly given the tremendous infrastructural challenges still besetting India. However, its emergence as a key growth sector has finally put India on the U.S. cognitive map. Call centers, for example, such as GE's outside Delhi, that permit U.S. companies to outsource their customer service functions are now a commonplace and unremarkable part of global business.

U.S.-India business flows are not limited to goods and services, though. Increasingly important has been the role of highly skilled, technologically trained Indian professionals. Trained professionals from India stepped into the United States and excelled. Some 50 percent of the recipients of H-1B (skilled worker) visas annually are Indian citizens. Other Indian entrepreneurs who came to the United States for graduate education have gone on to found innovative, headline-making companies, including Sun Microsystems, Hotmail, Novell, and Sycamore Networks.

The matter of overall direct investment, however, is mixed. U.S. FDI in India dropped off dramatically following the 1998 nuclear tests and the resulting U.S. sanctions and has never recovered to its 1995–97 levels.[4] India receives comparatively little FDI in comparison with its potential; a recent McKinsey and Company study estimates that India could receive as much as $100 billion within five years ($20 billion per year), but only if bureaucratic restrictions were eliminated. These restrictions include a whole range of factors, including lack of transparency, inconsistent regulatory environment, massive red tape, and inflexible labor markets. Infrastructure also remains an important disincentive to further U.S. investment in India.

Despite the unencouraging FDI situation, India took some important steps in the 1998–2000 period toward furthering the liberalization process. In 1999, India passed several historic deregulation bills that, if fully implemented, would provide a more open playing field, one more hospitable to direct investment. The telecommunications and insurance deregulation bills were the most anticipated, as they opened up to private investment two sectors that were previously part of the state. With the release of India's fiscal year 2001–2002 budget, India appeared to be committed to making progress on some of the outstanding regulatory problems (such as labor market inflexibility) that have kept U.S. investors from stampeding to India. A series of scandals in India, however, preoccupied policy makers from March through August 2001. As this volume went to press, the latest involved charges

---

4. U.S.-India Business Council, private communication.

of managerial graft in India's largest state-owned investment vehicle, Unit Trust of India. Also in August 2001, Standard and Poor's downgraded India's sovereign rating to one class above noninvestment grade, citing rising and unsustainable government debt as the motivating factor. The high-profile Dabhol power project in Maharashtra, Enron's signature India venture and the largest single private investment in India, saw an even higher-profile collapse in its agreement, and all other nascent power ventures between U.S. companies and Indian concerns subsequently evaporated.

On matters of trade policy, an increasing convergence has taken place between India and the United States. Historical ideological differences have withered away as the Bush administration first made it clear that it would not seek to link environmental and labor issues to trade and then explicitly courted India's support for World Trade Organization (WTO) talks. India decided to end quantitative restrictions in 2001, two years earlier than originally agreed, in a move welcomed by the United States. With India's agreement to recognize product rather than process patents—long a point of contention—a major intellectual property rights sticking point was removed, which could open the door for U.S. pharmaceutical companies to begin manufacturing or research investment in India down the road.[5]

The Matter of Equations: India, Pakistan, and the United States

Until July 1999, India perceived the United States as partial to Pakistan in a zero-sum game, or at the very least suspiciously unsupportive of India. This changed in 1999, which has led to an increasing level of trust and therefore potential for cooperation between the United States and India on matters at one time considered too sensitive for direct discussion. Two important moments brought about this change.

The first was Kargil. From May through June 1999, India and Pakistan fought a difficult undeclared war in an icy region of the Himalayas known as Kargil. The Kargil sector witnessed a quiet and unexpected attack from forces that Pakistan termed "irregulars" at the time. India

---

5. One specific area of dispute remains the production of antiretroviral drugs, the primary weapon in AIDS treatment and a category of drug unaffordable for the vast number of affected who reside in southern Africa. An Indian pharmaceutical company, Cipla, was the first to offer these drugs at prices that were more realistic (though by no means free).

launched a counterattack, maintaining that the attacking forces consisted of Pakistani military personnel as well as *mujahid* irregulars with direct backing from the Pakistani state. Against this background came a critical breakthrough for the U.S.-India relationship. In a last-minute face-saving visit of Pakistan's then prime minister Nawaz Sharif to Washington on July 4, 1999, President Clinton managed to convince him to effect a pullout from Kargil. India interpreted this gesture as the first instance in which the United States supported India in an India-Pakistan dispute; although the United States supported neither nation officially, the fact that it did not tilt toward Pakistan as it had during the previous two decades marked a major shift in the eyes of Indian foreign policy experts. As a result, India no longer bristles at the slightest mention of Kashmir by Americans; in fact, Clinton explicitly referred to the dispute over Kashmir during his speech to the Indian Joint Session of Parliament in New Delhi and received not words of protest or offense but instead a standing ovation.[6] This would have been unthinkable only a year earlier.

The Clinton visit to South Asia in March 2000 was in and of itself the second important moment that altered the Indian perception of the United States' approach to India and the South Asian region. In the run-up to the visit, many naysayers accused the visit of being "all symbolism and no substance." However, the symbolism of this visit was potently substantive: by sending a loud signal that the United States cared about and sought a new sort of relationship with India, Clinton won over many hardened hearts. Indian public opinion had long viewed the United States and U.S. politicians with deep suspicion, but the Clinton visit seemed to captivate India not only during the five days of the actual visit but for months afterward. The fact that his visit to Pakistan was merely a stop-over, and one surrounded by extraordinary security precautions (including a decoy plane)—along with the fact that the message he delivered to Pakistanis focused nearly exclusively on the merits of returning to democracy and maintaining restraint along the Line of Control—ultimately reassured India that the United States was sincere about seeking relationships with both India and Pakistan *on their own merits*, and without a policy of "tilting" toward either.

---

6. "Remarks by the President to the Indian Joint Session of Parliament," New Delhi, India, March 22, 2000, usinfo.state.gov/topical/global/environ/latest/00032202.htm.

Domestic Changes

The interests of the governments of India and the United States began to converge from late 1999 through the year 2000 as a result of domestic factors in both nations. On the Indian side, the reelection of the BJP to power in October 1999 (through the National Democratic Alliance, or NDA) reaffirmed the party's strength over the only other national political cal party in India, the Indian National Congress Party. Atal Bihari Vajpayee's resumption of the prime ministership provided a sense of stability after a three-year period of revolving-door governments, and political pundits began to talk of the alliance's lasting its full parliamentary term of five years. Vajpayee's moderate stance—in comparison with others in the BJP's top echelon—brought the BJP into political prominence from its near pariah position of ten years earlier, and Vajpayee's *personal* interest in establishing a better relationship with the United States was a key change. Many U.S. policy advisors viewed Vajpayee as someone the United States "could do business with." Vajpayee's desire to expand the relationship between India and the United States to one befitting "natural allies" is widely acknowledged as one of the legacies he will leave behind.

In addition, the BJP-led National Democratic Alliance government has proved to be the one that has actually begun to carry out the economic reforms begun in 1991 but in suspended animation since the mid-1990s. Though the Rashtriya Swayamsevak Sangh's rhetoric of autarkic self-reliance continues, its influence on the BJP's economic policy has been tempered both by the BJP's anticommunist ideology and by the push toward liberalization from other parties in the NDA coalition, such as the Telugu Desam Party. The camp interested in expanding ties with the United States prevailed, paving the way for the implementation and expansion of the economic reforms begun under the Congress Party's leadership. If in fact India continues its reform agenda, U.S.-India economic links would be poised to increase—links that would in the long term create a more stable and expanded relationship.

On the U.S. side, the entire Clinton family's interest in South Asia provided a real push to establish better U.S.-India ties. Hillary Rodham Clinton and Chelsea Clinton visited India, Bangladesh, and Pakistan in 1995. Their travels inspired President Clinton at a personal level to undertake his visit, and to meet with some of the same NGOs that had met with Hillary and Chelsea. Again, as with Prime Minister Vajpayee's personal interest in moving the relationship forward, a desire on the American side that went well beyond the bureaucracy of the State Department and stemmed from the Oval Office itself gave the year 2000 reciprocal visits and resulting agreements greater momentum.

The momentum of the Clinton administration continued in the first nine months of the Bush administration. High-level visits (by the deputy secretary of state and the U.S. trade representative) took place very early on in the new administration. The current administration views China's grand strategy with greater skepticism than the Clinton administration did, and in this sense its interests in Asia have converged with India's. Both the United States and India seek a constructive relationship with China, but both have concerns about Chinese long-term stability and longer-term strategic goals. The Bush administration also sees India as a partner in leading global trade round talks, and it is in a better position to "partner" with India on trade than the previous administration was since it has made clear that there will be no linking of labor or environmental concerns with trade issues. U.S. trade representative Robert Zoellick's July 2001 visit to India took a major step in the direction of partnership in trade fora by seeking to enlist India as a key proponent for the second WTO round, in hopes of averting an outcome similar to that in Seattle in 1999. Finally, in terms of policy changes on the U.S. front, the Bush administration rode into office with the explicit desire to dump the pursuit of the Comprehensive Test Ban Treaty—a key concern of the nonproliferation-focused Clinton administration—and just as important, the current administration has vocally declared its skepticism toward sanctions.

The rising prominence of the Indian American community in the United States has played a crucial role by creating a new channel of pressure for the United States to pay greater attention to India. India is now receiving more attention on Capitol Hill. One barometer of India's growing profile in Washington is that a full 25 percent of the U.S. House of Representatives is part of the Congressional Caucus on India and Indian Americans. The caucus was founded only in 1993, so its growing membership is an important marker of how U.S. lawmakers perceive India's (and Indian Americans') relevance and importance and how quickly that relevance and importance are increasing. That Indian Americans were the highest-earning ethnic group in 1990 and the second highest in 2000, according to the U.S. census, plays no small role in Capitol Hill's rising interest in the community. Coupled with the community's growing clout as a political voice and its potential for funding campaigns, this is likely to increase further still the focus on India and on the concerns of Indian Americans.

Global Culture

Less easy to pinpoint and harder to articulate are the flows of images and ideas that are pulling the imaginations of India and the United States increasingly close together. The growing circulation of images, ideas, and peoples in the last decade has created a stronger sense of shared worlds and shared preoccupations between the two nations. For the most part, this shared world is primarily urban and cosmopolitan: the youth cultures of urban America and urban India are now much more alike than different. Cosmopolitan forms of culture such as film, television, music, fashion, literature, and now the Internet are playing an interesting sort of diplomatic role, normalizing the two cultures with each other. At one time, this topic might have referred exclusively to the spread of American cultural products worldwide, but the last three or four years have witnessed an increasing boom in Indian cultural products in the United States.

Of particular note has been the phenomenon of the increasing attention paid to "Indian" literature in English in the United States. It is enabling a familiarization of American readers with the idea of India, however imagined. What once was a place viewed in literary terms only as the backdrop for English colonial narratives has now come into its own, on its own terms. That the *New York Times Book Review*, for example, fairly regularly features works with Indian themes and settings is one measure of this cultural normalization process at work.

In a related development, the movement of peoples between the United States and India has been on the increase in recent years. We may have still-thin private sector ties in the economic and civil society sectors, but the personal interactions between the two nations are demonstrably increasing. For example, applications for U.S. visas received by the American mission in India numbered 265,000 in 1997 but nearly doubled by the year 2000 to 495,000. The American mission estimates that this number will double again to one million applications by the year 2003.[7] Americans are also traveling to India more: comparable figures show a

---

7. Ambassador Richard K. Celeste, "Indo-U.S. Relations: Building a Dynamic Partnership for the 21st Century" (speech delivered at the Rajiv Gandhi Institute for Contemporary Studies, December 21, 2000).

rise in U.S. applicants for Indian visas from approximately 202,000 in 1997 to 244,000 in 2000.[8] Among this increase are surely substantial numbers of India-born naturalized U.S. citizens and their children—a growing percentage of the U.S. population that again forms part of a broader familiarization process.

It is perhaps too early to determine how important the role of culture will be in bringing India and the United States closer together, but cultural exchanges and increased study programs in addition to the increased circulation of material culture products are likely to continue building stronger and broader links between the two countries, moving the idea of India for Americans and the idea of America for Indians far beyond old stereotypes.

---

8. Tourism Office of India data, incorporating all categories of visa applications, telephone and fax communication, August 20, 2001.

Politics in India's Decentered Polity

John Echeverri-Gent

India enters the new millennium with a dramatically transformed political system. Until the 1990s, power and authority in the Indian polity were concentrated in the Congress Party. The Congress dominated the party system and determined the terms of partisan competition. The party played an important role in coordinating the exercise of authority within the central government and throughout India's federal system. Today, no single party has won a parliamentary majority for more than a decade. The inability of parties to win strong parliamentary majorities has encouraged national institutions such as the Supreme Court and Election Commission to be more assertive in their relations with the government. Economic reforms, in the balance, are decentralizing authority by curtailing central government *dirigisme*, establishing independent regulatory agencies, and shifting economic decision-making authority to the private sector. State governments are more active than ever in promoting economic development even while the central government takes measures to impose fiscal discipline on them. Together, these changes have decentered power and authority in India's polity.

The decentering of the Indian polity, encompassing its political institutions and party system, is the most prominent factor shaping the politics of the National Democratic Alliance (NDA) since its rise to power in October 1999. Decentering includes the "decentralization" of power— the horizontal dispersion of power among institutions at the same level of the federal system as well as the vertical dispersion from higher to lower levels. Decentering also includes the growing pluralism of politi-

The author wishes to thank Hal Gould, Rob Jenkins, Indira Rajaraman, Matthew Rudolph, Herman Schwartz, and Aseema Sinha for their comments on an earlier draft of this essay. Special thanks to Philip Oldenburg and Alyssa Ayres for their patience, encouragement, and insightful comments on multiple drafts of this text.

cal parties wielding power in India's federal system, especially the rise of "single-state" parties, or parties that win parliamentary seats in only one state.[1] Decentering means that power has been decentralized, that a growing range of actors wield it, and that the exercise of power takes place in increasingly diverse institutional settings.

A focus on decentering improves our understanding of the new dynamics of India's party and federal systems. Preoccupation with the fragmentation of the national party system obscures how partisan competition at the state level "makes" and breaks national alliances. The concept of decentering demonstrates that the operation of federal institutions is linked to the dynamics of the party system. The dispersion of power from the Congress Party to a wide range of parties has contributed to the horizontal and vertical decentralization of power throughout India's political system. As a result, decentering has created the need for new forms of coordination.

This chapter begins by examining India's general election in 1999 and recent changes in the party system. Next, it investigates the decentering of India's political institutions. Finally, it explores how the decentering of India's political system has shaped the politics and policies of the National Democratic Alliance since the 1999 elections.

The Decentering of India's Fragmented Party System

On October 13, 1999, the twenty-five-party National Democratic Alliance formed India's ninth government in ten years. In an effort to accommodate the varied political interests within the NDA, Prime Minister Atal Bihari Vajpayee presided over the induction of a seventy-member cabinet. The cabinet was the largest in Indian history, and its size increased even more during the following year. The 1999 elections were the third in three years and the fifth in ten years. The 543 seats that were contested in India's thirteenth general election were won by thirty-eight parties.[2] The distribution of Lok Sabha seats among

---

1. Single-state parties generally—but not always—coincide with "regional parties" in the general literature. I use the term *single-state parties* here because it more precisely denotes their scope and identity and because it is a better unit of analysis for examining how changes in the party system have affected Indian federalism.

2. All election data in this essay come from the Election Commission of India, *Statistical Report on General Elections* for the general elections in 1999, 1998, 1996, and 1991. These documents are available on the Election Commission of India's website at www.eci.gov.in. Data for elections prior to 1991 were collected from David Butler, Ashok

these parties was more fragmented than ever before. The number of "effective parties"—a statistic representing the degree to which the seats in a legislature are controlled by a few parties or dispersed among many[3]—reached 5.9, a level comparable to that of the most fragmented parliaments in the world.

The era of the single-dominant-party system increasingly seems to be an artifact of the independence movement in that it was only through the anticolonial struggle that the Congress Party gained the organizational and ideological resources that sustained its dominance through India's first forty years. Given India's remarkable social heterogeneity, it is not surprising that the decline of the Congress has resulted in political fragmentation at the national level. Winston Churchill once dismissed India as "merely a geographical expression . . . [that is] no more of a single country than the equator."[4] After all, India is more populous than Europe, and its people are arguably more diverse. India's population of one billion outnumbers the 700 million people living in Europe from Portugal to the Russian Federation. It has fifteen official languages and innumerable dialects, great religious pluralism, and culturally distinct states that are as large as or larger than many European countries by population and area.

The fragmentation of India's party system has increased dramatically since the mid-1980s, roughly coinciding with the electoral decline of the Congress. The 1989 elections marked a watershed. The number of parties contesting India's parliamentary elections averaged 42 prior to 1989 and 165 from 1989 to 1999. The average number of parties winning seats in the Lok Sabha grew from 20 prior to 1989 to 31 afterward.

Lahiri, and Prannoy Roy, *India Decides: Elections 1952–1995*, 3rd ed. (New Delhi: Books & Things, 1995).

3. The number of effective parties is now the standard measure of how concentrated legislative seats and vote shares are within a party system. It is the reciprocal of the Hirschman-Herfindahl index used in industrial organization literature to measure how concentrated sales are in a given industry. If there are N parties in a parliament and each party wins an identical number of seats, the number of effective parties is N. When some parties win more seats than others, the distribution of seats becomes more concentrated, and the statistic representing the number of effective parties declines. For instance, when the number of effective parties is 2.0, this means that the concentration is equal to that of two parties splitting all votes evenly. Different numbers of parties and different distributions of seats can lead to the same number of effective parties. See Markku Laakso and Rein Taagepera, "'Effective' Number of Parties: A Measure with Application to West Europe," *Comparative Political Studies* 12 (1979): 3–27.

4. Cited in Shashi Tharoor, *India from Midnight to the Millennium* (New York: Arcade, 1997), 7.

The fragmentation of parties as represented by the number of "effective parties" winning seats in Parliament also increased dramatically, from an average of 2.1 for the period prior to 1989 to an average of 5.0 from 1989 to 1999.

Despite the high levels of party-system fragmentation as a result of the 1999 elections, the Vajpayee government will almost certainly prove more stable than the previous four coalition governments that had ruled India since 1996. The 1999 elections were the first time in a decade that a preelection alliance had a majority of seats in Parliament. The ruling NDA increased its share of parliamentary seats from 276 to 305. The increase means that none of the Bharatiya Janata Party's (BJP's) allies control enough seats to bring down the government by defecting, as did the All India Anna Dravida Munnetra Kazhagam (AIADMK) in the spring of 1999. Perhaps just as important, the opposition is more fragmented and disorganized than ever before. It is difficult to envision how it might present a viable alternative to the NDA. Should defections cause the government to fall, there would almost certainly be new elections, an outcome that is not usually attractive for members of the ruling coalition.

Merely observing that India's party system has become highly frag-mented obscures other important changes in the party system. Although India's parties have always been sensitive to constituency-level factors such as caste in selecting candidates, their coalitional strategies increas-ingly derive from state-level considerations rather than national issues, especially when compared with the politics from 1971 through 1984, when the Congress and Janata parties ascended to power on the basis of the positions they took on national issues. The ascendance of single-state parties has increased the diversity of state-level party systems. The differentiation of state-level party systems requires the leaders of na-tional parties to follow distinct strategies from state to state, though some-times they still allow national considerations to determine strategy at the expense of state-level units. The rise of single-state parties has in-creased the diversity of parties winning seats in the national parliament and the number of parties whose parliamentary strategies are determined primarily by state-level considerations.

The Rise of Single-State Parties

We can begin to understand this aspect of decentering by noticing the divergence between the growing fragmentation of the party system at the national level and its continued cohesion at the subnational level. In contrast to the dramatic increases in fragmentation at the national level, the fragmentation as represented by the number of effective parties in terms of seats won at the state level has increased only slightly, from an average of 1.8 from 1952 through 1984 to an average of 2.4 from 1989 to 1999. Other measures indicate that there is even less fragmentation of vote shares at the constituency level.[5]

One factor contributing to the disparity in the degree of party-system fragmentation at the state and national levels is the proliferation of single-state parties. Single-state parties either are identified with regional cultures that do not transcend state boundaries, such as the Dravida Munnetra Kazhagam (DMK), the AIADMK, the Telugu Desam Party (TDP), the Shiromani Akali Dal, and the Shiv Sena, or are successful in state-level political arenas but unable to succeed in the politics in other states. Many of these parties are led by regional leaders such as Laloo Prasad Yadav, Biju Patnaik, Mulayam Singh Yadav, and Mamata Banerjee, each of whose personal following forms the core of party support but does not extend beyond state boundaries. These parties often were formed when regional leaders defected from declining national parties such as the Janata Party, the Janata Dal, and the Congress. Examples include the Rashtriya Janata Dal, the Biju Janata Dal, the Socialist Party, and the All India Trinamool Congress. The share of seats in the Lok Sabha controlled by single-state parties rose from a low of 7.2 percent in 1977 and 8.3 percent in 1980 to 33 percent in 1999.[6] At the same time, the vote share of single-state parties increased from 13.1 percent and 15.1 percent to 35.6 percent.

The increasing importance of single-state parties contributes to the growing diversity of party systems from state to state. A good indication of the diversity of state-level party systems is the increase in the number

---

5. The number of effective parties by vote share—a measure of the relative dispersion of the share of votes won by political parties—increased from just 2.7 to 2.8 over this period. For more on this measure, see Oliver Heath, "The Fractionalisation of Indian Parties," *Seminar* 480 (August 1999): 66–71. Pradeep Chhibber contends that India's single-member simple plurality electoral rule, the substantial policy authority that its Constitution allots to state governments, and the state-specific nature of social cleavages have always made the state level the strategic point of party strategy. For Chhibber, even the Congress Party has been "a coalition of state parties." The predominance of two-party systems at the state level provides strong support for Chhibber's contention. However, these factors have remained constant over time. They are insufficient to explain the growing fragmentation of the party system at the national level. See Pradeep K. Chhibber, *Democracy Without Associations* (Ann Arbor: University of Michigan Press, 1999).

6. Data for single-state parties include independents elected. These numbered nine (1.7 percent) in 1977, nine (1.7 percent) in 1980, and six (1.1 percent) in 1999.

of parties winning the most or the second most parliamentary seats in a state.[7] The number of parties in the "top two" list has increased considerably in recent years. The average number of parties included on the list jumped from 9.6 during the period from 1952 to 1984 to 14.8 during the period from 1989 to 1999, with the figure reaching 20 in 1998 and 18 in 1999. The increase is primarily attributable to the growing number of single-state parties joining the list. This number rose from just two in 1957 to fourteen in 1999.

The mobilization of the lower castes has increased the decentering of India's party system. As Yogendra Yadav has observed, India is now perhaps the world's only democracy in which the poor have higher rates of participation than the upper classes.[8] In 1999, the voter turnout of the Scheduled Caste (SC) communities was 2.2 percent higher than the national average. The biggest increase has been among the Scheduled Tribes (STs), whose participation has traditionally been below average. In 1999, their rate of participation was 0.4 percent above the national norm.[9] The mobilization of these groups has coincided with the decline of the Congress as a catchall party and the rise of parties with narrower social bases. The process began in the 1960s when Other Backward Classes (OBCs) in South India were mobilized by regional parties such as the DMK. OBC mobilization spread to North India. It bred defections from the Congress and the creation of new opposition parties. The mobilization of less affluent OBCs, SCs, and STs in the 1990s has led to the establishment of parties such as the Bahujan Samaj Party, the Samata Party, and the Samajwadi Party with narrower social bases. (See Christophe Jaffrelot's chapter in this volume.)

The decentering of India's party system has had complex consequences. Decentering has contributed to the decline of the "wave politics" that characterized the 1970s and 1980s. During this era, voters were mobilized on national issues that produced wide swings between pro- and anti-Congress votes. In the 1990s, government performance supplanted national issues as the most important voter consideration.

---

7. I have eliminated from this calculation all second-place parties that won one seat and less than 10 percent of the state's votes.

8. Yogendra Yadav, "Politics," in *India Briefing: A Transformative Fifty Years*, ed. Marshall Bouton and Philip Oldenburg (Armonk, NY: M.E. Sharpe, 1999), 25.

9. Heath, "Fractionalisation of Indian Parties."

State government performance is frequently an important factor affecting national parliamentary outcomes. For instance, in the 1999 elections, the poor performance of state governments run by the BJP and its NDA allies outweighed the national issue of Kargil and Atal Bihari Vajpayee's attractive leadership qualities in Karnataka, Punjab, and Uttar Pradesh. In Andhra Pradesh, while the BJP exerts a limited ideological appeal, its political successes were aided by its alliance with the popular government of the Telugu Desam Party. And the success of the NDA in Bihar, Rajasthan, and West Bengal was due more to the foibles of opposition-led state governments than to national-level issues. Maharashtra is the exception that proves the rule. The split of the Congress due to the falling out between Sonia Gandhi and Sharad Pawar—after Gandhi thwarted Pawar's ambitions on the national scene and Pawar subsequently disputed her qualifications to be prime minister—enabled the coalition between the Shiv Sena and the BJP to minimize its losses despite the weak performance of the coalition's state government. However, the elections demonstrated that Pawar and his new Nationalist Congress Party had little following outside of Maharashtra. What began as a national issue was transformed into a single-state conflict.

Decentering has also increased the profile of state-level leaders at the national level. It is true that during the 1960s state-level leaders played a critical role within the Congress Party. However, their differences were resolved inside the Congress. Under Indira Gandhi, state leaders were placed at the beck and call of national leaders even when, as in the case of Sanjay Gandhi, they held no elected office. State leaders wielded considerably more power in the coalition-based politics of the 1990s. The most flagrant abuse of this power was exercised when Jayalalitha, the leader of the AIADMK, an erstwhile member of the BJP-led coalition that formed the government at the center in March 1998, brought down the government twelve months later by withdrawing from the coalition.

The decentering of the party system simultaneously promotes party-system fragmentation and coalition building. Fragmentation at the national level creates incentives for local leaders to break from their parties because it increases the possibility that these leaders, as heads of newly formed parties, can become central government ministers and use the resources of their ministries to expand their support. Mamata Banerjee's formation of the Trinamool Congress is a good example of this process.

Simultaneously, state-level competition can foster shared interests and partisan alliances that sustain cooperation at the national level. Examples include alliances between the BJP and TDP in Andhra Pradesh and the BJP and Samata Party in Bihar.

The decentering of the party system also promotes stability by moderating the more extreme views of coalition members. The BJP's muting of its stance on building the Ramjanmabhoomi Mandir, abrogating the special status of Kashmir, and imposing a uniform civil code reflects the pressures to moderate its positions that stem from the imperatives of coalition building. The capacity of parties to manage coalitions is an important factor affecting whether decentralization promotes stability or instability. The experience of the BJP provides the basis for some optimism in this regard.

Patterns of Coalition and Competition

Many analysts speculate that India will develop a bipolar coalitional structure with the BJP and the Congress forming the cores of rival coalitions. The total number of seats controlled by the BJP and Congress coalitions increased from 63 percent in 1996 to 78 percent in 1998 and then to 80 percent in 1999. However, the growth of the number of seats won by the BJP and its allies accounted for all of the increase. While the share of seats won by the BJP-led coalition increased from 36 percent in 1996 to more than 55 percent, that of the Congress-led coalition declined from 27 percent to 25 percent. The fact that the changes in the number of seats won by the BJP and Congress ran in opposite directions from their vote shares suggests how important coalition strategy has become in India's decentered party system.

The BJP paradoxically strengthened its position as India's leading party while suffering a decline in electoral support. Its overall vote share diminished from 25.6 percent to 23.8 percent, and the 182 parliamentary seats that it won in 1999 equaled its total in 1998. Coalition strategy is the key to the combination of the BJP's success and the deterioration of its electoral performance. The BJP has adjusted to the fragmented and increasingly decentered structure of India's party system better than any other party. Cementing coalition partners meant that the party was obliged to contest forty-nine fewer seats than in 1998. The sacrifice greatly strengthened the NDA government. Its parliamentary delegation increased by almost fifty seats even as its vote share declined from 42 to 41 percent. The success of the BJP in crafting the NDA is a remarkable accomplishment considering that as late as 1996, when the president asked the BJP to form a government, its pariah status was so entrenched that India's office-hungry parties spurned its entreaties to join its government.

The BJP has traditionally been a party of northern and western India, but the 1999 elections continued its expansion to other parts of the country. In 1989, 97 percent of the seats it won in Parliament were from seven states in the north and west: Delhi, Gujarat, Madhya Pradesh, Rajasthan, Uttar Pradesh, Bihar, and Maharashtra. In 1991 and 1996, these states provided 92 percent of the BJP's parliamentary seats, and their share declined to 85 percent in 1998. The portion of the BJP's parliamentary seats provided by these core states dropped to 75 percent in 1999. The states in which BJP expansion has been most successful are Orissa in the east and Andhra Pradesh and Karnataka in the south. There is little question that strategic alliances with popular regional leaders played a crucial role in the BJP's 1999 electoral successes in Orissa and Andhra Pradesh. Even though the party sacrificed the interests of its Karnataka unit by allying with members of the unpopular state government in order to support the newly formed Janata Dal (United) in other parts of the country, Karnataka remains an important beachhead in South India.

Another key factor in the BJP's geographical expansion has been its moderation of Hindu nationalism, which is identified with the Brahminical culture of North India. Indeed, although *hindutva* greatly increased support for the BJP in the north and west during the late 1980s and early 1990s, the party's expansion in the south and east has coincided with the BJP's jettisoning of its more militant demands and its positioning of itself as a party of moderation and competence. The implicit shelving of its militant Hindu nationalism was highlighted in 1999 when the BJP submerged its identity under the banner of the National Democratic Alliance and campaigned exclusively on the moderate NDA campaign manifesto rather than issuing its own.

The BJP and its allies appear to be coalescing into a social bloc grounded primarily in the upper classes of Indian society. Polling at the time of the 1999 elections showed that the party was supported by 46 percent of the upper castes and 30 percent of the dominant peasant castes.[10] When the electorate was divided into economic strata, the survey found that the BJP was supported by 40 percent of the vote from those with "very high economic status" and 32 percent of those with "high economic status." The BJP's figures for upper castes and for very high and high economic status were the greatest of any political party. The BJP's support steadily declines as we move down social and economic hierarchies. In the last few years, corporate India has become increasingly supportive of the BJP.[11] Since 1998, the party has become the favorite for business contributions. In addition, the BJP and its affiliated organizations have been very successful in establishing links with affluent sections of the Indian diaspora. The support of the BJP's NDA allies generally complements the party's social base. The allies receive strong backing from dominant peasant castes, with 22 percent support according to the 1999 survey. They also receive substantial support, 23 percent according to the survey, from OBC groups in the middle echelons of Indian society. Combined support for the BJP and its NDA allies is strongest among groups with the highest social status and incomes.

In contrast to the BJP, the Congress suffered from its strategy to go it alone as articulated by its All India Congress Committee meeting in Pachmarhi in September 1998. In the 1999 elections, the Congress lost 29 seats, reducing its total to 114, the worst in its history. This decline occurred despite the Congress's increased vote share, from 25.8 percent in 1998 to 28.3 percent in 1999.

At a time when the decentering of India's party system required greater sensitivity to state-level factors, power was increasingly centralized into the hands of Sonia Gandhi and her coterie of advisors. This contributed to the poor strategic judgment exercised by the Congress prior to the September 1999 general elections. The Congress snatched defeat from

10. The data in this paragraph are from Yogendra Yadav with Sanjay Kumar and Oliver Heath, "The BJP's New Social Bloc," *Frontline* 16, no. 23 (November 6, 1999), www.the-hindu.com/fline/fl1623/16230310.htm (accessed October 22, 2000). For similar data for the 1996 and 1998 general elections, see Subrata K. Mitra and V.B. Singh, *Democracy and Social Change in India* (New Delhi: Sage, 1999), 132–40.

11. Business voters give more support to the BJP than to any other party, with the BJP coalition receiving 33 and 38 percent of the business votes in the 1996 and 1998 elections. The Congress and its allies came in second, winning 23 and 26 percent. See Mitra and Singh, *Democracy and Social Change*, 134. For business's preference for the BJP in regard to campaign finance, see Sukumar Muralidharan and Sudha Mahalingam, "Big Business and the Elections," *Frontline* 16, no. 16 (July 31, 1999), www.the-hindu.com/fline/fl1616/16160140.htm (accessed October 22, 2000). See also C.P. Chadrasekhar, "Friends of the BJP," *Frontline* 16, no. 16 (July 31, 1999), www.the-hindu.com/fline/fl1616/16160140.htm (accessed October 22, 2000).

the jaws of victory with an unrelenting sequence of mistakes. The party was riding high after an impressive set of victories in Madhya Pradesh, Rajasthan, and Delhi in the November 1998 state legislative elections. A December 1998 poll published in *India Today* found that if elections had been held at that time, the Congress would have won 45 percent of the vote and 305 Lok Sabha seats. Then came the deluge of errors. In April 1999, the Congress attempted to exploit the AIADMK's sordid defection from the BJP coalition by trying to form a government without facing elections. This was the third time in two years that the Congress had tried this tactic. Each time it failed. Each time the party's image was further tarnished by the impression that its leaders were more interested in holding office than in representing the public will.

During the spring of 1999, Sonia Gandhi mishandled a challenge from Sharad Pawar, a Congress Party stalwart from Maharashtra whom Gandhi feared as a rival for party leadership. Pawar responded to Gandhi's efforts to undercut his power within the party by writing an open letter asserting that it was inappropriate for a foreign-born citizen such as Sonia Gandhi to become India's prime minister. Pawar then split from the Congress, taking much of the Maharashtra party organization with him.

Sonia Gandhi's ill-advised choices of political allies damaged the party's prospects even more. Particularly unfortunate was the alliance with the AIADMK, whose leader, Jayalalitha, brought down the BJP-led coalition after its leadership refused to stop her prosecution for corruption. The Congress's alliance with Laloo Prasad Yadav, another regional leader who had been arrested for his role in Bihar's $280-million cattle fodder scandal, also did little to support the Congress pledge of competent and clean governance.

Despite leading the Congress to its worst defeat in history at the national level, Sonia Gandhi and her advisors retain firm control over the party. They exercise their control in a manner that discourages intraparty democracy and the constructive airing of differences—processes that are particularly useful for developing effective strategy in a decentered party system. This was highlighted by the elections for party president in the fall of 2000, when Jitendra P. Prasad challenged Sonia Gandhi. Even though the outcome was never in doubt, Gandhi's coterie ostracized Prasad and manipulated the election process to ensure that the weak challenger's showing would be minuscule. The centralization of power and erosion of intraparty democracy was again manifested in January 2001, when leaders of the Congress authorized Gandhi to pick the entire Congress Working Committee membership rather than hold elections for twelve of its twenty-four members, as was previous practice.

At the same time that the Congress has been defeated at the national level, it has experienced remarkable success at the state level. It won three of four state elections held simultaneously with the 1999 national elections, and it was a member of victorious coalitions in three of four state elections and in the Union Territory of Pondicherry in May 2001. These victories had less to do with Sonia Gandhi's leadership than with the performance of state governments and local patterns of coalitions. The Congress's victories create the possibility of the emergence of greater voice and autonomy within party affairs for victorious state leaders. Should state leaders such as A.K. Anthony, Ashok Gehlot, S.M. Krishna, and Digvijay Singh be able to loosen the stranglehold over the party exerted by Sonia Gandhi and her advisors, it may help to rejuvenate the Congress. Should Gandhi and her coterie quash their autonomy and silence their voices, the Congress Party may suffer new desertions by state leaders, and it will continue to have difficulty developing a strategy that achieves national success through adjustments to the diverse political conditions in India's states.

The Decentering of India's Political Institutions

The transformation of India's party system, the activation of its civil society, and its reorientation to the global economy have produced important changes in the configuration of power among India's political institutions even though the laws of the Indian Constitution have not been altered fundamentally. At the national level, power has been dispersed from Parliament and the cabinet to the president, the Supreme and High Courts, and the Election Commission. Simultaneously, economic reforms are transforming state intervention from *dirigisme* to regulation. *Dirigiste* interventions interfere with markets to dictate economic outcomes. Regulation involves enforcing a set of rules whose incentives and norms are designed to make markets operate efficiently and equitably. *Dirigisme* centralizes power when central government intervention determines distributional outcomes. Under regulation, in contrast, rules act as decision-making parameters that allow for more choice by market participants. The transition from *dirigisme* to regulation can be seen in the central government's creation of independent regulatory agencies to promote market-driven development. Changes in India's fiscal federalism have been more ambiguous, as state governments now have more autonomy to promote economic development while the central government has imposed new measures to improve fiscal discipline in the states.

Increased Assertiveness by the President, Supreme Court, and Election Commission

The electoral decline of the Congress Party and the association of the Rajiv Gandhi and Narasimha Rao governments with a series of corruption scandals coincided with the growth of a constituency for good governance. One source of this constituency is India's expanding middle class. Another is the mobilization of nongovernmental organizations (NGOs) and social movements in the name of defending the public interest. The potency of the anticorruption constituency can be seen in the anti-incumbent proclivities of the Indian electorate. Only two of nine national governments have won reelection since 1971. Twenty-four of thirty-four state government ruling parties lost elections from 1993 to 2001.

By merging the principle of parliamentary sovereignty with that of judicial review, the Indian Constitution has laid the basis for decades of discord between the executive and judiciary branches.[12] The fragmentation of the party system since 1989 has weakened the executive branch by preventing governments from controlling the two-thirds parliamentary majority necessary to amend the Constitution—a weapon that was frequently resorted to in the days of Congress dominance to overturn disagreeable Supreme Court decisions. In 1993, the Supreme Court usurped the government's control over the appointment and transfer of Supreme and High Court justices by obliging India's president to follow the counsel of a panel of the five senior most Supreme Court justices rather than that of the prime minister. The Supreme Court further weakened the government in response to the 1996 *hawala* scandal, in which leading politicians from the ruling and opposition parties were indicted for taking illegal payoffs. It overturned a 1988 government directive ordering the Central Bureau of Intelligence (CBI), India's primary investigative agency, not to investigate a government department without the government's approval. The court placed the CBI's investigations

---

12. Lloyd I. Rudolph and Susanne Hoeber Rudolph, "Redoing the Constitutional Design: From an Interventionist to a Regulatory State," in *Against the Odds: India's Democracy at Fifty*, ed. Atul Kohli (Cambridge: Cambridge University Press, forthcoming 2001). The discussion in the following three paragraphs draws from this manuscript.

under its own supervision and ultimately enhanced the agency's independence from the prime minister and cabinet.

The fragmentation of the party system and the growing constituency for political reform have dispersed power from the government to the president and Election Commission. The election of hung parliaments from 1989 to 1998 enhanced the president's discretion to ask parties to form governments, though all presidents have followed the precedent set in 1989 by R. Venkataraman by asking the party with the most seats in the Lok Sabha. In 1999, President K.R. Narayanan extended presidential power through his acts to delimit the authority of the caretaker government that he appointed for the six-month interim before the 1999 elections. He made pointed inquiries about its new telecommunications policy, and by receiving opposition party requests for a Rajya Sabha debate about the caretaker's actions during the Kargil crisis, he encouraged the government to meet with the opposition to discuss its policy.

Presidents had been effectively obligated to follow the advice of the prime minister and his council of ministers until the end of the 1980s, though the Forty-Fourth Amendment in 1978 enabled the president to return legislation for reconsideration, with the provision that acts that are sent to the president a second time must be signed. In 1987, President Venkataraman took unprecedented action by returning a legislative bill that authorized the government to open the mail of individuals. His action convinced the government to withdraw the legislation. The power was used again in October 1997, when President Narayanan convinced the United Front government to back down from its decision to invoke the provisions of Article 356 to impose central government rule on the state of Uttar Pradesh. The increasing assertiveness of the president has remained an important factor in discouraging the central government from abusing its power under Article 356.

With the 1991 appointment of the flamboyant T.N. Sheshan as chief election commissioner, India's Election Commission took its active supervision of Indian elections to a new level. It imposed a code of conduct on India's parties during the last three national elections that, among other things, barred government authorities from announcing policies that involve financial enticements to constituencies at any time during a campaign. During the 1999 campaign, the Election Commission overturned several governmental decisions on these grounds, though it acquiesced to the Vajpayee government's controversial decisions to award a 10 percent increase in support prices for ten agricultural commodities and a 5 percent increase in the adjustment for inflation, or "dearness allowance," for central government employees. Beginning in 1993, the commission began to compel all of India's parties to hold internal elections. It enforced strict—many would say unrealistic—limits on campaign spending. To limit intimidation and violence in voting, the commission began using central government security forces and sent out 1,500 observer teams equipped with video cameras. The Election Commission overreached its authority with its ruling to ban the public dissemination of the results of polling surveys during the 1999 campaign, and its decision was overturned by the Supreme Court.

The Rise of Independent Regulatory Agencies

The Government of India has established a number of independent regulatory agencies with the objective of developing markets to attract and efficiently allocate private investment, domestic and foreign. The earliest and most developed independent regulatory agency is in the financial sector. Until 1992, India's stock exchanges were overseen by the Controller of Capital Issues (CCI) within the Ministry of Finance. The CCI determined which firms could access the stock markets and the number and price of shares they could issue. In 1992, the CCI was abolished and the Securities and Exchange Board of India (SEBI) was given legal sanction. SEBI is designed to develop and regulate India's stock markets in a fashion similar to that of the U.S. Securities and Exchange Commission. It is central to the transformation of Indian stock exchanges from institutions with archaic market infrastructure to sites of trading technologies that include satellite-linked computerized trading systems and dematerialized depositories as modern as any in the world. Constructing effective independent regulatory agencies requires the development of new institutional capacities, especially the capacity to monitor the actions of market participants and impose sanctions against those who violate regulatory procedures. SEBI has made important strides along these lines, but the scandals in March 2001 involving insider trading, rampant speculation, and fraudulent financial practices demonstrate that India has a considerable distance to go before it attains effective regulation of its equity markets.

The development of independent regulatory agencies is central to India's strategy to attract private investment to help meet the country's infrastructural needs. It is also vital to resolving the burgeoning fiscal problems of India's central and state governments, since independent regulatory agencies are increasingly regarded as means to increase government revenues by depoliticizing the process of determining the pricing of public services.[13] The government has recently created new independent regulatory agencies in four sectors: telecommunications, power, ports, and insurance. The Telecom Regulatory Authority of India (TRAI) was established in 1997 to promote investment in the telecom sector and regulate the market for telecom service providers. The Electricity Regulatory Commissions Act of 1998 authorized the creation of the Central Electricity Regulatory Commission and of state electricity regulatory commissions. By the beginning of 2000, seven states had created electricity regulatory commissions. In April 1997, the Tariff Authority for Major Ports began functioning to regulate the charges levied by private sector providers of port facilities, and in 1999 Parliament passed legislation creating the Insurance Regulatory and Development Authority. These fledgling agencies are only beginning to develop effective regulatory capacity, and their independence from the NDA government remains limited, as is demonstrated by the government's overruling of TRAI's opposition to the switch from license fees to revenue sharing in the telecom sector during the summer of 1999.

Decentering and the New Politics of Fiscal Federalism

State governments have accumulated ever more serious fiscal problems just as the decentralization of authority within India's governmental institutions is increasing their importance for economic development. Indian state governments' aggregate gross fiscal deficit rose from a five-year average of 2.7 percent of gross domestic product (GDP) from 1993–94 to 1997–98 to 4.2 percent in 1998–99 and 4.9 percent in 1999–2000, the highest ever. More troublesome is that the states' revenue deficit, after never having risen to more than 1 percent of GDP over the period from 1971–72 to 1995–96, grew to 2.5 percent of GDP in 1998–99 and 3.7 percent in 1999–2000. Fiscal problems seem to be the worst in the least affluent states. The average ratio of fiscal deficit to gross state domestic product in India's three poorest states—Bihar, Uttar Pradesh, and Orissa—increased from 4.7 percent

13. Rakesh Mohan, "Fiscal Correction for Economic Growth," *Economic and Political Weekly* (June 10, 2000): 2027–36.

in 1993–94 to 7 percent in 1997–98.[14] The increase in fiscal deficits has been accompanied by a deterioration in the quality of expenditures. Interest payments as a percentage of total revenue receipts have steadily increased from 7.5 percent in 1980–81 to 21.3 percent in 1999–2000, while development expenditures have declined from 19.6 percent in 1980–81 to 11.5 percent in 1996–97.[15]

The roots of the states' fiscal problems are grounded in two factors: (1) a system of fiscal federalism that encourages fiscal profligacy by state governments and (2) the increased competition in state politics following the 1967 elections, which gave rise to populism. Fiscal federalism in India includes two mechanisms that redistribute resources from central to state governments. The central government, through its Planning Commission, finances developmental projects of state governments. Planning Commission loans are allotted to the states on the basis of the "Gadgil formula," which accounts for population, poverty, and revenue mobilization. Additionally, the Reserve Bank of India has traditionally arranged for state governments to borrow from capital markets at interest rates identical for each state regardless of their fiscal circumstances and subject to limits determined by the central government. These administrative arrangements mean that the cost and availability of credit to state governments have been unrelated to whether they have put their loans to productive use.

The second mechanism for redistributing resources from central to state governments is the finance commissions convened by the central government. Because it allocates more buoyant tax revenues to the central government than to the state governments, the Indian Constitution calls for convening a finance commission every five years to redistribute some of these revenues to the states. Until recently, the finance commissions have taken a "gap-filling" approach that determines the amount of funds to be awarded to each state on the basis of the gap between its revenues and its nonplan expenditures. This approach has encouraged states to increase their nonplan expenditures while giving them little incentive to raise revenues.

---

14. The increase for Bihar was from 4.0 percent to 6.2 percent. Uttar Pradesh jumped from 4.5 to 8.6 percent, and Orissa grew from 5.7 to 6.3 percent. World Bank, *India: Reducing Poverty, Accelerating Development* (New Delhi: Oxford University Press, 2000), 144, annex table 3.1.

15. Reserve Bank of India, *Annual Report 1999–2000*, table IV.5, www.rbi.org.in (accessed June 17, 2001); Ashok K. Lahiri, "Sub-National Public Finance in India," *Economic and Political Weekly* (April 29, 2000): 1539–49.

It is within this institutional framework that populism came to domi-
nate the terms of partisan competition at the state level. In their eager-
ness to win elections, politicians made campaign promises that were
fiscally irresponsible. Subsidies increased while tax revenues lagged
behind. Explicit and implicit subsidies provided by state governments
now amount to an estimated 9.9 percent of GDP.[16] Most of these subsidies go to power, irrigation, transport, and higher education, where user
charges are low, collections are weak, and costs are inflated by over-
staffing and inefficiencies. Particularly troubling is the power sector,
where the losses of state electricity boards, which are responsible for
the distribution of electricity, grew from 9.8 percent of state plan expenditure in 1992–93 to 18 percent in 1998–99. User charges for irrigation
pay for only 20 percent of the maintenance cost of the system. State
subsidies encourage inefficiency, and they benefit the more affluent. Since
state governments have been unwilling to improve their tax bases, they
have paid for these subsidies with growing fiscal deficits and reductions
in spending on social and economic infrastructure.

The central government has also contributed to the fiscal problems of
the states. The cascading effect of the central government's implementation of the high salary increases recommended by the Fifth Pay Commission in 1997 is a major factor in the states' most recent financial problems.
Efforts to reduce the fiscal deficit of the central government have resulted
in a decline in transfers to the states. Transfers as a proportion of GDP
dropped to 3.6 percent in 1998–99, compared with 4.8 percent in 1990–
91. Since the implementation of the Gadgil formula in 1969, the Planning
Commission has routinely underestimated the support necessary to meet
the demands on the states' revenue expenditures in the form of administrative costs and transfers that accompany the state plans. This, along with
the costs imposed by the proliferation of centrally sponsored schemes,
has contributed to the deterioration of the states' revenue accounts. Finally, reforms to liberalize interest rate controls have increased the cost of
borrowing for the central and state governments.

State governments attempt to circumvent their budget constraints in
three ways. First, they take out loans from the National Small Savings
Fund and the Public Provident Fund collected in post offices and banks
and held in the public accounts of the central government. These high-

---

16. The Ministry of Finance found that subsidies amounted to 14.4 percent of GDP in
1994–95. Nearly 69 percent of all subsidies come from state governments. See Lahiri,
"Sub-National Public Finance," 1543.

cost loans are made available to each state in proportion to the share of savings that has been collected within the state. The loans have grown from Rs. 50 billion in 1993–94 to Rs. 237 billion in 1998–99. State governments also skirt budget constraints by issuing guarantees to state public sector enterprises to enable them to raise money from the market rather than draw upon state resources—often to finance the construction of infrastructure without adequate provision for cost recovery. The guarantees issued have increased from Rs. 403 billion in March 1992 to Rs. 796 billion in September 1997, the equivalent of 9.1 percent of the states' net domestic product. Finally, states resort to ways and means advances and overdrafts from the Reserve Bank of India to manage their liquidity problems and improve the appearance of their balance sheets at the end of the fiscal year. Many states made extraordinary use of these measures in order to cope with the burden imposed by the hefty pay increases that accompanied the implementation of the Fifth Pay Commission recommendations.[17]

While India's states have become mired in fiscal problems, economic liberalization has increased the incentives for state governments to pursue their own initiatives. Prior to the reforms, India's central government exercised more *dirigiste* economic controls than virtually any other noncommunist state. Nearly all industrial projects needed licenses from the central government to begin new projects or expand the capacity of existing ones.[18] Central government approval was required for all foreign investment projects on a case-by-case basis before 1991, and there was a 40 percent ceiling on foreign equity. Today, all but six industries are free of licensing. Private firms are permitted to operate in all but three strategic sectors. Reforms provide for automatic approval for foreign direct investment (FDI) for projects in many sectors. One hundred percent FDI is allowed in industries such as power, pharmaceuticals, and hotels and tourism, with ceilings at levels of 51 percent and above for most other sectors.

The lifting of central government controls has greatly increased the mobility of private capital at a time when the economy is driven more than ever by private investment. The share of the private sector in gross domestic capital formation increased from an average of 54 percent for the decade of the 1980s to 71 percent in 1997–98. By the end of the

17. World Bank, *India: Reducing Poverty*, 37; Lahiri, "Sub-National Public Finance," 1540–41.
18. Small-scale industries were required to obtain licenses from state governments.

1990s, the investment component of state plans on average accounted for 9 percent of total investment.[19] This shift has created incentives for states to reorient their perspectives from dependence on the central government to efforts to attract private investment. This reorientation can also be seen in reforms that encourage states to raise funding from private markets. In 1998–99, the Reserve Bank of India established a debt auction system through which state governments can directly access the market at low rates of interest. The 1999 Insurance Regulatory and Development Authority Act and other efforts to develop India's bond markets will further reduce the relative importance of central government funding for state finances. We can also see the declining importance of central government financing in the rise of foreign investment compared with central assistance. In 1990–91, the $103 million that India received in total foreign investment was less than 2 percent of the $6.1 billion in central assistance provided to state and union territory plans. For the triennium ending with fiscal year 1999–2000, India received an annual average of FDI valued at $2.7 billion. This was 37 percent of the annual average of central assistance for state and union territory plans during this period.[20]

The liberalization of central controls and the progressive turn to mobile private capital in order to finance development has encouraged many states to implement economic reforms in order to attract investment. Andhra Pradesh, under its high-profile chief minister Chandrababu Naidu, has been a leader in state-level reforms. The state has undertaken an ambitious program to reform the power sector by unbundling its state electricity board into separate generation and transmission companies. Distribution is expected to be privatized by 2003. Andhra Pradesh has also begun ambitious programs to eradicate illiteracy and promote technical education. The energetic efforts of the "CEO of Andhra Pradesh" have landed a number of high-profile foreign investment projects.

---

19. Computed from Ministry of Finance, *Indian Economic Survey, 1999–2000*, table 1.4, www.nic.in/indiabudget/es99–2000/app1.5.pdf (accessed January 14, 2001).

20. The data on FDI are from *Reserve Bank of India Bulletin* (January 12, 2001), table 44, www.rbi.org.in/index.dll/2?SectionHomepage?fromdate=01/12/01&todate=01/12/01&s1secid=1001&s2secid=1001 (accessed June 15, 2001). The data on central assistance for state/UT plans are from Ministry of Finance, *Indian Economic Survey 1999–2000*, table 2.11, www.nic.in/indiabudget/es99–2000/app2.11.pdf (accessed June 15, 2001); and Planning Commission, Government of India, *Basic Data on Financing of the Central Plan (1984–85 to 1998–99)*, table 1, planningcommission.nic.in/t1.htm (accessed January 14, 2001). The central assistance figures were converted into dollars on the basis of exchange rates provided in World Bank, *India: Reducing Poverty*.

Microsoft chose Hyderabad for its second development research center outside the United States. Naidu convinced India's top business houses to select Andhra Pradesh for the site of the Indian School of Business, designed to train top management for corporate India with the cooperation of Northwestern University's Kellogg Graduate School of Management and the University of Pennsylvania's Wharton School. Naidu has also secured more than $3 billion in World Bank funding.

The tactics of this shrewd politician demonstrate the political constraints on state-level reforms. Andhra Pradesh has incurred substantial fiscal deficits during Naidu's tenure. These are in part due to Naidu's ambitious developmental plans, but they are also a consequence of his support for populist programs, which becomes more salient prior to elections. Naidu's efforts to alleviate Andhra Pradesh's fiscal problems are impressive but limited by powerful political interests. He has attempted to improve government productivity by promoting the use of new information technologies and increasing the government's capacity to monitor and evaluate administrative services. Naidu has authorized government departments to impose user fees. He has initiated reforms that permit the downsizing or closure of failing public enterprises. Naidu also has curbed subsidies for rice, electricity, and irrigation, even though he has used his leverage in the NDA to oppose the reduction of central government subsidies for food and fertilizer.

State governments find themselves engaged in an interstate competition to attract domestic and foreign investment. The diversity of investment climates is quantified and ranked by the Indian business magazine *Business Today* and the Confederation of Indian Industries, a dynamic national business association. Favorable policy regimes attract corporate investment, and the impact of state government policy on private investment decisions will continue to grow because infrastructure and human capital—policy domains predominantly under state government authority—are the primary determinants of investment location. The increasing efficiency of India's financial markets threatens to exacerbate the disparities as the financial system redirects savings to better-performing states. The days when Indian governments will issue bonds that are rated by credit agencies on the basis of state government performance are at hand. Even less-mobile forms of investment such as household savings appear responsive to differential state performance. As of the end of March 1998, the credit-deposit ratios of poor performers such as Bihar and Uttar Pradesh were only 27 and 31 percent, respectively, well below the 55 percent national average. The credit-deposit ratios for good performers, including Karnataka, Andhra Pradesh, and Maharashtra, ranged between 69 and 72 percent, with Tamil Nadu achieving a rate of 90 percent.[21]

At the same time that India's economic reforms have curtailed central government *dirigisme* and encouraged state governments to take developmental initiatives, the central government has altered the incentives of India's fiscal federalism to impose greater fiscal discipline on the states. In the spring of 1999, the Ministry of Finance negotiated arrangements with a committee of the National Development Council to provide financial aid to state governments under extraordinary fiscal stress in return for their signing a memorandum of understanding that specified fiscal reforms creating greater discipline. Nine state governments eventually signed these memoranda.[22] This episode served as a prelude to the recommendations of the Eleventh Finance Commission.

When the central government convened the Eleventh Finance Commission on July 3, 1998, it expanded its terms of reference by asking the commission to review state finances and suggest ways in which the states might restructure their finances to restore budgetary stability. On April 24, 2000, the central government further requested that the commission draw up a fiscal reform program to reduce the revenue deficits of the states. In addition, it asked the commission to recommend ways to link the states' implementation of the deficit reduction program to the grants that the central government provided to the state governments to cover their nonplan revenue deficits. The commission submitted its report on July 7, 2000, before it had time to formulate a fiscal reform program for the state governments. The recommendations for the reform program were included in the commission's supplementary report on August 31, 2000. The central government accepted the general report in the summer of 2000. It accepted the supplementary report in December.

The recommendations of the Eleventh Finance Commission created considerable controversy, demonstrating that the decentering of India's polity has made fiscal federalism more contentious. Previous finance commissions had based their recommendations for distributing central government revenues among India's states on technocratic formulas that

21. Montek S. Ahluwalia, "Economic Performance of States in Post Reforms Period," *Economic and Political Weekly* (May 6, 2000): 1644.
22. The data in this paragraph are from Lahiri, "Sub-National Public Finance," 1540–41.

aroused little political controversy. The eleventh commission added a new variable for fiscal deficit reduction and altered the weighting of the variables in the formula—population, per capita income, area, infra-structure, and tax mobilization—to provide more funding to poorer states. In an unprecedented act, Andhra Pradesh chief minister Chandrababu Naidu led a group of government leaders from eight wealthier states to New Delhi on August 21, 2000, to protest the commission's recommen-dations. Naidu contended that they gave short shrift to the "performing and reforming" states. The protest led by Naidu suggests that single-state parties may have more difficulty than national parties in accepting the redistribution of funds from state to state.

The supplementary report recommended reforms that pose important changes for India's fiscal federalism. It urged that 15 percent of the revenue-deficit grants that initially were rewarded to fifteen chronic revenue-deficit states be reallocated and combined with matching funds from the central government to create a Rs. 106 billion "incentive fund" to reward fiscal reform in all states. The objective was to eliminate all revenue deficits of state governments by 2004–2005 and reduce the states' gross fiscal deficit to 2.5 percent of GDP. The recommendations set up a monitoring group composed of officials from the central government's planning commission and finance ministry and from each state govern-ment. The monitoring agency was charged with designing fiscal reform programs for each state, and it was authorized to release incentive funds conditional on the states' performance.

How did the central government alter the liberal provisions for state governments and the decentralizing tendencies of India's decentered polity without inciting a revolt of the single-state parties? Globalization and the requisites of reform have motivated efforts to centralize control over fiscal policy in many developing countries. In India, rising interest costs limit central and state government public investment and raise pri-vate sector capital costs, thereby disadvantaging India in global compe-tition. Continued deficits threaten to lower the Government of India's credit rating and increase its costs of borrowing. They also impede im-portant financial sector reforms. The state governments' acceptance of the incentive fund was facilitated by their previous experience with memoranda of understanding. Many states endorsed the idea of using central government funds to reward fiscal reforms at the National De-velopment Council meeting of chief ministers in February 2000. The new incentive fund helped to placate wealthier states such as Andhra

Pradesh by making them eligible for additional funding. Even revenue-deficit states became eligible for matching funds. Paradoxically, the decentering of India's polity contributed to the central government's imposition of fiscal discipline on state governments. By pitting the states in competition for private investment, it creates incentives for the states to be more fiscally responsible. Coalition politics and the fragmentation of Parliament limit the possibilities for reducing the central government's fiscal deficit. The Finance Commission offers a more tractable opportunity because the central government has preponderant power—it appoints and determines the terms of reference of the commission—in a more politically insulated process.

The BJP: Operating Strategically in India's Decentered Polity

Politics and public policy in India's decentered polity are shaped by three major factors: the decentering of the party system, globalization, and the political activation of nonparty organizations. Coalition politics is a central feature of governance in India's decentered polity. The political and policy initiatives undertaken by the BJP, the largest partner in the ruling NDA, must be balanced with the need to secure the consent of its coalition partners. Globalization creates a different set of incentives. The opportunities and constraints it presents have encouraged the NDA to continue the project of restructuring the Indian state and its economic policy regime by reducing central government *dirigisme*, rolling back barriers to international trade and capital flows, and reforming fiscal and monetary policy so as to improve India's international competitiveness. These changes have altered the political economy of the state by encouraging increased activism on the part of India's business community while inciting resistance from groups that benefited from previous institutions and policies. Some of the groups resisting the BJP's economic reforms are linked to the party itself through their membership in the Sangh Parivar, a family of organizations centered on the Rashtriya Swayamsevak Sangh (RSS; National Volunteer Association), a militant organization with a national network of cadres dedicated to promoting Hindu nationalism. The RSS and affiliated organizations such as the Swadeshi Jagaran Manch (Self-Reliance Awareness Movement), Viswa Hindu Parishad (VHP; World Hindu Council), Bharatiya Mazdoor Sangh (Indian Workers' Federation), and Bharatiya Kisan Sangh (Indian Farmers' Union) have attempted to impose their vision of Hindu nationalism on the BJP at the same time that the party has endeavored to redefine it in a manner that is compatible with the opportunities presented by globalization and effective governance in India's decentered polity.

The Rise of Vajpayee and the Moderation of the BJP's Hindu Nationalism

Coalition politics redistributed power within the BJP in favor of Prime Minister Atal Bihari Vajpayee and his moderate supporters. Even though the prime minister's association with the RSS goes back decades, many observers have found his moderation out of step with the mainstream of the BJP. Vajpayee supporters outside the BJP often explain their backing by noting that Vajpayee is "the right man in the wrong party." After Vajpayee led a disastrous 1984 electoral campaign in which the BJP won only two parliamentary seats, L.K. Advani rejuvenated the party by aligning it with militant Hindu nationalism. It may be misleading to distinguish a pragmatic strategist such as Advani as a hard-liner relative to Vajpayee's moderation. Nevertheless, Advani generally takes positions closer to the strident *hindutva* of the RSS, and the two played very different roles in the defining issue of Hindu nationalism in the early 1990s—the militants' campaign to replace the Babri Masjid with a temple to celebrate the putative birthplace of the god Ram. Advani was the leader of the movement that climaxed in the violent destruction of the mosque on December 6, 1992, while Vajpayee criticized this action. The political backlash suffered by the BJP after the destruction of the Babri Masjid led Advani to moderate the party's position. The failure of the party to gain coalition partners after it was asked to form a government in 1996 and its efforts to expand its electoral support beyond its strongholds in northern and western India also encouraged the BJP to recast *hindutva* in a more moderate form. As a result, Advani supported Vajpayee as prime minister in 1996, and he readily accepted Vajpayee's leadership of the government when the BJP-led alliance ascended to power in 1998. It has been from his position as prime minister beginning in 1998 that Vajpayee has extended his control over the BJP and nudged Advani from his preeminence.

Vajpayee's assertion of control over the party can be traced back to the BJP convention in Bangalore in January 1999, when the prime minister stymied opposition to his economic reforms and rebuffed the complaints of BJP president Kushabhau Thakre—an Advani loyalist—that the party had not been adequately consulted about the reforms. In November 1999, Vajpayee supported the ouster of Advani protégé Kalyan Singh as chief minister of Uttar Pradesh, India's largest state. By the August 2000 BJP party conference in Nagpur, Vajpayee replaced Thakre with his own choice, Bangaru Laxman, the first BJP president ever from South India and the first *dalit*, or Scheduled Caste member, to be president of the party. The powerful general secretaries of the BJP were also reorganized, with Advani supporters such as K.N. Govindacharya—a *bête noire* of Vajpayee because of his opposition to the government's economic reforms and his labeling of the prime minister as the moderate "mask" of the party—being replaced by supporters of the prime minister. Key Advani supporters such as Sushma Swaraj and Uma Bharati were allowed to languish outside the government for most of 2000, while others such as Pramod Mahajan and Arun Jaitley realigned themselves to support Vajpayee. The politics of the NDA even obliged Advani to reinvent himself as a moderate in order to become more acceptable to the BJP's allies. Opposing the prime minister in the name of *hindutva* would be the undoing of this project.

Vajpayee has attempted to redefine *hindutva* during his tenure as prime minister. The BJP's concept of *hindutva* is based on three principles. The first is cultural nationalism as embodied in the party slogan "One nation, one people, and one culture." This principle is based on the understanding that the Indian nation, despite its social diversity, shares a distinct cultural identity associated with the values and beliefs of Hinduism as understood by the party and its supporters. The second principle is "positive secularism," defined as "justice for all, appeasement of none." This principle is founded on the conviction that the long reign of the Congress Party was bolstered by its cynical pandering to religious minorities that divided the nation. The third principle is *swadeshi*, which the BJP's 1998 election manifesto discusses as a pragmatic approach to economic policy guided wholly by consideration of national interests. In the eyes of many BJP supporters, *swadeshi* is closely linked to the party's cultural nationalism. For instance, the July 1997 BJP economic resolution—the last adopted by the BJP's National Executive before the party joined the NDA—criticized "the false slogan of globalisation, the fatal attraction of unrestrained consumerism, the aping of the West, the concern for comfort of the few at the cost of the vast millions, the lurking dangers to our cultural values and the emerging threat to our sovereignty."[23]

The BJP's advocacy of cultural nationalism and positive secularism has led it to support a number of controversial policies. Prominent among these has been its backing of a uniform civil code that would replace the legal protection of customary Islamic and Hindu law in civil affairs with a single code for all citizens. The BJP has also opposed the provisions in Article 370 of the Indian Constitution granting special autonomy to the state of Kashmir—India's only Muslim-majority state. The opposition to these positions among the BJP's allies in the NDA has obliged the party to jettison them. Not only has Prime Minister Atal Bihari Vajpayee given up talk of abolishing Article 370, his government has begun a peace initiative with Muslim leaders that may well lead to even greater autonomy for Kashmir.

With BJP hard-liner Murli Manohar Joshi serving as minister for human resource development, the principles of *hindutva* have made their greatest advances in education and cultural affairs. In November 2000, Joshi announced a national curriculum for schools that was refashioned to promote a better appreciation of aspects of Hindu culture including Vedic sciences, the Upanishads, yoga, and Indian systems of medicine such as Ayurveda. Earlier, Joshi had formed a committee headed by former chief justice J.S. Verma to recommend the fundamental duties of Indian citizens reflecting India's national interests. The committee urged that the fundamental duties be incorporated into the curriculum. Joshi has also succeeded in placing advocates of *hindutva* in the most important senior administrative positions in India's system of higher education, including the heads of the University Grants Commission, the Indian Council of Social Science Research, and the National Council of Educational Research and Training. These officials are overseeing a redistribution of resources in favor of institutions propagating *hindutva*.

Economic Reforms: Incentives and Constraints in India's Decentered Polity

The NDA government has initiated a series of economic reforms in response to the opportunities and challenges presented by globalization. The increasing availability of foreign capital, the expanding opportuni-

---

23. Cited in Harish Khare, "New Economy, Old Pains," *Hindu* (November 29, 2000).

ties presented by foreign trade for economic growth and technological development, the spread of global norms for private and public "best practices," and the growing authority of international institutions such as the World Trade Organization have encouraged India to initiate reforms. The recommendations of a series of government committees and commissions have provided ideas to serve as grist for the reform mill. Nevertheless, coalition politics and the resistance of societal interests, including militant Hindu groups belonging to the Sangh Parivar, have trammeled the NDA's reforms, at times creating a substantial gap between reform rhetoric and reality.

Prime Minister Vajpayee made a series of moves shortly after the BJP-led coalition formed the government in 1998 that have had a formative impact on its economic reforms. Resistance from the RSS obliged Vajpayee to pass over his close associate Jaswant Singh as finance minister and appoint Yashwant Sinha, a relative newcomer to the BJP without a strong political base. When Sinha issued a disappointing first budget on June 1, 1998, and was then forced by political opposition to reverse his proposals to increase petroleum and urea prices, Vajpayee began to look for other channels to promote economic reform. In August 1998, he shifted N.K. Singh from the Ministry of Finance to the Prime Minister's Office (PMO) as secretary. Twelve days after Singh's shift, the PMO announced the formation of the Economic Advisory Council, consisting of ten high-powered, reform-minded economists, and the Council on Trade and Industry, including twelve of the country's leading industrialists. The two councils have been the source of many of the ideas behind the Vajpayee government's economic reforms, and under the stewardship of N.K. Singh and Brajesh Mishra, the high-profile primary secretary to the prime minister, the PMO has been an important agent of economic reform, sometimes alienating government ministries in the process.

The 305-seat Lok Sabha majority that the NDA won in the 1999 elections gave hope that the government would make the difficult decisions necessary for implementing economic reform. Yashwant Sinha's budget for fiscal year 2001–2002 was widely acclaimed for its reform initiatives. The finance minister announced that he had met his target of reducing the government's fiscal deficit from 5.6 percent to 5.1 percent of GDP, and he promised to trim the deficit to 4.7 percent in 2001–2002. Sinha pledged to introduce a second generation of reforms that had previously seemed politically unfeasible. He vowed to amend the Industrial Disputes Act to increase the size of firms permitted to lay off workers without government permission from those with less than 100 employees to those with up to 1,000 employees. At the same time, Sinha promised to increase workers' severance pay from fifteen to forty-five days for every year of employment. The finance minister also urged revision of the Contract Labor Act to facilitate outsourcing and temporary contract hires. Sinha promised to repeal the Sick Industrial Companies Act to make it easier to close down companies. He made a bold pledge to privatize twenty-seven public sector enterprises and earn more than $2.5 billion in the next year. Finally, he won support for extending reforms to the agricultural sector by promising measures to strengthen the institutional structure for rural finance, promote agribusiness, and expand cold storage.

Despite the finance minister's good intentions, the NDA's capacity to deliver many of these economic reforms is questionable. Coalition politics within the alliance poses a formidable problem for efforts to reduce the fiscal deficit. One of the objectives of participating in the NDA for single-state parties is to secure more resources from the central government to assist their efforts in promoting development and building political support. The leaders of these parties are loath to see reductions in subsidies and the budgets of NDA ministries that they control. Some of the most vociferous opposition to the subsidy cuts have come from leaders of important NDA coalition partners such as Chandrababu Naidu. Alliance partners in agricultural states such as Haryana's Om Prakash Chautala and Punjab's Prakash Singh Badal have succeeded in raising minimum support prices for food grains well beyond the recommendations of the Commission on Agricultural Costs and Prices and the Ministries of Agriculture and Food, even as the unprecedented stocks of the Food Corporation of India rot away. The NDA is attempting to fashion a solution to these problems by drawing up the Fiscal Responsibility Act, which would impose mandatory ceilings on the fiscal deficit.

The NDA's ambitious goals for privatization demonstrate other political constraints. In the summer of 1999, it created the Ministry of Disinvestment to put organizational muscle behind its program. Rather than merely selling minority shares to raise revenue as previous governments had, the NDA has offered strategic control over public sector enterprises to firms whose managerial synergies promise to make them more profitable. Despite these changes, progress in privatization has been disappointing. In fiscal year 2000–2001, the NDA succeeded in privatizing at most a quarter of its $2.1 billion objective. Part of the problem is that NDA ministers often oppose the privatization of public sector enterprises under their authority since it means losing control over capital, jobs, and prestige. It is hard enough to gain the acquiescence of ministers when there is a single ruling party, but when control over ministries is divided up among multiple coalition partners, the consequent "not-in-my-backyard" attitude creates even more formidable barriers. The Cabinet Committee on Disinvestment has been convened to make final decisions about privatization, but ministers still succeed in either delaying or overturning the committee's decisions. Communication Minister Ram Vilas Paswan of the Lok Shakti Dal delayed efforts to sell shares of the telecommunications companies VSNL and MTNL before he compelled a reduction in the shares that would be sold. Shiv Sena leader Manohar Joshi has delayed efforts to privatize the automobile giant Maruti Udyog Ltd. Even BJP stalwart Ram Naik, as minister of petroleum and natural gas, has repeatedly resisted the privatization of the oil companies Indo-Burmah Petroleum and Indian Oil Corporation. The leaders of single-state parties outside the government resist the privatization of local plants in order to limit austerity in their local economies. Chandrababu Naidu may be a big promoter of reform in his state, but he single-handedly forced the government to postpone disinvestment of Rashtriya Ispat Nigam Ltd., a central-government-owned steel company based in his state.

The resistance of labor and opposition parties presents another barrier to privatization. On March 2, 2001, the NDA struck a deal to sell 51 percent of Bharat Aluminum Company Ltd. (Balco) to Sterlite Industries for Rs. 5.5 billion. Seven thousand workers at Balco's production facility in the state of Chattisgarh immediately went on strike to protest the sale and prevent the new management from operating the plant. The BJP's own labor federation, the Bharatiya Mazdoor Sangh, joined the strike, and its leader, Dattopant Thengadi, condemned the sale of Balco as "fraud committed by bureaucrats." Ajit Jogi, the Congress Party chief minister of Chattisgarh, charged that the NDA had grossly undervalued Balco as the result of bribes to central government officials. Jogi proposed that Chattisgarh purchase Balco on the same terms as Sterlite. The NDA rejected his offer. The matter became even more complicated when SEBI ruled that Sterlite was involved in insider trading and price manipulation. It barred the company from raising funds from India's capital markets. A May 8, 2001, Supreme Court decision finally brought the parties together for a compromise. Nevertheless, the difficulties of privatizing Balco dramatize the political problems of privatization through strategic sales. In some cases, the government may try to avoid the controversies over corporate favoritism and insufficient valuation of public sector equity through public sale of equity, as it decided to do in June 2001 in the case of the Shipping Corporation of India.

March 31, 2001, was a landmark for Indian trade policy as Commerce Minister Murasoli Maran announced the elimination of quantitative restrictions on the import of 715 commodities and thereby ended all quantitative controls on imports. India is one of the last countries to end quantitative restrictions. Its fears that imports would overwhelm the politically powerful agricultural and small-scale industry sectors were finally overcome by its commitment to the World Trade Organization and negotiations with the United States leading to a trade agreement that was signed during President Clinton's visit in March 2000. Shortly after the signing of this agreement, Indian industrialists began to complain about an influx of cheaply priced Chinese imports. The government responded to the outcry by initiating antidumping investigations against Chinese sports shoes, toys, and dry-cell batteries. It imposed the requirement that Chinese imports secure Bureau of Indian Standards certification and mark all products with retail prices. The government also conducted raids across the country and confiscated Chinese goods that failed to meet the requirements. The new export-import policy announced by the commerce minister includes further safeguards for Indian producers. Maran announced that he would create a "war room" to monitor imports of 300 sensitive items in order to protect Indian producers from dumping. He also created other nontariff barriers by requiring that all imports of sensitive commodities such as rice, wheat, urea, and petroleum products be conducted by state trading corporations and restricting the import of automobiles to India to the port of Mumbai (formerly known as Bombay). Maran's ambitious target that India reach 1 percent of world trade in 2004 by increasing exports 18 percent annually demonstrates the NDA's commitment to further opening of the Indian economy. Domestic politics has made it a plodding process, but resistance has diminished as the economic opening weakens its opponents and strengthens its supporters.

Telecommunications Reform: Favoritism or Flexibility?

India's rapidly growing telecommunications sector has seen dramatic policy changes in the last few years. A history of public sector monopoly and a major scandal involving kickbacks by private sector equipment and service providers who entered basic and cellular services after early reforms provide the backdrop to the recent changes. Expensive licensing fees and the continued privileges of the Department of Telecommunications—the public sector service provider—resulted in huge losses for private sector companies. By 1999, the cellular phone industry was losing $92 million every month, and it and the six private sector firms licensed for basic services owed almost $900 million in license fees.[24]

It was at this point that the PMO intervened, in part because the Department of Telecommunications, with its immense economic interest in the sector, proved to be an ineffective agent of change, but also in response to the lobby of many of India's most powerful corporations that had entered the sector. The PMO's push for telecom reform began with the December 1998 recommendations of a subcommittee of the Council on Trade and Industry headed by Ratan Tata. In August 1999, the PMO enunciated a new telecommunications policy similar to these recommendations. It alleviated the losses of private sector firms by allowing them to shift from licensing fees to revenue sharing. The Vajpayee government also split the Department of Telecommunications into smaller functional units. On August 15, 2000, the government opened domestic long-distance service to the private sector, though existing basic service providers retained exclusive long-distance rights within their regional domains on the dubious grounds that to open up short-haul long-distance service would diminish incentives to expand services to the "rural masses."

During the fall of 2000, the PMO organized several meetings at which it was decided to support policy changes to permit basic providers to use "wireless in local loop" (WiLL) technology to provide limited wireless service within their jurisdictions even though implementing the measure would undercut the 1999 telecom policy's exclusive allotment of wireless telephone service to cellular companies. On January 8, 2001, a reorganized Telecom Regulatory Authority of India, under new chairman M.S. Verma, reversed its June 1999 rejection of WiLL technology and recommended that WiLL be introduced. On January 27, 2001, Telecom Minister Ram Vilas Paswan announced that basic producers would be allowed to use WiLL technology to provide limited wireless service and that the basic service sector would be opened to all providers. The new policy benefits companies, such as Reliance Industries,

---

24. The data in this paragraph come from Pradipta Bagchi, *Telecommunications Reform and the State in India: The Contradiction of Private Control and Government Competition*, CASI Occasional Paper, no. 13 (Philadelphia: University of Pennsylvania, 2000).

that are aggressively expanding into basic services. It incited an uproar from the powerful Cellular Operators Association of India, whose leaders appealed to the prime minister to review the decision. Vajpayee referred the matter to his cabinet's Group of Ministers on Telecom and Information Technology. The group recommended a compromise that satisfied no one. The dramatic policy changes in the competitive and rapidly growing $3-billion sector have incited allegations that the government favors some industrialists over others. At the same time, the changes demonstrate that the government is capable of remarkable flexibility in order to improve its policies.

The March 2001 Tehelka scandal increased the challenges that India's decentered polity presents to the NDA. Two investigative reporters for a nine-month-old Internet magazine, Tehelka.com, posed as defense merchants and made video recordings of Bangaru Laxman, the president of the BJP, taking an apparent bribe. They also recorded Jaya Jaitley, the president of the Samata Party, taking money in the living room of defense minister and NDA convenor George Fernandes. In the ensuing uproar, Laxman, Jaitley, and Fernandes were obliged to resign from their positions. Opposition parties, NDA allies, and Hindu militant organizations also attacked the PMO's Brajesh Mishra, who was prominently mentioned in the tapes, and N.K. Singh for their alleged links to Indian corporations. Singh was later transferred to the Planning Commission. In the wake of the scandal, the Congress Party adopted more confrontational tactics against the NDA. Relations among NDA allies have been strained as key partners, including the TDP and Shiv Sena, have shunned rallies organized by the BJP to build support against the vehement Congress attacks. Facing elections in her West Bengal base in less than two months, Mamata Banerjee withdrew her Trinamool Congress from the NDA; however, the move failed to pay off, and her party fared poorly in the May 2001 elections. The 262 members of Parliament whose parties continued with the NDA government retained a parliamentary majority only with the support of the twenty-nine members of Parliament from the Telugu Desam Party, which remained outside the government.

Conclusion

This chapter has described the process of decentering that has prevailed in the party system and state institutions that constitute the Indian polity. No longer is the power in India's party system concentrated in the Congress Party, as it was for India's first forty years. Instead it is widely dispersed among a diverse array of parties, an increasing number of which have power bases confined to single states. The transformation of the party system has occurred at a time when globalization has incited a decentralization of power by creating incentives for a transition from *dirigisme* to regulation. Instead of intervening to dictate market outcomes, the state regulates the procedures of market institutions and consequently enables greater private sector autonomy. This transformation has begun to redistribute power from government ministries to independent regulatory agencies and private sector firms.

The decentering of power in India's political system has created greater flux in Indian politics than at any other time since independence. The end of Congress Party domination, the rise of single-state parties, the differentiation of state party systems, the diffusion of power across central government institutions, and the relative increase in the autonomy and power of state governments mean that partisan strategy is increasingly determined at the state rather than the national level. National parties must be increasingly sensitive to variations among the states if they are to fashion winning national strategies. Single-state parties generally give primacy to state rather than national considerations even when they serve as key players at the national level. Their strategic decisions increase the fluidity of Indian politics. Parties such as the Telugu Desam and the Trinamool Congress aligned with the BJP to gain leverage over central government resources and improve their prospects against their local rivals. The Trinamool Congress split with the NDA because the Tehelka scandal threatened to undermine its prospects in the May 2001 West Bengal elections.

Governance in India's decentered polity requires new forms of political coordination. For India's first forty years, coordination largely occurred within the Congress Party. Now it must take place across a much more diverse range of parties and institutions. The NDA's preelection alliance and common manifesto have resolved some coordination problems. The central government must also find ways to coordinate the policies of increasingly assertive state governments in a range of policy domains requiring the cooperation of the states. The Vajpayee government's unprecedented use of the PMO and an estimated thirty-five cabinet committees has helped to resolve the coordination problems presented by the twenty-five-party coalition government. By overcoming cabinet ministers' resistance to reform, making use of the expertise of leaders in the private sector, and promoting solutions to problems that transcend ministerial boundaries, the PMO offers a valuable instrument of governance. At the same time, serious questions have been raised about the undue influence over the PMO of some of the most powerful corporations in India. Even if the government remains above the entreaties of individual firms, the increasing activism of corporate India and the preponderantly elite nature of the BJP's political support may lead the government to neglect the changes in education, public health, and infrastructure that are necessary for widespread participation in the benefits of reform. The challenge of India's decentered polity is to create effective mechanisms of political coordination that are democratically accountable.

The Indian Economy: Pushing Ahead and Pulling Apart

Joydeep Mukherji

India's economy will become more prosperous and more diverse in the coming years. Economic liberalization during the last decade has progressed in tandem with a loosening of the once tightly centralized political system, setting the stage for bigger gaps in economic performance between different regions of the country and between different sectors of the economy. The extent to which India benefits from more internal competition in markets, ideas, and the policies of its various levels of government will depend on the flexibility of its institutions and on the quality of its political and economic leadership. Failure to manage growing economic divergence and regional differences could place great strain on the country's democratic institutions. India's more than one billion people are becoming more aware that they are behind other countries in progress and development, and thus more impatient for change.

India's economic policies remained remarkably insulated from global trends until quite recently. After independence in 1947, the country embarked upon a domestically oriented growth strategy that downplayed the role of foreign trade and promoted industries sheltered behind high trade barriers. The strategy ignored exports and was based on "a misidentification of foreign trade with imperialism and of free trade with the failure of colonial authorities to promote industrialization."[1] The following decades saw record growth in world trade volumes, which benefited other Asian exporting countries such as Korea and Taiwan but had no impact on Indian economic strategy. Nor did the success of outward-oriented economies in the 1980s, such as those of Thailand,

---

1. T.N. Srinivasan, *Eight Lectures on India's Economic Reforms* (New Delhi: Oxford University Press, 2000), 223.

Malaysia, and Indonesia, based on active promotion of the private sector and attraction of foreign investment into export sectors, have much impact. India continued to restrict its private sector, maintain the highest trade barriers outside the communist world, and ban foreign investment in most sectors. The remarkable success of China's economic reform, which started in 1978, also had little impact, at least until recently.

India's splendid economic isolation from global trade and its pursuit of unsustainable economic policies, bolstered by foreign loans, led it to the verge of defaulting on its foreign debt in 1991. Since then, successive governments have undertaken gradual reform to expand the role of market forces in the economy, lowering trade barriers and largely abolishing the earlier system of industrial licensing and detailed control over the business decisions of the private sector.[2] Prior to the reform, India's twenty-nine state governments had limited ability to attract either private or public investment other than through lobbying in Delhi. Liberalization has begun to remove politics from business decisions. It has enhanced the importance of state governments in setting policies to attract private investment. Policy competition among state governments has been complemented by intensifying competition within most industries and by growing foreign competition as India has lowered its barriers to trade and foreign investment. The level of competition in the marketplace, as well as in the policies of state governments, will only intensify in the coming years. This offers the best hope that India's private and public institutions, which largely ignored the lessons from other successful Asian economies, will learn from their own experiences. As a result, they may become more flexible, more responsive, and more able to generate the wealth that India sorely lacks.

The Results of Reform

The size of India's economy, as measured by gross national product (GNP), reached $442 billion in 1999, making it the eleventh biggest in the world. On a per capita basis, though, GNP was only $450, or 162nd in the world. Using purchasing power parity (adjusting the nominal numbers for the purchasing power of Indians who buy goods and services in their own currency at domestic prices), India emerges as the world's

---

2. The background and objectives of the reform are described by Kirit S. Parikh in "Economy," in *India Briefing: A Transformative Fifty Years*, eds Marshall Bouton and Philip Oldenburg (Armonk, NY: M.E. Sharpe, 1999).

fourth-largest economy, behind the United States, China, and Japan. Following the same adjustment, per capita GNP rises to $2,149, which is still 153rd globally.[3]

India's economic performance since the beginning of reform in the early 1990s is impressive when compared with its own past but is still well below its potential. Economic growth during the postreform era has averaged 6.5 percent annually, compared with 5.8 percent during the 1980s. While the increase may appear marginal, it is based on better economic underpinnings. The growth of the 1980s relied heavily on external borrowing, with foreign debt rising to around $80 billion from $20 billion over the decade. Failure to restructure the economy and boost its productivity left India vulnerable in 1991 when high oil prices led to a balance of payments crisis. Subsequently, growth has been based more on domestic liberalization that has enhanced the role of the private sector.

Reform introduced competition by easing restrictions on domestic and foreign business, as well as on rules for foreign direct investment. The number of industries "reserved" for public sector enterprises was gradually cut to three (defense, atomic energy, and railway transport). Government licensing for businesses was reduced to only six strategic, social, and environmentally sensitive sectors. Barriers to foreign trade were reduced. The weighted average tariff for imports was cut to around 30 percent at the end of the decade from 128 percent in 1991. Nontariff barriers to imports, such as licensing requirements and quotas, were gradually reduced, with the last quotas abolished in April 2001.

Deregulation and greater autonomy for the Indian private sector led to higher growth and a marked improvement in the quality of domestic goods and services. India began to belatedly open its economy to the international market. As a result, merchandise exports and imports in total rose to 21 percent of gross domestic product (GDP) in fiscal year 1999 (which ended on March 31, 2000) from 15.6 percent in fiscal year 1990. India's current account balance, which includes trade in goods and services but excludes lending and foreign investment, remained within a modest deficit of below 2 percent of GDP during the 1990s, compared with a peak of 3.1 percent of GDP in fiscal year 1990 and around 2.5 percent of GDP in the late 1980s. Foreign direct investment

---

3. World Bank, *World Development Report 2000* (Washington, DC: Oxford University Press, 2000), table 1.

has approached $3 billion annually in recent years, compared with an average $200 million in 1985–91. That, plus foreign investment in Indian stock and debt markets, provided foreign exchange to pay for the current account deficit and reduced the need for external borrowing. It also helped boost India's foreign exchange reserves above $40 billion in 2001 (compared with just $1 billion in June 1991).

The private sector, including both firms and households, saved more of its income during the first decade of reform and increased its investment. India's domestic savings rate, a measure of the total financial and nonfinancial resources that are available for investment, rose marginally during the decade to average nearly 24 percent of GDP. Growing government budget deficits meant that private firms and households were responsible for almost the entire amount of domestic savings in the country by fiscal year 1998. Better economic policies helped raise the level of domestic investment to almost 25 percent of GDP during the decade (the gap between the domestic investment rate and savings rate reflects foreign savings injected into the economy). In recent years, almost two-thirds of domestic investment has come from the private sector.

The economy benefited from more investment and, more important, from better investment. Growth was based on higher efficiency. For example, the incremental capital output ratio, a measure of the amount of capital invested each year compared with the increase in total output, fell from 4.4 in 1990 to 3.4 in 1998, according to the Reserve Bank of India.[4] This was largely due to better productivity in the service sector, which uses less capital. The World Bank estimates that total factor productivity, the increase in output that exceeds the amount that can be attributed to added use of labor, capital, and other inputs, grew about 1.3–1.5 percent annually for the period 1979–97. The same measure is estimated to have grown at a higher rate of 2.4–2.8 percent during 1994–96, indicating an increase in later years due to reform.[5]

The positive impact of reform and deregulation was reflected in the greater economic dynamism that resulted from more competition. Within a couple of years after the sector was opened to competition, private

4. Reserve Bank of India, *Annual Report 1999–2000* (Mumbai: Reserve Bank of India, 2000), 18.
5. World Bank, *India: Policies to Reduce Poverty and Accelerate Sustainable Growth* (Washington, DC: World Bank, January 31, 2000), 130.

firms accounted for around half the traffic in domestic air travel. Government-owned ports faced new competition from private and foreign investors who entered into new ports in the states of Gujarat and Andhra Pradesh and expanded existing facilities in Maharashtra. The auto industry, once dominated by two companies, now has nearly a dozen firms producing a wider range of better-quality vehicles. Similar changes have transformed the consumer electronics and many other sectors.

Competition has begun to force India's previously sluggish and cosseted business firms to restructure their operations. This is reflected in part in growing mergers and acquisitions. A new code for companies seeking to take over other companies was introduced in 1997, and the first successful hostile takeover was accomplished in 1998. The value of mergers and acquisitions more than doubled to $9.2 billion in 2000, with foreign companies and their local subsidiaries accounting for less than half of this value, unlike in the previous year. Much of the activity was in the cement, telecommunications, and engineering sectors, where deregulation has forced firms to acquire larger production capacities to reduce unit costs. Consolidation is especially evident in the cement industry, which has been forced to cut costs, raise production, and create efficient, modern plants that enjoy economies of scale. Cement output rose 50 percent during 1995–2000 as firms undid the overdiversification of business lines that was a legacy of the licensing era.

The impact of reform was also felt in the once tightly controlled and government-dominated financial market. Companies found new sources of fund-raising as capital markets grew and new lenders and investors emerged. Previously, firms had to rely largely on government-controlled banks and other financial institutions, as well as on a heavily regulated stock market in which the government had to approve all new listings. Capital market reform helped boost the market value of Indian stocks nearly 500 percent during the period 1990–99 to reach $184 billion, while the number of listed companies more than doubled to over 5,800. Many old firms lost their dominant positions in the more competitive environment to rising new firms. Nearly half the companies listed in the top 100 in terms of stock market capitalization (the market price of all the company's listed shares) in 1990 had dropped off that list by 1998, often replaced by firms that had not existed a decade earlier. Estimates by India's National Council for Applied Economic Research suggest that nearly 8 percent of Indian households own shares or debentures and that 23 million Indians have invested in mutual funds. Capital market development has been complemented by the gradual entry of new Indian private sector and foreign banks into the government-dominated lending business. Private sector banks now hold 20 percent of total deposits, compared with around 11 percent in 1992. They have successfully targeted the more lucrative segment of the consumer market, as well as businesses that seek to lower their costs through new financial products and the use of better technology to manage financial transactions. India's financial markets are no longer the exclusive domain of large domestic businesses and government officials.

Despite the improvement, India's economy remains weak. Economic reform has improved the condition of the private sector and given Indians a sense that prosperity is possible. Nevertheless, it has neglected to address the serious problems of India's large public sector. Successive governments have failed utterly to reduce the country's large budget deficit. As a result, India's economic path is still not entirely sustainable, since the diminished reliance on external debt, which grew by only $20 billion during the 1990s, has been offset by heavy domestic borrowing by all levels of government. The total debt of India's state and national governments stands at around 66 percent of GDP. Interest payments on the central government's own debt consume just under half of its total revenues, one of the highest percentages among countries with a sovereign credit rating. The combined budget deficit of the state and national governments has hovered around 10 percent of GDP in recent years, about the same as in 1990, when India nearly defaulted on its external debt. Just over half the deficit is at the central government level, but the states' combined budget deficit has been rising in recent years.

The long-term impact of budget deficits depends, in part, on how productively the money is spent. Unfortunately, a rising share of government spending has been devoted to current expenditure, not to investment that might generate revenues in the future or improve the country's long-term growth prospects. About 82 percent of state government expenditures are devoted to current spending, mainly for salaries, subsidies, pensions, and interest payments. As a result, states are unable to invest in providing better infrastructure, as well as health care and education for their citizens. Large government deficits and falling public investment dilute the sustainability of recent economic growth by failing to strengthen the pillars of future growth.

The Politics of Reform

India has proceeded more slowly with its economic reform than China and many Latin American countries. To a large extent, the slow pace reflects the failure of India's political leadership, cutting across all parties, to build a strong consensus in favor of difficult but necessary changes in policy. Reform and liberalization were thrust upon India's political class because of a balance of payments crisis. In the words of one analyst, "The fact that reform has been driven by bankruptcy more than ideology has consequences. Politicians have moved towards the market more in confused sorrow than ideological triumph."[6] India's politicians and bureaucrats, along with many other people who influence policy, did not decisively reject the old economic model by embarking on reform. Rather, they sought to fix it. In that sense, India's failure to build stable macroeconomic foundations for future growth, by correcting unsustainable budget deficits and the ensuing rise in government debt, is a political failure.

The initial goal of reform was to stabilize the economy to avoid a default on external debt. Subsequently, the government moved to change the basic parameters of the economy. Gradually, a consensus emerged on the benefits of reform and on measures to boost private sector autonomy and economic growth. Thanks to four national elections during the last decade, dozens of India's political parties, ranging from national parties such as the Bharatiya Janata Party and the Congress Party to almost all the smaller regional and caste-based parties, including communists, have been in government. All parties explicitly or implicitly endorsed liberalization while in office, though not always while in opposition. Over time, political momentum has increased for creating a very different economy based on market forces. Political disputes are no longer over whether to reform but over the pace and strategy of reform. However, the weak political impulse behind economic reform continues to constrain its pace.

The slow pace of reform in India, compared with its pace in dictatorships such as China or in many democracies in Latin America during the 1990s, reflects genuine disagreement within the country and the complexities of changing policies within a vibrantly democratic federal state.

---

6. Swaminathan S.A. Aiyar, *India's Economic Prospects: The Promise of Services*, CASI Occasional Paper, no. 9 (Philadelphia: University of Pennsylvania, 1999), 5.

Unlike in China, reform in India did not result in a burst of success in agriculture or in any other large sector that could create a formidable political constituency for further liberalization and encourage the country's leadership to proceed faster. Though poverty has decreased in recent years, the decline has not been sufficient to generate substantial political support for a more rapid pace of reform, nor did reform emerge after a period of hyperinflation that seriously undermined public support for previous policies, as in Argentina and Brazil. Moreover, it was not India's fate to be led during the 1990s by prime ministers with a clear vision on economic matters. Finally, issues of caste and communal identity, not economic policy, dominated politics during the decade.

Economic reform has not been a major public issue during recent elections. A growing section of India's urban population supports reform because of its direct benefits for the members of this group. Many of them also perceive that reform is good for the country as a whole and is needed for India to catch up to the industrialized world. Many, if not most, Indians do not translate their discontent with a low standard of living into support for economic liberalization. For example, 47 percent of those polled by the magazine *India Today* in early 2001 felt that nonperforming public sector enterprises should not be sold, while only 34 percent were in favor of privatizing them.[7] According to polls conducted during the 1996 elections, less than 20 percent of the electorate had any knowledge of economic reform, compared with the 90 percent who held an opinion on the issue of job and education quotas based on caste.[8]

Awareness has undoubtedly increased since then but is still likely low, partly because political parties do not campaign on clear differences in economic ideology. Major politicians and parties do not define themselves by economic policies; hence, electoral identities do not coincide with economic views, and divisions within parties on economic issues are often far deeper than divisions between them. As a result, there is neither strong political support in India for deep reform nor widespread opposition against it. Over time, however, economic reform is becoming less of an elite concern. Public recognition of the need to make painful decisions affecting the government's own finances, as well as those of the companies it runs, will likely grow, though slowly.

---

7. *India Today* (New Delhi), January 5, 2001.
8. Yogendra Yadav and Y.B. Singh, "Maturing of a Democracy," *India Today*, August 15, 1996.

The change in mind-set has been very slow. Reform started with public sector monopolies and heavily regulated and licensed private sector firms. The government has moved from direct control over different sectors of the economy toward indirect control through new regulatory bodies, such as the Securities and Exchange Board of India, the Telecommunications Regulatory Authority of India, the Tariff Authority for Major Ports, the Central Electricity Regulatory Commission and its state-level counterparts, and the Insurance Regulatory and Development Authority. Political interference, poorly drafted laws, and a general reluctance to cede control have slowed the process, but it cannot be reversed. Organized labor has typically opposed reform, with very few exceptions, fearing that deregulation and privatization would result in the loss of its own political power. The prospect of job losses in a country with no formal social safety net also constrains the pace of labor and industrial reform.

The weak political impulse behind reform has often allowed the bureaucracy to undermine measures that threaten to erode its discretionary authority. Despite liberalization, the government continues to discourage competition in areas opened to the private sector by creating new entry barriers and restrictions. For example, until recently the Department of Telecommunications successfully and openly defied official government policy by undermining all attempts at opening the telecommunications sector to private participation. For several years, it used every administrative and legal method possible to restrict the powers of the new regulatory body designed to set telecommunications tariffs and fix conditions for service providers. The growing unaccountability of the bureaucracy, including senior officials, allowed the department to ignore the political consensus in the country in favor of opening the sector to private firms. While a dramatic personal intervention by the prime minister in mid-2000 finally pushed the reform ahead, the department (along with its successor entities) clings to its old ways. Similar to other departments and ministries facing the loss of direct control over their economic fiefdoms, it continues to find ways to restrict the number of firms allowed to enter a newly deregulated field. The bureaucracy, sometimes in cooperation with large domestic firms and politicians who have been funded by them, continues to create high entry barriers, such as huge up-front payments for licenses and high and typically meaningless thresholds for minimum net worth for eligible companies, along with numerous and cumbersome approvals for routine business decisions. The effect has been to preclude greater competition; assist large Indian, and sometimes foreign, companies; and preserve the discretionary powers of bureaucrats and politicians.

Despite these obstacles, both the political consensus behind reform and the momentum behind liberalization policies should strengthen in the coming years. India has a sophisticated political class that governs through well-developed formal and informal institutions. Its tactics range from public advocacy of specific reform measures to reform by stealth and compromise with powerful opponents. Political leaders at all levels have skillfully used tactics of "divide and rule," outright obfuscation, threats, and enticements as well as open advocacy to pursue reform within the country's complex but functioning democracy.[9]

Reform has often proceeded with small steps that weaken, but do not seriously hurt, powerful opposing interest groups while slowly nurturing new interest groups that stand to benefit from deeper measures. Initial cuts in trade barriers, for example, gradually created a business lobby in favor of trade liberalization to counterbalance other industrialists that opposed them. The provision of a generous voluntary retirement plan to public sector bank employees, along with other measures to increase the level of competition from private sector banks, has gradually weakened trade union resistance to reform. Such tactics have, in some industries, moderated labor's opposition to privatization. With skillful political manipulation and incremental change, "the incentives thrown up by economic reform can result in unpredictable political realignments."[10]

Maintaining the political sustainability of reform will constrain its pace. Politicians will seek new sources of illicit income as old ones disappear through liberalization. Spending on elections and on maintaining patronage networks forces all Indian politicians to raise vastly more money than is permitted under India's unworkable campaign finance laws. Politicians and bureaucrats may firmly believe that all important, and most unimportant, decisions must receive their approval, but the growing middle class and the increasingly influential media think otherwise. Perhaps more important, reform will continue because no party or group has offered any alternative solution to India's economic problems. Finally, reform in many sectors, including privatization, will be compelled by the growing financial distress of India's central and state governments.

9. Rob Jenkins, *Democratic Politics and Economic Reform in India* (Cambridge: Cambridge University Press, 1999).

10. Ibid., 73.

Competition and Regional Differentiation

The economic performance of India's different regions and states, and of its different industries, will diverge more in the coming years as liberalization proceeds. Some states and municipalities will prosper more than others. Several states have already taken advantage of their newfound ability to pursue policies promoting private investment and economic growth, while others hesitate or advance timidly. Similar differences are likely to emerge in the rural local governments that all states are supposed to establish on a sound footing in the coming years. Added to that, the private sector is likely to perform better than the public sector in terms of expanding output and creating new jobs, although large pockets of the private sector may suffer from growing competition. India's financial sector will also become more diverse, with efficient modern institutions with first-rate technology and good management competing with crippled public sector institutions beset with political handicaps.

Such differences may seem only normal in a country with over a billion people, various distinct regions, and diverse social and cultural traditions. Nevertheless, the gap in performance will create political and institutional tensions in a country that is still emerging from its centralized tradition since independence. Fiscal policy, especially the sharing of tax revenues between the central and state governments, as well as between different states, will become more politicized. These differences will become apparent to all Indians, not just the elite.

Will such divergence in economic performance and in policies help or hurt the country? The answer depends on how India's public and private institutions, its leadership, and its voters react. States may try to emulate successful policies in other states or try to block reform by intervening at the national level. A bigger, more dynamic and productive private sector could encourage politicians to tackle the sensitive issue of public sector reform or serve as an excuse to ignore the problem. Public policy will determine how institutions respond to the new environment of greater competition and more autonomy. For example, without fiscal accountability, competition among the states could result in disastrous budget deficits and potential debt defaults. Conversely, fiscal decentralization accompanied by proper incentives that make states more responsible for their own financial fate could lead to better public finances. Greater competition could spur the banks to improve their performance and raise profitability. However, failure to reform the weak public sector banks and strengthen regulatory and prudential standards could lead some of them to make reckless lending decisions based on the expectation that the government will always be ready to bail them out. Similarly, cutting trade barriers should hasten India's integration into the world economy, lower costs, improve the quality of goods and services available to consumers and businesses, and boost income. However, the introduction of more competition from abroad without improving the country's poor infrastructure, especially in electricity production, could keep domestic production costs high while imports become cheaper, handicapping local producers.

States

India's twenty-nine state governments will increasingly shape its economic future. Many of the states are bigger than most countries (the largest, Uttar Pradesh, would be the fifth most populous country in the world on its own). Under India's federal constitution, states hold either exclusive or shared responsibility in most of the sectors that are crucial for development and prosperity. For example, states account for around 85 percent of all public spending on education and 75 percent on health. Moreover, they are largely responsible for providing irrigation, building rural roads, and supplying electricity. As the central government proceeds gradually in reforming trade, fiscal, and financial sector policy, the focus of reform will shift more toward the states. This will create new challenges since state governments are still by and large less capable than the central government of providing competent management, with some exceptions. Bureaucratic red tape and corruption are just as bad or worse at the state level.

A recent study provides the dimensions of the growing diversity among the states.[11] Based on fourteen major states that account for 95 percent of the population, the results indicate that the disparity in economic growth rates at the state level widened during the 1990s. Per capita GDP grew in the range of 2.1–3.9 percent across the states during the 1980s but between 1.1 percent and 7.6 percent during the 1990s (see figure 1). Among the six poorest states (as measured by the percentage of the population below the poverty line in 1994), the mean GDP growth rate remained 2.9 percent during both periods. For the richer states, how-

---

11. M.S. Ahluwalia, "The Economic Performance of the States: A Disaggregated View," Twelfth NCAER Golden Jubilee Lecture, New Delhi, January 12, 2000.

Figure 1

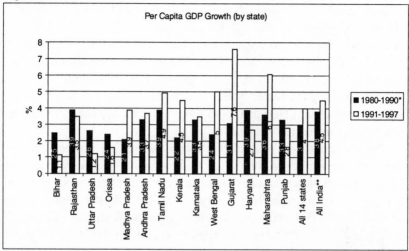

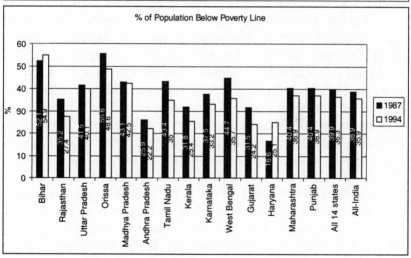

* Refers to fiscal year ending on March 31 of subsequent year.
** All-India per capita GDP growth figures for 1980-91 and 1992-97.
Note: Data for Punjab includes Haryana.
Source: M.S. Ahluwalia, "The Economic Performance of the States: A Disaggregated View," Twelfth NCAER Golden Jubilee Lecture, New Delhi, January 12, 2000, Table 4.

ever, the mean growth rate rose to 4.3 percent from 3.2 percent. Nationally, economic growth accelerated during the 1990s, but it actually decelerated in seven states. Some states have been booming like the newly industrializing countries of East and Southeast Asia. For example, the economies of the coastal states of Maharashtra and Gujarat grew at an astonishing 8 percent and 9.6 percent, respectively, during 1991–97. Alarmingly, India's two biggest states, Uttar Pradesh and Bihar (prior to the creation of two new states carved out of them in 2000), suffered the lowest per capita growth. Although growth rates diverged, the richest did not always grow faster. The two richest states in the decade prior to reform, Punjab and Haryana, both grew more slowly than the national average in the postreform period.

The pattern of growth reflects many factors but increasingly depends on the quality of state-level leadership and its ability to provide public infrastructure. Better governance attracts more investment from the private sector, which is likely to assume a larger share of total investment in the country in the coming years. With more liberalization, policies will be more important than political lobbying in directing investment and creating new jobs. For example, some states have taken the lead in overhauling their bankrupt electricity boards, which typically provide power at low or no cost while racking up huge losses. As of 2000, only fourteen states had taken the first step toward reform by establishing electricity regulatory commissions. Only six had begun to restructure their power sectors, separating the generation, transmission, and distribution tasks into separate entities, setting power rates on a nonpolitical basis, and facilitating the private sector investment that is needed to expand capacity. With national electricity demand estimated to exceed supply by 10–20 percent, the benefits of electricity reform will be immense to the handful of states that first overcome their power shortage and provide reliable power to new industries as well as to households. Successful energy reform in a few states could seriously divert the flow of new investment away from the laggards, unless they respond quickly. The ability to provide a better level of public infrastructure, including roads, ports, and airports, will play a bigger role in shaping economic growth across India's different regions and states.

Many states have gone further than the national government in opening their economies to the private sector. Some, such as Gujarat, have developed good working relationships between potential investors and the state bureaucracy in order to reduce the delays and the obstacles that typically plague all business ventures in India. Gujarat, along with Andhra Pradesh, has been a leader in attracting private investment into new ports.

Some states have quietly privatized more of their public sector enterprises than the central government has. For example, the poor and badly governed state of Bihar had sold three sugar mills to the private sector by 2000, while the central government had managed to sell only one bakery. Andhra Pradesh has taken the lead in introducing information technology (IT) into governance, linking state government offices electronically and delivering government services through the Internet. Ironically, one of the most effective uses of IT has been quick provision of the certificate that attests to an individual's caste affiliation through local offices throughout the state, an essential document in getting employment and education benefits. Some state chief ministers favor private investment in new colleges and schools for IT training to benefit industries in their own states, while others remain opposed because of the hostility of local bureaucrats and teachers' unions. As with power reform, some states will be better able to utilize Internet and electronic communications to wire up government offices, place data such as land records on-line, hasten decision making, and increase transparency. As a result, they are likely to attract more investment and create faster economic growth.

Policy differences at the state level are already reflected at the national level, where regional political parties enjoy power through coalition governments. Proreform coalitions between state leaders and some national leaders may become more common in the future to battle opponents of reform within the national government, as well as in other political parties and domestic lobbies. For example, the chief minister of Andhra Pradesh, Chandrababu Naidu, played an instrumental role in implementing recent policies to allow Indian IT companies greater access to international communications networks, opening the telecommunications sector to competition and private investment. The state leader worked with Prime Minister Vajpayee and a few ministers in Delhi to overcome the opposition of bureaucrats, ideologues within the Bharatiya Janata Party, and unions to change national policies.

The growing importance of state governments, and their need for more resources, is generating greater tension in the allocation of national government revenues. Every five years the central government appoints a finance commission to recommend changes in the formula governing the transfer of revenues to the states. Following the report of the eleventh such commission in 2000, several of the more developed states, including Andhra Pradesh, Kerala, Tamil Nadu, and Maharashtra, formally protested the commission's formula. The proposed formula still gives more money to states with more poverty, faster population growth, poorer public finances, and worse physical infrastructure. The principle of transferring more to those who are in the worst position clashes with the principle of rewarding those states that have made an effort to improve their financial and social performance. The allocation is based on measures of policy failure more than on success, as low income and high population growth merit more central transfers. The transfer formula appears more just in a centralized system in which states have little ability to influence events, but, with more local autonomy, it has now become a negative incentive. Political wrangling over transfers is likely to intensify as regional parties in Delhi pursue agendas based on their states' needs. In that regard, it is worth noting that Uttar Pradesh and Bihar (including the new states carved out of both in 2000) have the largest contingent in the national parliament and have among the weakest of state governments.

The divergence in policies and economic performance goes below the level of states to include local governments, whose role was strengthened by the seventy-third and seventy-fourth amendments to the Constitution in 1992. The amendments enhanced the powers of states along with those of urban municipalities and rural governing bodies called *panchayats*. States retain discretion over which powers and responsibilities will be transferred to or shared with local governments. As a result, there will be more divergence across states in the level of devolution of power to local authorities as states implement decentralization. States are supposed to set up their own finance commissions composed of experts to recommend the details of financial devolution. Over time, local governments are likely to assume more responsibility in primary health care, education, and rural employment schemes. The effectiveness of local governments will vary across states, since most of their money will come from financially weak state governments with little cash to spare. Some states, such as Kerala and West Bengal, have more-developed *panchayat* systems, while others are less able to deliver services through local governments.

Trends Within Public Enterprises and the Private Sector

The gaps in performance between states will be complemented by a gap between the public and private sectors. The contrast between the dynamism of the private sector and the sluggishness of the public sector is indicated by the rapid success of the private cable television industry, which has connected around 25 million viewers just in the last few years. This exceeds the number of taxpayers in India and just about equals the number of telephones provided by public sector enterprises during the last fifty-three years.

Public sector firms are typically overstaffed, while private firms in the "organized" (i.e., formally registered and documented) sector are reluctant to hire more workers owing to archaic labor laws. Cumbersome restrictions on hiring and firing raise the cost of labor relative to capital, inducing firms to substitute capital for labor in a country with over a billion people and mass unemployment. Total employment in the organized sector, including both the public and private sectors, grew less than 1 percent during the 1990s despite per capita GDP growth of around 4 percent.[12] Much of the added output came from firms using "contract" labor or other methods to contain the number of full-time workers on their official payroll. The contrast between the formal sector and the much larger informal sector, which is largely bereft of legal and regulatory protection, can be stark. Workers in the latter typically have little or no job security, must work very hard, and get low pay compared with their counterparts in the public sector and in parts of the formal private sector. The informal sector is often quite dynamic and nimble, but its growth is constrained by policies and institutions geared toward the formal sector.

The Public Sector

Much of the public sector, including nearly 240 enterprises owned by the central government and more owned by state governments, will continue to perform poorly, increasingly assuming a welfare role for workers and communities rather than making a contribution to the economy. Nearly 100 central government enterprises report losses. Only ten firms, eight in energy and two in telecommunications, account for two-thirds of the sector's entire profits. All the profitable enterprises benefit from laws and regulations that restrict or in some instances prohibit competition. Deregulation and the introduction of competition is likely to reduce those profits in the coming years, while political opposition to job losses is likely to postpone the painful restructuring necessary to turn around the remain-

---

12. Government of India, *Economic Survey 1999–2000* (Delhi: Government of India, 2000).

ing public enterprises that are capable of becoming profitable.

The failure to privatize has been one of the biggest shortcomings of the first decade of reform. Although meant to reduce the size of the public sector, India's privatization program has actually enlarged it thanks to the bureaucracy's success in undermining the process. The issue has been studied extensively but with little result, other than the creation of a new ministry and more positions for senior bureaucrats. In 1996, the government created the Disinvestment Commission, which submitted recommendations on 43 of the central government's 240 enterprises. They were largely ignored. The commission was replaced in 1999 by the Department of Disinvestment, whose recommendations have to be approved by the Cabinet Committee on Disinvestment. The process gives ample time and opportunity for an opponent of any sale, typically the government department threatened with the loss of a captive enterprise, to scuttle it. Not surprisingly, the central government had sold only one bakery to the private sector by the end of 2000.

The public sector accounts for around two-thirds of all employment in the formal sector of the economy, or nearly 30 million people. Its share has barely shifted during the last decade despite faster growth in the private sector, indicating both the burgeoning of economic activity in the informal sector and the reluctance of private employers to formally expand their full-time payroll because of the heavier regulatory and cost burden that would result. According to the World Bank's *Development Report*, the share of national output emanating from state-owned enterprises remained at 13.4 percent during 1990–97, the same as in the previous five years. As the government dithers on privatization, competition is eroding the market value of public sector companies, ultimately diminishing their chances of being sold.

The Private Sector

Not all parts of the private sector are likely to thrive equally as a result of economic reform. The service sector, the fastest growing in recent years (accounting now for over half of GDP), is likely to maintain its lead over most of heavy and much of light industry. Such industries are more constrained by the legacy of bad policies, poor physical infrastructure, and the still heavy burden of regulation. India's serious infrastructure problems will constrain industry more than many service sectors. Technological development has allowed for easier communication with the outside world, facilitating the export of services more than that of goods. As a result, service and research-intensive sectors such as information technology, communications, entertainment, pharmaceuticals, biotechnology, and back-office operations will do well in the coming years.

The expansion of the service sector is generally less dependent on difficult policy decisions, such as liberalizing labor laws. It can typically use semiskilled and skilled labor and thus avoid many of the problems of unionized workforces. It also uses capital less intensively than most industries. These advantages, combined with India's large pool of trained manpower, should allow some sectors to thrive in the coming years through developing state-of-the-art technology even as much of industry and most Indians live with antiquated technology. For example, India is likely to export more and better software systems for hospital management and information systems while only a few modern hospitals in India use such technology. Such technology will connect doctors, hospitals, and insurance companies abroad, while many Indians remain deprived of basic health care.

The IT sector, along with its related activities, is likely to continue its rapid growth of recent years. The sector employs about 350,000 people and is expected to generate about $9 billion in exports in fiscal year 2001. Nearly 200 of the 500 largest firms in the United States purchase software from Indian companies. India is estimated to account for around 80 percent of the offshore IT services market. Over the coming years, the industry will continue to move from simpler to more complicated tasks as it gains more expertise. India is likely to realize more of its great potential in undertaking back-office work for foreign companies, such as accounting, data processing, call centers, customer correspondence, medical transcription, reservations handling, and ticketing. Thirteen international airlines have shifted their back-office work to India, and more may follow. Other multinationals are likely to follow the example of firms such as Nortel Networks and expand their software and engineering research in India.

While a few sectors of the economy operate at the frontier of technology, many others will remain impervious to the twenty-first century, as shown by the contrast between the jute industry and the IT sector. The jute industry is sustained by government protection. Its ancient and largely bankrupt mills survive through financial assistance from public sector banks. The IT sector receives almost no funding from the banks or other government institutions. The government restricts the use of synthetic fibers to create a protected market, mandating the use of jute bags for packing sugar and food grains and raising costs for purchasers. In contrast, the IT sector is fiercely competitive, and buyers can choose their technology and products. The protection given to the jute industry has eliminated any pressure to innovate, improve quality, or cater to market demands. Most jute mills are located in West Bengal, whose government has responded to the demands of the owners and the unions by successfully lobbying the national government to prop up the industry. Not surprisingly, one result is that some mills actually use technology that is a hundred years old. The IT sector is developing new technology for the world market. The government has established a fund, administered by bureaucrats, to upgrade the jute industry's ancient technology. It is not likely to succeed because, among other reasons, private mill owners are unlikely to invest more of their own money into a stagnant business. Venture capital funds, often from abroad, facilitate the introduction of new technology in the IT sector. Finally, the jute industry is trying to shed workers slowly, while the IT sector complains of a labor shortage.

More than four decades of a closed, regulated economy have left a legacy that will not disappear soon. Many firms have become overly accustomed to a sheltered business environment and lenient creditors. A number of companies, especially in manufacturing, have remained blissfully ignorant of the impact of future competition on their industry, from both domestic and foreign companies, and have been sluggish to invest, modernize, and build an efficient scale of operations. The lack of workable bankruptcy laws and the still high barriers against corporate takeovers have insulated inefficient owners and management from the consequences of their business failures. The absence until recently of "creative destruction," the essence of a capitalist economy, accounts for much of the obsolescence of Indian industry.

Bad Government and Poor Policies

Poor government policies continue to keep India from reaching its potential. The economic success of countries in East and Southeast Asia during the last four decades indicates that mass poverty can be overcome through proper policies. The new dynamism within India in recent years gives hope that the country can follow the same path, though perhaps somewhat more slowly. The obstacles to prosperity are many in India, but they are not insuperable.

Poor Institutional Framework

India's institutional framework remains weak, compounding the problems of poor human capital and inadequate physical infrastructure. On paper, the country's legal, accounting, and regulatory framework is impressive compared with those of most developing countries. In practice, these institutions work poorly.

The legal system is in shambles, with over 28 million cases pending.[13] It typically takes ten to twenty years to obtain and enforce a decision. The system is less of an obstacle for the rich and the powerful, but it effectively excludes most Indians, for whom it is too costly and too slow. While justice often prevails, it often comes too late even for wealthy investors. Cogentrix Energy, a U.S. energy firm, successfully overcame eight public interest litigations filed against its proposed power project in the state of Karnataka, but it pulled out of India in frustration at the delays. Weak enforceability of contracts and ownership rights limits the growth of small business, which is especially vulnerable to arbitrary and illegal measures taken by government officials or larger competitors. Larger companies have developed their own ways, legal and otherwise, to stabilize their business environment. The gaps in the levels of law and order in different states, and between different segments of the economy, may widen. Growing lawlessness depresses economic growth and stifles the rise of small business, especially in the worst-governed parts of India. The modern software and technology parks appearing in the southern and western parts of India host IT companies governed by modern laws on electronic commerce, while other parts of India, especially in Bihar and Uttar Pradesh, are effectively under the brutal rule of local mafias.

Hindu philosophy acknowledges that all entities must die, but they are promised many rebirths. Ironically, modern Indian industrial policy is just the opposite. Bankruptcy and liquidation are near impossible. Companies whose losses erase their net worth are sent into a quagmire called the Board of Industrial and Financial Reconstruction, a quasi-judicial bureaucratic body that effectively provides full protection from creditors to the owners and managers who led the company into bankruptcy. A typical case languishes in the board for fifty-two months. It is a process designed to fail. Nearly 80 percent of the 4,000 or so companies brought to the board since 1987 are still languishing under bureau-

---

13. World Bank, *India: Policies to Reduce Poverty*, 45.

cratic scrutiny, with creditors unable to recoup any money. Creditors typically cannot use the legal system to compel repayment of debt or to seize the collateral offered by defaulted borrowers. Ongoing deregulation, especially in the banking sector, will generate more political pressure for the government to amend these laws and put an end to the ability of Indian debtors to default on their loans with impunity.

Agricultural Policies

Economic reform has largely ignored the agricultural sector, which employs most of the labor force. The successful delicensing of industry during the 1990s has not been repeated in agriculture. Restrictions on the sale and movement of crops within the country, and sometimes within states, are still common. State governments regularly intervene in agricultural markets, often to artificially lower the cost of an input (such as cotton or oil seeds) purchased by powerful local agroprocessing firms. Laws that force farmers to sell their crops to specified buyers and intermediaries hinder the growth of a domestic market in agriculture, benefiting an army of middlemen between farmers and final purchasers. Declining public investment, especially in rural roads and irrigation, compounds the problem.

Government policies in other sectors have indirectly hurt agriculture by depressing the price received by farmers and worsening their terms of trade with the industrial sector. Trade barriers raise the price of industrial and consumer goods, which farmers purchase, above world prices. Restrictions on exports often keep domestic agricultural prices below world prices. The result is an implicit tax on the agricultural sector. Recent cuts in import tariffs have reduced the burden of this tax, with the agricultural price index increasing 16 percent relative to the manufactured price index during 1990–98.[14]

The government has been reluctant to give Indian farmers world prices for their crops partly because of the impact it would have on both the urban poor and those rural dwellers who are net purchasers of food. However, faster economic growth and falling poverty depend on boosting both the income and the output of the agricultural sector, which in turn requires price reform to reduce the implicit taxation. Various bottlenecks, such as the lack of irrigation, credit, high-yielding seeds, rural

---

14. Government of India, *Economic Survey 1999–2000*, table 5.13.

roads to markets, and electricity, limit the extent to which farmers can increase their output in response to higher crop prices (better terms of trade). To the extent that these bottlenecks can be eased, farm output can be increased by a higher amount with a smaller increase in agricultural prices, minimizing the impact on the nonfarming poor of agricultural liberalization. Policies to give farmers easier access to inputs and to markets would minimize the added cost to poor consumers and increase the income of most farmers.[15]

Prospects for agricultural growth appear mixed in the near term. Ongoing industrial reform, especially more competition, will help the agricultural sector indirectly, but the dearth of public investment in irrigation, rural roads, and electricity will constrain its growth. Recent experiments in some states to transfer management of irrigation networks from indifferent bureaucrats to the users of the water may, if successful, raise the efficiency of existing projects and help boost output and income. Moreover, better telecommunications should improve the spread of information to farmers, especially on market prices for their products. This could enhance their ability to bargain with the middlemen who purchase their crops for sale in urban markets and could lead to growing political demand for higher prices.

Budget Deficits and Government Debt

Growing budget deficits and mounting government debt keep India poor. High GDP growth has been accompanied by eroding budget balances at the central and state levels, indicating that India cannot grow its way out of its problems. Cash-strapped governments have already pruned their pitifully low investment budgets. Disturbingly, there appears to be no correlation between the health of state government finances and the rate of economic growth in the state, reflecting serious problems in tax collections and poor spending decisions.[16] Some faster-growing states, such as Maharashtra and West Bengal, actually collected less in tax revenue as a share of state-level GDP at the end of the 1990s than at the beginning. Failure to correct these trends could undermine the country's ability to pay its debt.

---

15. Ashok Gulati, "Indian Agriculture in an Open Economy," in *India's Economic Reforms and Development: Essays for Manmohan Singh*, ed. I.J. Ahluwalia and I.M.D. Little (Delhi: Oxford University Press, 1998).

16. M.S. Ahluwalia, "Economic Performance of the States."

Despite many initiatives to boost collections by cutting high tax rates and making sales and excise taxes less complicated, Indian governments at all levels collect less tax revenue today as a share of GDP than at the beginning of the last decade. Total tax collections fell marginally to 14.1 percent of GDP from 14.2 percent during the decade. Indirect taxes, largely from customs and excise duties, fell to 10.5 percent of GDP in fiscal year 1999 from 11.3 percent in 1993. The fall is due in part to trade liberalization and tax simplification but also to many tax loopholes and exemptions. Despite a doubling in recent years of the number of taxpayers to nearly 25 million, direct tax revenues (from corporate and personal income tax) barely increased to 3.6 percent of GDP from 2.9 percent during the 1990s, not enough to compensate for the decline in indirect tax collections. Unlike other developing countries undertaking reform during the previous decade, India was not able to introduce a value-added tax. On the spending side, political pressure has prevented the government from reducing its vast payroll and large subsidies, which are usually mistargeted and inefficient.

The state governments are also financially weak. The level of central government loans and grants to the states (as a share of GDP) has declined over time. States have increasingly relied on short-term loans from the central bank, leading the bank to issue stop-payment orders periodically because the states have exceeded their borrowing limits. State governments have increasingly issued guarantees on debt raised by entities under their control to circumvent restrictions on their own borrowing.

India's fiscal problems are linked to its federal constitution and may become a bigger issue in national politics in the coming decade. The financial architecture of India's federal system compares favorably with that of other similar countries (such as Canada and Australia), but the actual practice is worse. More than 60 percent of consolidated government revenues flow to the central government as they arise largely from personal and corporate income taxes, customs taxes, and some excise taxes that are most efficiently collected nationally. However, around 60 percent of total government spending (net of intergovernmental transfers) is at the state level, requiring large transfers from the central government. Some of the funds are transferred under tax-sharing formulas developed periodically by the Finance Commission, and the rest is transferred through the central government's Planning Commission as loans and grants. Despite its sound design and transparency, the system works poorly. Revenues are hurt by badly designed taxes, poor coordination between the state and central governments, and massive tax evasion.

Agriculture accounts for around one-third of the economy's output but still attracts no income tax, thanks to the political clout of affluent rural voters at the state level. Much of the service sector also escapes taxation. Central government transfers are made with little regard for creating incentives for state governments to match their new spending with better revenue efforts of their own. All state governments have an incentive to spend more and seek more central funding as the system undermines the accountability of governments at all levels for their taxing and spending decisions. Failure to develop a mechanism to prevent states from embarking on unsustainable fiscal policies could result in spiraling debt. Periodic loan forgiveness by the central government also creates an expectation that debts owed to the central government can always be negotiated.

Fortunately, some states have recognized their budget problems and are attempting to improve their tax systems, control wasteful, untargeted subsidies, and recover costs for services they provide. Uttar Pradesh and Andhra Pradesh have entered into multiyear structural reform programs with the World Bank. However, progress will be slow, as the country's political leadership has not generated public support, or even grudging consent, for austerity measures. Hence, political opponents will continue to vociferously oppose reform measures that correct unworkable populist schemes even when they privately support them. For example, the opposition Congress Party in Andhra Pradesh and the Bharatiya Janata Party in Karnataka oppose power sector reforms started by the state governments despite supporting them at the national level. Other states have different economic priorities. Less developed states such as Bihar and Assam typically demand more central government subsidies, populist schemes, and public sector jobs. Unlike Maharashtra, Gujarat, and Andhra Pradesh, they have not shifted their focus toward providing public infrastructure, such as roads, telecommunications, and ports, nor toward industrial development and policies to nurture service industries such as IT.

The total annual borrowing requirement for the wider public sector, including all levels of government and the enterprises they own, is estimated to be around 12 percent of GDP. It consumes almost half the flow of domestic savings available in the country, spending most of it very badly and severely reducing the resources available for investment by households and private firms. The country pays a heavy cost in terms of the economic growth and job creation that is forgone because of the misuse of its own resources by the public sector. Public support for public sector workers has fallen in recent years. In 2000, strikes by employees of the Uttar Pradesh state electricity board, civil servants in Rajasthan, and the central Department of Telecommunications elicited little or no public sympathy. While this might portend eroding political opposition to public sector restructuring, including privatization, the fear of job losses and of corruption in the divestment process constrains public support for such measures.

Foreign Investment and Exports

One of the biggest contrasts between India and its more prosperous neighbors to the east is the paucity of foreign investment in the country, especially in its export sectors. Total flows of foreign investment are estimated to exceed $1 trillion globally in 2000, of which India receives less than $3 billion. A growing share of production in all countries is being undertaken by multinationals, which now account for 10 percent of global GDP, compared with 5 percent in 1982.[17] Investment by foreigners accounts for a growing share of total investment in both China and India in the last decade but is heavier in the former. Foreign investment accounted for 17 percent of total capital formation in China in 1996, up from 7.4 percent in 1991. In India, it rose to only 2.9 percent from 0.4 percent during the same period. The value of the accumulated stock of foreign investment in China is now around 30 percent of GDP, compared with 8 percent in India. Net foreign direct investment averaged only 0.6 percent of GDP during 1996–2000 in India, lower than in Brazil (3.2 percent), China (3.7 percent), Malaysia (3.4 percent), and Mexico (2.6 percent).

The experience of other Asian countries shows that the importance of foreign investment reaches well beyond the actual money brought into the country. Foreign investors either produce or are linked with over 60 percent of all exports from China. The technology, skills, and international marketing networks they provide are largely responsible for the 250 percent growth in Chinese exports during the last decade as well as the more than 200 percent growth in Philippine exports. The lack of export-oriented foreign investment is one reason that Indian exports grew

---

17. United Nations Conference on Trade and Development, *World Investment Report 2000* (Geneva: United Nations, 2000), 4.

only 130 percent during the same period. In contrast to the situation in China and much of Southeast Asia, foreign investors have largely targeted their production to India's protected domestic market.

India's failure to attract foreign investment into an export platform for the global market reflects both its political reluctance and its poor infrastructure. The rules, archaic procedures, and habits of governance inherited from earlier years of centralized control still block the development of a dynamic export sector for most goods. They raise the cost of doing business, generate redundant paperwork, and delay the movement of inputs and outputs required in sectors such as electronics.

Progress in removing the visible, and the sometimes more difficult invisible, barriers to investment will be slow. For example, a recent study indicated that it took more time to process air cargo at India's airports than to transport it to foreign destinations.[18] The same study estimated that unclaimed cargo, some languishing for years, fills one-third of the valuable storage space in airport terminals, thanks to the noncommercial orientation of the public sector authorities managing the facility. The average turnaround time for a ship in an Indian port is around seven or eight days, compared with less than a day in Singapore.[19]

Clogged physical infrastructure and outdated procedures and policies pose a lesser and diminishing constraint on the IT sector, which remains a growing exception to the normal rules in India. With recent advances in technology combined with liberalization in the telecommunications sector, India stands poised to benefit from rapidly growing service exports in the manner in which others benefited from manufacturing exports in the 1980s and 1990s.

The Financial Sector

Financial sector reform has given lenders more discretion to make their own lending decisions and set their own interest rates while borrowers have gained access to more potential lenders and investors. Prior to reform, more than 80 percent of bank lending was preempted in some manner by the government. In 1990, over 53 percent of bank deposits were taken by the public sector, either through a cash reserve require-

---

18. "Too Many Bottlenecks Hinder Air Cargo Growth," *Economic Times*, September 27, 2000.

19. M.S. Ahluwalia, "Infrastructure Development in India's Reforms," in *India's Economic Reforms and Development*, ed. Ahluwalia and Little, 111.

ment (monies deposited with the central bank) or a statutory liquidity ratio (money invested in government debt paper). In addition, banks had to lend additional amounts to "priority sectors," special categories of borrowers, giving them very little discretion in allocating their funds. Interest rates were also controlled in detail and did not play a role in linking different financial markets with each other or Indian markets with global markets.

Most interest rate controls have been lifted, and both cash reserve and statutory liquidity ratios have been gradually reduced so that they now preempt just over 30 percent of all deposits. Lending to priority sector borrowers continues, but the government is likely to dilute its impact by expanding the list of industries falling within that definition. Nonbank financial companies, many of them in the leasing business, have joined new foreign and Indian private sector banks in competing with the dominant government-owned commercial banks. Competition will increase further with the growth of mutual funds and venture capital funds and the imminent expansion of the insurance industry following the liberalization of the industry in 2000 to end the public sector's monopoly. The market for long-term lending will probably deepen as the insurance industry expands. The likely emergence of private pension funds should also boost the flow of savings into domestic capital markets.

Reform has offered more scope for better-run financial institutions but has not seriously addressed the problems of the worst ones. As a result, the gap in performance and financial results between the better private and foreign banks and the worst public sector banks will likely widen in the coming years. The former will use more sophisticated technology, implement better risk management systems, and develop better credit skills. Gross nonperforming loans (prior to provisions the banks may have made to absorb losses) are around 15 percent of total loans for the commercial banks as a whole, compared with 23 percent in 1993. Some of the more viable public sector banks may gradually improve their operations and financial performance, taking advantage of their large deposit bases and physical presence in most parts of the country. Over time, continued GDP growth may alleviate the burden of their nonperforming loans and strengthen their profitability. The government's decision to reduce its ownership in selected public sector banks to below 51 percent could also help in bringing a commercial orientation to the operations of those banks. However, a handful of weak public sector banks are likely to continue receiving public funds to bail them out. These institutions, beset with strong unions, a civil service work culture, and weak and politicized management, may fare worse in a more competitive environment. The laggards, once described as being "too Indian to fail," will exert pressure on the government to constrain the pace of reform.

The contrast between the best and the worst will become more apparent as India's financial sector increasingly connects with external markets. Growing foreign portfolio investment in Indian markets has raised the level of foreign ownership of Indian financial institutions that are listed on local stock exchanges. Domestic banks, such as ICICI Bank, have begun to list their shares in overseas markets. The incentive to tap the deep pockets of global investors has led more Indian banks and companies to modernize their financial reporting to meet international standards in accounting and disclosure of information. While the flow of foreign funds buying assets in India is likely to grow, Indian funds, including mutual funds, are just beginning to buy financial assets abroad. The Indian government still retains control over capital flows, but they are likely to become less effective with the country's growing integration into global capital markets.

The impact of government budget deficits spills over into India's financial institutions, constraining their ability to act as efficient intermediaries between lenders and borrowers. Despite large reductions in the cash reserve and statutory liquidity ratios, banks continue to lend much of their money to the government. Government debt has accounted for around 36–40 percent of bank assets throughout the last decade. Commercial bank credit to the government grew faster than credit to commercial entities during the 1990s. Over half of the funds received by the commercial banks as new deposits during 1999 were used to purchase government debt paper, compared with less than one-third in the previous year.

Corruption

India's failure to build stronger political support for reform measures is related to failures of governance. Corruption has become such an integral part of the economic and administrative system that it is more than just an added cost of doing business. It shapes the course of government policies, influences the likelihood of their implementation, and constrains the pace of reform. For example, it poses one of the biggest obstacles to power sector reform. An estimated 40 percent of the power generated by state electricity boards is stolen. The network of entrenched interests, from businesses and consumers stealing the power to public employees extracting bribes to facilitate the theft, is a major obstacle to reform. Theft makes it difficult for would-be reformers to convince their voters of the necessity to raise power tariffs, since people perceive that only the honest, or those with little clout, will pay more while others continue to steal. The ability of "insiders" in the power sector to block privatization is replicated in many other sectors.

On a larger scale, corruption has undermined the ability of the government to provide basic services such as schooling and health care, as much of the money is pilfered or misappropriated. Corruption has also become firmly embedded in the private sector, permeating its dealings with the government, other companies, and customers and even its internal operations. It is not likely to recede as long as the legal system remains largely unworkable and most law enforcement agencies politicized and ineffective.

Poverty

India has the world's largest pool of desperately poor people. The recent acceleration in economic growth is slowly cutting the rate of poverty, but not by much. According to the Planning Commission, 26 percent of the population (or about 260 million) was defined as "poor" by India's low standards in 2000, down from 36 percent in 1993–94. The poverty estimates, though, suffer from many of the limitations inherent in any sampling technique and may not be fully comparable over time. While economic growth has undoubtedly contributed to falling poverty rates, the improvements are still very modest compared with the record of East and Southeast Asia (especially China). Social indicators improved modestly during the 1990s, with population growth averaging 1.8 percent during 1990–99, compared with 2.1 percent during 1980–90. The number of births per woman fell to 3.2 in 1998 from 5 in 1980 (still higher than the number for low-income countries as a whole, which fell to 3.1 from 4.3). In 1998, life expectancy at birth for boys was sixty-two years and for girls sixty-four years. However, 24 percent of males and 56 percent of females over seven years of age were illiterate.

With nearly 75 percent of India's poor living in rural areas, agricultural growth plays the key role in reducing poverty. According to some estimates, wages for unskilled male agricultural labor grew at an average annual rate of 2.4 percent in 1991–98, compared with 4.6 percent during 1980–90.[20] This may indicate that agricultural growth in recent years has had a lesser impact on rural poverty than before, but more data are needed to be certain. The success of the "Green Revolution," the introduction of high-yield seeds that dramatically increased farm production and raised the demand for rural labor, was largely responsible for the impressive fall in poverty seen in the northern states of Punjab and Haryana in the 1970s and 1980s. High-yield seeds require irrigated land, which increased to 32 percent of the total cropped land in 1995–97, compared with 23 percent in 1979–81.[21] As a result, crop yields have increased. The average yield of food grains rose from 1,023 kilograms per hectare in 1980 to 1,380 in 1990 and to 1,611 in 1998.[22] The Green Revolution spread to West Bengal in the 1990s and may reach Assam in the current decade, and it remains a strong precursor to poverty reduction.

The large number of poor people in the country reflects widespread poverty as well as income inequality. According to one measure of inequality, the Gini coefficient, income is distributed roughly as unequally in India as in China and the United States. According to this measure, in which 0 represents perfect income equality and 1 indicates the most extreme inequality, India scored .38 in 1997, compared with .4 for China, .36 for the United Kingdom, and .41 for the United States.[23]

Hope for the Future

The momentum behind India's economic reform will grow. The positive impact of measures already implemented is gradually building political support for bolder steps. Growing public awareness of India's poor economic performance compared with most countries, along with an early taste of prosperity from one decade of reform, has generated demands for economic growth that no political party can ignore. All major parties now consider GDP growth of 5 percent per annum as inadequate, in sharp contrast to the prereform years. Even if much of India's political class remains ambivalent about diluting direct political and

---

20. World Bank, *India: Policies to Reduce Poverty*, 8.
21. World Bank, *World Development Report 2000*.
22. World Bank, *India: Policies to Reduce Poverty*, 246.
23. World Bank, *World Development Report 2000*, 282–83.

bureaucratic control over economic decisions, politicians are becoming more pragmatic and less ideological.

The absence of viable alternatives to reform will outweigh disagreements over its pace and extent. Over time, the accumulation of success stories will strengthen the momentum behind liberalization, slowly eroding ideological resistance from both leftists and Hindu nationalists (who recently have borrowed much of their economic ideology from their leftist opponents). India's insecurity about opening the economy to foreigners, the product of a long colonial history, will likely be assuaged as younger Indians see reform and liberalization as paths to greater prosperity and security. Similarly, India's lingering ambivalence about the wisdom of leaving most production decisions to market forces will likely abate, though slowly.

The political base for reform should be strengthened by the benefits flowing from recent policy changes. Several hundred million people, including the poor and rural dwellers, stand to benefit directly from long-delayed reform in the telecommunications industry, which will extend phone service, reduce India's very high long-distance calling rates, and cut long waiting lists for phone connections. Growing success in sectors such as IT bolsters support for liberalization in other sectors. The political impact of IT exceeds its direct economic impact. It remains the most prominent economic success story in India since independence, along with the Green Revolution. The extraordinary attention average Indians give to IT reflects both the relative lack of success in other areas and the aspirations attached to it. The number of direct beneficiaries of IT is still small, but it has become the symbol of the country's drive to modernize. Such aspirations provide an opportunity for political leaders to change public discourse about reform and economic policy and to use the IT example to overcome obstacles in other sectors.

For example, foreign investment in Indian IT generates no hostility, partly because it is seen as a sector in which Indians can thrive (see "From Bangalore to Silicon Valley and Back: How the Indian Diaspora in the United States Is Changing India" by Sadanand Dhume in this volume). The success of nonresident Indians in Silicon Valley provides the impulse for much of the capital flowing into Indian IT. Nonresident Indians have successfully lobbied the Indian government for measures to reduce barriers to venture capital inflows and facilitate more investment in the sector. IT is encouraging more risk taking in Indian business and changing corporate culture through modern forms of governance. Several Indian IT firms have listed their shares in foreign stock markets, adopting international standards for accounting and setting the example for others. Indian companies have purchased software firms in the United States to expand their business reach. Foreign investment is now becoming a two-way flow, easing concerns about it in India.

India's growing pharmaceutical industry may follow the IT example. Some of its more dynamic firms are already using low-cost skilled labor in India to develop products for export markets in the United States and Europe. In addition, a few Indian firms have bought American firms and are expanding operations in their target markets. The industry is moving from producing generic drugs cheaply to inventing new drugs. The adoption of product patent laws by 2005 under commitments made to the World Trade Organization should spur some of India's 20,000 drug firms to invest in research and development to develop new patents, as they will lose their legal protection to copy patented foreign drugs. The success of IT and pharmaceuticals will likely be copied by India's burgeoning entertainment industry. Its traditional exports of movies, songs, and shows will be complemented by new exports in channels such as multimedia and animation, generating a growing flow of content to fill the airwaves throughout Asia and Africa and in niche markets in developed countries.

The growing clout of sectors that stand to benefit from more reform, such as IT, telecommunications, and pharmaceuticals, as well as that of exporters in general, will generate pressure for further economic liberalization. India's large private sector has sometimes been ambivalent about liberalization. Business leaders lobby in private for measures to reduce government control over their own operations, but many remain opposed to measures that would expose them to more competition, either from foreign investment or from imports resulting from lower trade barriers. Business lobbying has played a key role in keeping regulatory caps on foreign investment in many sectors, forcing foreign firms to seek domestic partners and artificially reducing their bargaining power with potential Indian partners. The more farsighted Indian firms have made use of the diminishing protection they still enjoy against foreign competitors to prepare themselves for the future, restructuring their businesses to acquire new technology and cut costs. Many have expanded their horizons beyond India, looking overseas for either export or investment opportunities. Others have not. The gap between the best and the worst in corporate India will grow. The former will push for faster reform, which the latter can delay but not block.

Indian business is likely to advocate reform more forcefully as it increasingly perceives liberalization as essential to its own ability to compete in an environment that will inevitably become more competitive. The political influence of the business community has increased in recent years, partly as a result of changing cultural perceptions that are slowly eroding prejudices against business and economic gain. This increased influence is also due to the growing amount of money that businesses provide to politicians and political parties, much of which is illegal under India's unworkable laws for campaign financing. Needless to say, such contributions provide unfair benefits to the donors and distort decision making in many areas. However, they can also become an effective counterweight to bureaucratic resistance to liberalization, especially when the business donors stand ready to benefit from it.

The disproportionate political clout of India's confident and growing middle class, and the media that increasingly reflect its economic aspirations, should complement the support of the business community for deeper reform. Policies over the last decade have already created a strong constituency for reform in urban consumers and others who have experienced an immediate increase in their income. Future governments, regardless of their political stripe, will come under more pressure from these groups to push for reform. The weight of political forces will likely place more emphasis on internal reform that favors domestic business than on external liberalization or measures that ease the path for foreign investors.

As reform spreads to the states, its progress will depend less on individual leaders and the central government in general. Competition among the states has already decentralized the impulses in favor of reform. The success or failure of different policies in different states will be clearly visible to most Indians in the coming years, unlike the success of other Asian countries that largely bypassed public perception. Thanks to growing literacy and easier communication, success stories in a few states, especially those that involve generating jobs and reducing poverty, will soon spread to others. For example, innovative policies to promote rural education in the state of Madhya Pradesh and bring IT to the villages in Tamil Nadu are more likely nowadays to be copied or adapted by other states. Economic change may influence cultural attitudes as well. Some faster-growing states may begin to see poverty as something to be eradicated rather than simply managed. Over time, public expectations regarding the acceptable pace of economic change could increase.

India's deeply entrenched economic problems preclude the kind of explosive economic growth seen in some of the "tiger" economies in East and Southeast Asia. Nevertheless, ongoing steps to promote a market economy and competition will boost productivity and sustain economic growth. Financial necessity more than ideology will increasingly drive all Indian governments to privatize their public sector enterprises. As a result, a greater share of the flow of domestic savings should be available in future years to firms in the private sector that are subject to market discipline in their spending decisions. Steps to correct large government budget deficits, deregulate, modernize outdated laws and bureaucratic procedures, and cautiously liberalize agriculture can sustain economic growth at its recent pace of around 6 percent, or even at a slightly higher pace.

This growth scenario has implications beyond the economy. Poverty is likely to decline, though gradually. Demands for enlarged job quotas in the public sector for "backward" and "low"-caste people are likely to grow in the absence of a rapid increase in job creation elsewhere in the economy. Employment in the cash-strapped public sector, however, will remain stagnant, as most new jobs will be created in the private sector. This raises the likelihood that caste-based job quotas will be extended to the private sector as a political compromise. Even under optimistic scenarios, the financial weakness of the central government is likely to persist for many years, thanks to its heavy debt burden. Its poor budgetary position will limit the government's ability to pay for expensive programs to fulfill strategic ambitions, as the economy is not likely to deliver sufficient prosperity to its more demanding citizens and still leave large surpluses for other purposes.

The political challenge of managing growing prosperity and economic disparity will be handled by India's vast political class of nearly 800 elected officials at the national level, around 41,000 in state legislatures, and about 3 million in municipal, village, and regional governments. India has made a more successful investment in political development and democracy than in economic growth and better living standards for its people since independence. Now, as economic issues become more pressing, it remains to be seen whether the political investment will be equal to the task. The early signs are encouraging. The country's institutional framework retains suppleness, despite the inflexibility of some public institutions. It has provided policy stability during a decade characterized by weak coalitions, many national elections, and social changes that have led to the emergence of "backward" and "low"-caste leaders at all levels of government. For all its weaknesses and corruption, the political system provides well-developed channels for resolving disputes in a largely peaceful and orderly manner, if not very quickly. India's greatest hidden asset may well be a sophisticated political class that has mastered the art of bargaining and compromise. This certainly slows the pace of change, but it gives hope that regional tensions and economic disparities will be managed within the constitutional framework.

Competition among the states has begun to spur some local leaders to imitate the successful policies of others. Chief ministers now vie with one another to attract the IT industry to their states. More important than the modest direct impact of such investment is that it signals a constructive political response to promote progress and modernization to meet growing demands from voters. Several states have entered into reform programs to strengthen their finances with international lenders such as the World Bank and the Asian Development Bank, and more may follow. India's middle class, which now extends into the countryside, is growing in size and confidence. It will become even better informed and educated in the future and less tolerant of the failures of the bureaucracy and the public sector, as well as of the pleas for special treatment from parts of the private sector. Political support for the public sector has been falling in recent years, especially for its unionized workers, who are increasingly perceived to be corrupt and undeserving of their sheltered status. Democracy will sink deeper roots in India in the coming years. Will the country's public and private institutions manage the strains of diversity and raise living standards while keeping the federal state united? On balance, the prospects look pretty good.

From Bangalore to Silicon Valley and Back: How the Indian Diaspora in the United States Is Changing India

Sadanand Dhume

Students at a shimmering new business school use sophisticated computers with high-speed connections to the Internet. Some of their classes are taught by professors from the University of Pennsylvania's Wharton School, Northwestern University's Kellogg School, and the London School of Business. In order to be admitted, the students must take the GMAT, the same test required of students at most business schools in the United States. But the young M.B.A. students are not sitting in Boston, Houston, or Detroit: they are at the Indian School of Business on the outskirts of the southern Indian city of Hyderabad.

The school is the brainchild of Rajat Gupta, the Indian-born managing partner of the international management consultancy McKinsey and Company.[1] It is also yet another example of the growing influence on India of the Indian diaspora in the United States. The longer-term trends that have made that influence possible are not about to disappear. On October 18, 2000, while returning from Egypt on Air Force One after a round of Middle East peace talks, President Clinton signed into law a bill that almost doubled the number of nonimmigrant H-1B (work) visas to be issued to 195,000 a year for the next three years. "The growing demand for workers with high-tech skills is a dramatic illustration of the need to 'put people first' and increase our investments in education and training," said Clinton in a statement. "In today's knowledge-based economy, what you earn depends on what you learn."[2]

I'd like to thank Alyssa Ayres and Phil Oldenburg for their patience and for their critical insights. I'd also like to thank my editors at the *Far Eastern Economic Review* for their unfailing encouragement and commitment to covering the impact of the Indian diaspora on India.

1. Jonathan Karp, "McKinsey Executive's Plan Displays Rising Clout of Nation's Emigrants," *Wall Street Journal*, March 23, 2000.

2. "Clinton Signs Law Advancing Skilled Workers' Visa Numbers," Associated Press Newswire, October 18, 2000.

In the United States, the new law was seen as a victory for high-technology companies. New-economy giants such as Oracle, Texas Instruments, Microsoft, and Sun Microsystems had lobbied hard for the right to hire more foreign workers to feed the nearly insatiable demand for technically skilled manpower—the legion of software programmers, Web designers, and engineers needed to keep the new economy humming.

But the consequences of this legislation will be felt just as acutely half a world away from Silicon Valley and Seattle—in Delhi and Bangalore, in Mumbai, Hyderabad, and Chennai (formerly known as Madras). In recent years, about four in ten H-1B visas have gone to Indians.[3] Should this trend continue, a crude calculation suggests that in the next three years alone as many as 250,000 Indians, most of them software professionals, will likely wing their way to U.S. shores, adding to the already 1.7-million-strong Indian community there. The economic downturn in the United States in 2001 may reduce this estimate in the short term, but the long-term trend is not likely to be reversed.

Of course, Indian Americans—I use the term loosely to include both U.S. citizens of Indian ancestry and Indian nationals living and working in the United States—are but a small part of a diaspora estimated at about 18 million worldwide. Other countries have larger Indian communities, either in terms of absolute numbers (Malaysia) or in terms of percentage of the population (Britain, South Africa, Mauritius, Suriname, Guyana, Fiji, Singapore, and many of the Persian Gulf states).

Despite their large numbers, though, for the most part Indians in these countries lack the influence over India that success in increasingly globalized new-economy industries and political clout in the world's most powerful country give their fellow immigrants in the United States. The timing, place, and nature of immigration have all influenced this. The flow of nineteenth-century and early-twentieth-century Indians who left to work on the sugar estates of Suriname and Guyana, the tea and rubber plantations of Southeast Asia, and the railroad projects of Africa was largely one way. Postwar immigrants to the United Kingdom and to the Persian Gulf states have had more of an impact. Workers in the Gulf states have long sent home remittances. And some Sikhs and Kashmiris in the United Kingdom have helped fuel support for separatist move-

---

3. See Sadanand Dhume, Deidre Sheehan, Shada Islam, and Dan Biers, "Brain Game," *Far Eastern Economic Review* (*FEER*), November 2, 2000. Indians are followed by Chinese (10 percent) and Filipinos (3 percent).

ments in Indian Punjab and Kashmir. But even these more recent emigrants—with a few exceptions such as international steel baron L.N. Mittal and industrialists such as the Hinduja brothers and Swaraj Paul—do not enjoy quite the same profile as their counterparts in the United States. Indian immigrants in the United Kingdom are mainly working class. Quite simply, no country in the world except the United States has attracted large numbers of highly educated, technically skilled professionals and allowed them to succeed in so short a period of time. Germany's failed effort to jump-start a so-called green card scheme is testimony to this fact.

To sum up, though emigration from India is nothing new, never before has the overseas Indian community been as engaged with India's state, its markets, and its civil society. The end of the Cold War and the solidification of the United States' economic, cultural, and technological preeminence have given the Indian diaspora there an outsize voice in India compared with Indians in less-developed economies. The Tamil entrepreneur in Silicon Valley is given a hearing by Indian government officials and business leaders. The Tamil worker on a rubber plantation in Malaysia is not.

The nature of Indian immigration to the United States—with its preponderance of highly educated professionals, many with scientific skills—has further abetted this process. Finally, the rise of a wealthy entrepreneurial class of Indians in globalized new-economy technology industries has given these Indian Americans greater opportunity to influence India than, say, wealthy Indian doctors or motel owners in the United States.

This chapter attempts to explain the consequences of this stepped-up interaction between the wealthy, highly educated, and increasingly entrepreneurial Indian diaspora in the United States and India. How is the increasingly thick web of links between places as far apart as Hyderabad and Seattle, as Mumbai and New York, shaping the world's second most populous nation? After briefly sketching the history of Indian immigration to the United States, the chapter will examine how the rise of the new economy in the United States has led to a dramatic increase in both the number of ethnic Indians living there and the collective wealth the community commands. It will explain how they are affecting India's economy and influencing policy. It will also look at how the first stirrings of a philanthropic spirit have the potential to shape India in new and exciting ways. Finally, it will examine how wealth, and with it the proximity to political power, is helping the Indian diaspora emerge as an important driver of U.S. policy toward the subcontinent.

A Brief History of Indian Immigration to the United States

Currently, the United States is home to nearly 1.7 million persons of Indian origin.[4] Of these, about 25 percent are U.S. citizens, and more than half live in just five states: California, New York, New Jersey, Illinois, and Texas. California alone is home to 315,000, or about one in five, Indian Americans. Santa Clara County, with its concentration of high-technology firms, had about 66,000 Indian Americans in 2000, a staggering 231 percent increase over the number in 1990. About three-fourths of Indians in the U.S. workforce are college graduates, compared with 55 percent of immigrants from China and about a third of all Americans. According to the 1990 census, the average per capita income of Indian families in the United States was $60,093, compared with $41,110 for non-Hispanic white families and a national average of about $30,000. Even if its rate of growth slows by half in the next decade, by 2010 the Indian American community will have swelled to nearly 2.7 million.

The first Indian presence in the United States is usually traced to the early part of the twentieth century, when peasants from Punjab province (now divided between India and Pakistan) began arriving on the West Coast seeking work in Washington's lumber mills and California's agricultural fields.[5] These early immigrants were hardly welcome. Their presence was fought, successfully, by the Asiatic Exclusion League and other organizations. Up against legislative roadblocks that made it impossible to own or lease land, the community dwindled. The number of Indians in California fell from about 10,000 in 1914 to fewer than 1,500 in 1940. In 1946, Congress gave Indians the right to become naturalized U.S. citizens and allowed a small number into the country each year. Between 1948 and 1965, another 7,000 Indians immigrated to the United States.[6]

---

4. The 2000 census puts the figure at 1,678,765. See www.iacfpa.org.
5. See Vinay Lal, "Establishing Roots, Engendering Awareness: A Political History of Asian Indians in the United States," in *Live Like the Banyan Tree: Images of the Indian American Experience*, ed. Leela Prasad (Philadelphia: Balch Institute for Ethnic Studies, 1999), 42–48.
6. Ibid.

The trickle became a flow with the passage by Congress of the Immigration and Naturalization Act of 1965, known as the Hart-Celler Act. Hart-Celler abolished nation-of-origin restrictions that had long favored European immigrants and replaced them with criteria based on kinship ties, refugee status, and, most crucially for Indians, "needed skills." Over the next ten years, the number of Indians in the United States swelled as doctors, architects, scientists, and other skilled professionals abandoned socialist India to seek their fortunes in the land of promise.[7] By 1975, their numbers had increased to over 175,000. In 1980, the Census Bureau claimed that the more than 360,000 Indians in the United States formed the most highly educated, highly skilled, and highly paid group of new immigrants.

Indian immigration continued to increase in the 1980s as professionals continued to pour in and as families continued to be united. The earlier professional class was joined by growing numbers of lower-income workers, such as taxicab drivers and newspaper kiosk owners. The 1986 Immigration Reform and Control Act gave another boost to immigration by granting amnesty to thousands of formerly illegal immigrants.[8] In 1990, it received yet another push when the number of visas granted annually to skilled workers was almost tripled, from 54,000 to 140,000.[9]

The more liberal visa regulations coincided with the birth of a new generation of high-technology industries in Silicon Valley.[10] With its vast network of engineering schools—including the six world-class Indian Institutes of Technology—churning out tens of thousands of English-speaking graduates, India was uniquely positioned to feed the United States' soon-to-explode hunger for technically skilled manpower. Between 1990 and 2000, the Indian American population increased 106 percent to nearly 1.7 million, making Indians the fastest growing of all Asian American groups.

The integration of India into the global economy will continue to shrink the distance between New Delhi and New York, Hyderabad and Houston, Bangalore and Boston. Moreover, the ubiquity of air travel

---

7. Though India's constitution was amended in 1976 to officially make it a socialist republic (see alfa.nic.in/const/preamble.html), its economic system has always been mixed.

8. Louis Freedberg and Ramon G. McLeod, "The Other Side of the Law," *San Francisco Chronicle*, October 13, 1998, put the total number of formerly illegal immigrants (from all countries) who were granted amnesty under the 1986 law at 2.8 million.

9. AnnaLee Saxenian, *Silicon Valley's New Immigrant Entrepreneurs* (Public Policy Institute of California, 1999).

10. Ibid.

and the proliferation of e-mail and of news and e-commerce sites on the World Wide Web will ensure that the act of emigration no longer necessarily means (largely) shutting out one world to become part of another.

This is not to suggest that 1.7 million Indian Americans are in any position to steer the destiny of one billion Indians or to divert the United States' foreign policy from the pursuit of its own rational self-interest. As in the past, the vast majority of Indians remain untouched and unaffected by those of their compatriots who choose to leave. The odds of the Indian American connection altering the life or prospects of an ambitious technology entrepreneur in Bangalore are much higher than those of its altering the life of a landless laborer in Bihar.

Yet there is no denying that Indians in the United States have the numbers, the wealth, and the glamour to affect India more substantially than any other group of Indian immigrants to any other country. If this connection were shown on an airline map, a single thin line linking New Delhi to Washington or Mumbai to New York would have been replaced by several thick lines linking people, places, and institutions half a world away more intimately than ever before.

The Impact on the Economy

Two recent developments have the potential to transform the Indian American diaspora's so far anemic role in India's economy. India's booming technology sector has given overseas Indians (and others) a sound economic incentive to invest in India. At the same time, the freshly minted Indian-owned technology companies in the United States have the cash, the expertise, and the connections India's own technology companies need in order to become more powerful engines of economic growth. They have the potential to do for India's tech sector what access to U.S. markets did for East Asian manufacturing companies a generation earlier.

Of course, not all the increasingly strong links between India's technology companies and the United States can be ascribed to the presence, much less to the efforts, of the large overseas Indian community. It is probably correct to assume that the United States would be important to Indian tech companies—for example, as a market and a source of capital—even if its overseas Indian community didn't exist. It is also next to impossible to clearly establish the precise boundary between the role of Indian Americans and the role of the United States per se in India's technology boom. But, with this caveat in mind, most observers would agree that India's technology industries would not be nearly as vibrant or as well integrated with the United States as they are if it weren't for the Indian diaspora.

The first part of this section briefly contrasts the meager role overseas Indians have played in the Indian economy thus far with the role of overseas Chinese in China. The second part explains how technology industries are beginning to change this. Finally, the third part looks at how ripples from the technology boom are being felt in other parts of the Indian economy.

Overseas Indians Versus Overseas Chinese

Indian Americans are hardly the first of India's scattered diaspora communities to contribute to its economy. The post-1973 OPEC oil boom sucked hundreds of thousands of Indian workers to the Persian Gulf states. Their remittances gave the Indian economy much-needed hard cash and the luxury of a little balance-of-payments breathing space.

Yet, apart from the limited importance of Gulf worker remittances,[11] overseas Indians as a group have so far done comparatively little for the Indian economy. In the fiscal year ended March 31, 2000, foreign direct investment (FDI) flows from *all* overseas Indians totaled a meager $83 million, or 3 percent of total FDI that year. This is down from the mid-1990s, when overseas Indian investment hit $600 million, or 30 percent of FDI.[12] In contrast, in the last two decades overseas Chinese, mainly from Hong Kong and Taiwan, have poured billions of dollars into China's eastern seaboard, helping transform it into an international manufacturing powerhouse.[13]

The paltry FDI flows into India reflect more than one truth. First, despite embarking on economic reforms since 1991, India has remained a manufacturing backwater. Poor infrastructure and miles of regulatory red tape have ensured that FDI inflows have remained a trickle when compared with those to China and the rest of East Asia. Perhaps just as important has been the occupational profile of the overseas Indian com-

---

11. An indirect effect of the Indians in the Persian Gulf states was that the return of many thousands of them to India following the Gulf War of 1991 helped lead to the balance-of-payments crisis that forced India toward economic reforms. Those reforms, as discussed in this chapter, opened the door for the growth of India's software services sector and the potential for greater Indian American participation in the Indian economy.

12. Dan Biers and Sadanand Dhume, "In India, a Bit of California," *FEER*, November 2, 2000.

13. Ibid.

munity. There has always been an entrepreneurial class of overseas Indians—including Sindhi traders as well as the Patels, who control much of the motel industry in the United States—but, more generally, educated Indian immigrants have looked for the security of jobs in big corporations or for professional success as doctors, scientists, or accountants. As a community, Indians have not been as business oriented as the Chinese, who, for example, control a substantial chunk of business in Southeast Asia.

The boom in India's software industry and the rise of a powerful and entrepreneurial group of Indian high-tech millionaires in the United States have the potential to change this. For perhaps the first time, there is both a business opportunity and a community of overseas Indian entrepreneurs in a position to take advantage of it.

The Technology Story

Indians in Silicon Valley

Indian immigration to California accelerated after the annual cap on H-1B visas for skilled workers was raised from 54,000 to 140,000 in 1990. Between 1990 and 2000, the population of Indians in the state doubled to nearly 315,000. Many of these immigrants were software engineers first "bodyshopped" by Indian companies such as Tata Consultancy Services to work on short-term on-site projects at cut-rate prices. They then used these jobs as springboards to better-paying jobs with U.S. firms.

Ironically, this influx of Indians chasing the capitalist dream can be traced back to the policies of Jawaharlal Nehru, India's first prime minister and a firm believer in state planning. Nehru dreamed of propelling India toward economic development on the backs of thousands of highly trained scientists and engineers, who would build dams, bridges, and power plants for the newly independent nation. Compared with other developing countries in Asia such as Korea and Indonesia, the Government of India has neglected primary education and instead devoted a disproportionately large slice of its education outlays to building a vast network of engineering universities and other high-quality tertiary-education facilities.[14]

The crowning achievement of Nehru's ambitious project was the cre-

---

14. Some examples are the Indian Institutes of Management (IIMs) and several highly competitive medical schools, which also supply a large pool of Indian immigrants to the United States.

ation of five (now six) Indian Institutes of Technology (IITs).[15] Students across India compete for about 3,000 places each year by sitting for an examination that places heavy emphasis on mathematics and physics. Only about 3 percent make the cut, compared with an 11–18 percent acceptance rate at Ivy League universities in the United States.[16]

Many IIT students see their education as a (one-way) ticket to America. By one estimate, about 20,000 IIT graduates, almost 20 percent of those who have graduated since the system's inception, live in the United States.[17] In recent years, virtually every graduate with a sought-after major such as computer science has headed to the United States. It is not uncommon for IIT class reunions to be held in San Francisco or Seattle rather than in Delhi, Mumbai, or Chennai.

IIT graduates make up only a tiny sliver of the Indian immigrant population in the United States, but they are unusually high profile. Among them are Rajat Gupta, managing partner of McKinsey; Rakesh Gangwal, CEO of US Airways; Sun Microsystems cofounder Vinod Khosla; Sabeer Bhatia, who sold Hotmail to Microsoft in 1997 for $400 million; Kanwal Rekhi, founder of Excelan; Vinod Gupta, whose InfoUSA is the United States' leading provider of business and consumer databases; and Arun Netravali, the president of Bell Labs. The success of many IIT graduates has helped open doors for other Indians in Silicon Valley. It has also helped them organize by providing a core of professional loyalty. And they remain at the forefront of those giving back to India—as entrepreneurs willing to invest, as role models, and, increasingly, as philanthropists.

The early Indian presence in Silicon Valley was largely professional rather than managerial or entrepreneurial. In other words, more often than not Indians were doing technical work rather than managing companies, let alone owning them. In 1990, Indian immigrants (98 percent of whom had come to the United States after 1965) made up 2 percent of Silicon Valley's technology professionals but less than 1 percent of its managers. Many Indian technology professionals felt that there was a glass ceiling preventing them from reaching the highest levels of management in U.S. companies.[18]

---

15. Alexander Salkever, *Technical Sutra*, www.salon.com (accessed December 6, 1999). The IITs are in Delhi, Mumbai, Chennai, Kanpur, Kharagpur, and Gauhati.
16. Melanie Warner, "The Indians of Silicon Valley," *Fortune*, May 15, 2000.
17. Salkever, *Technical Sutra.*
18. Saxenian, *Silicon Valley's New Immigrant Entrepreneurs.*

TiE: The IndUS Entrepreneurs

In the 1990s, Indians in Silicon Valley began to organize. As the story goes, in late 1992 a small group of successful Valley Indians gathered for a meeting with N. Vittal, then India's secretary of electronics. He was late, and while they were waiting members of the group began sharing their difficulties in running their businesses. They promised to meet again to network and to share ideas. This was the beginning of The IndUS Entrepreneurs, or TiE, the premier Indian mentoring and networking association. For the first two years it remained an informal group, but in 1994 TiE became a formal organization. Its early members included several first-generation technology entrepreneurs, such as Suhas Patil, the founder of Cirrus Logic and a former professor at MIT; Prabhu Goel, the founder of Gateway Design Automation; and Kanwal Rekhi, who founded and ran Excelan before selling it to Novell for $210 million in 1989.

In the nine years since it was founded, TiE has emerged as the cornerstone of a network of contacts that has allowed Indians to emerge as top players in Silicon Valley.[19] K.B. Chandrasekhar of Exodus Communications is perhaps the foremost example of how TiE has helped spawn entrepreneurs, who in turn have become investors themselves. Chandrasekhar approached Rekhi for funding for his struggling startup in 1995. Five years later, a good chunk of the World Wide Web's traffic was running on servers managed by Exodus, and Rekhi's initial investment of $1 million had ballooned in value to $130 million.[20]

To sum up, by the late 1990s the Internet boom and the growth of mentoring networks had helped transform the Indian community in Silicon Valley by creating a clutch of high-profile (and high-net-worth) successes. By 1998, the professional profile of Indians in the Valley had changed. Though many remained in engineering jobs, a growing number had moved up to middle- and senior-level management positions. Most crucially, 7 percent of all high-tech firms in the Valley were run by Indian entrepreneurs.[21] In May 2000, *Fortune* magazine estimated that Bay Area Indian immigrants had created companies worth $235 billion. To put this in perspective, that's nearly half as much as India's gross domestic product that year.

---

19. See Murray Hiebert, "Guiding Lights," *FEER*, October 19, 2000.
20. Warner, "Indians of Silicon Valley."
21. Saxenian, *Silicon Valley's New Immigrant Entrepreneurs*.

*Meanwhile in India: Laying the Groundwork for Economic
Integration with the United States*

On March 12, 1999, a Bangalore-based company became the first Indian firm to begin trading on a U.S. stock exchange when it listed on the technology-dominated Nasdaq. If there is one single moment that defines the coming of age of India's technology industry, it is probably Infosys Technologies' listing. Though Infosys is widely regarded as India's most successful and best-managed software services company, its evolution nonetheless reflects broader changes in the industry that have put it on the radar screen of international investors—including the Indian Americans who have flocked to Bangalore in recent years looking for the next big success.

Infosys was founded in 1981 by N.R. Narayana Murthy, a soft-spoken engineer and IIT graduate, and six of his colleagues. They borrowed part of the seed capital, the princely sum of Rs. 10,000 (then about $1,000) from their wives. This was back in the days of India's infamous "license-permit Raj." It took Infosys eighteen months to get a license to set up the company. In the mid-1980s, Infosys, like other early players in India's infant software services industry, such as Wipro and Tata Consultancy Services, made its money by bodyshopping, or sending its programmers on short-term contracts to the United States and Europe to help customize software for clients on-site.

The business climate in India took a dramatic turn for the better in 1991 after Prime Minister P.V. Narasimha Rao and Finance Minister Manmohan Singh began slashing red tape and liberalizing the economy. Among other things, Infosys no longer needed permission from a bureaucrat in Delhi to import a computer. Meanwhile, the government created software technology parks, providing them with tax credits and relatively advanced infrastructure such as high-speed satellite links for data transmission.[22]

Throughout the 1990s, India's software services industry exports grew 50 percent a year. In the fiscal year ended March 31, 1998, they were worth $1.7 billion. Three years later they had grown to about $8.3 billion, according to the National Association of Software and Service Companies, an industry booster. Nasscom's target for software exports in 2008 is $50 billion, which is more than all Indian exports in 2000. Standard and Poor's calls India's software exports the modern-day equivalent of growing oil reserves.

---

22. Nayan Chanda, "Gates and Gandhi," *FEER*, August 24, 2000.

Not surprisingly, this extraordinary explosion of software growth has created a lot of wealth. Infosys's own growth has been ahead of the curve. In the five years to 1999, its earnings rose at an annual rate of 66 percent to reach $17.5 million on revenues of $122.1 million. At their peak in March 2000, Infosys shares were trading at $375, more than eleven times the offer price of a year earlier. According to Credit Suisse First Boston, in a decade Infosys's revenues could reach $9 billion.

Connecting the Dots: Silicon Valley Comes to India

As software exports have become an increasingly important engine of growth for India's economy, so too have India's connection with America and, to an increasing extent, Indian Americans. India's technology industry has been closely linked to the United States from its inception in the mid-1980s. Whether for bodyshopping, Y2K, or e-commerce, the United States has always been by far the most important market. But the birth of a small but vibrant technology sector in India and the parallel rise of Indian American entrepreneurs have created conditions that could lead to a deepening and widening of the sector and the emergence of cities such as Bangalore, Hyderabad, and Chennai as important centers of technological innovation.

U.S. technology firms began making their presence felt in Bangalore in the mid-1980s. Attracted by India's competitively priced scientific brainpower, companies such as Hewlett-Packard and Texas Instruments began farming out small amounts of research to newly set up units in Bangalore. But the tech boom of the late 1990s has ensured that this is no longer a novelty. Hewlett-Packard and Texas Instruments have been joined by other giants such as Microsoft and Oracle, both of which develop software in Hyderabad. Bell Labs, the research arm of Lucent Technologies, has opened research centers in both Hyderabad and Bangalore. In September 2000, Jack Welch of GE inaugurated a sprawling concrete-and-glass laboratory that will focus on everything from plastics and polymers to metallurgy, mathematical modeling, and software. GE officials expect the center's staff to grow from 600 to 2,600 scientists in three years and say that the Bangalore center will eventually become GE's largest research lab in the world.[23]

Again, it's impossible to quantify how much of this interest was spurred by Indians in Silicon Valley, though their presence clearly helped in at

---

23. Sadanand Dhume, "GE's Indian Dream," *FEER*, September 21, 2000.

least two ways: by creating an awareness of Indian technical talent and by creating a pool of skilled persons, some of whom wanted to return to India for personal reasons, that companies could draw on.[24] (The same is true, though to a lesser extent, of India's pharmaceuticals sector.)

Indian Americans are now taking a qualitatively different interest in India's technology sector. They are motivated partly by philanthropy— the idea of giving back to the land of their birth and education after having succeeded beyond anyone's wildest expectations in America. But the growing credibility of India's own technology industry and the potential to make huge profits by spotting and investing in the next hot Bangalore start-up are bigger spurs.

Some members of the Indian Silicon Valley elite have made the journey from penniless geek to entrepreneur to angel investor in a matter of years. By May 2000, Chandrasekhar, whose stake in Exodus was then valued at about $700 million, had helped fund about twenty start-ups. Bhatia of Hotmail fame had invested in seventeen.[25] The majority of these investments were in U.S. start-ups, but by 2000 India had begun to attract attention, too. Chandrasekhar has invested in Aztec Software, a small Bangalore start-up, Bhatia has also invested in fledgling Indian companies, and Rekhi has invested indirectly in Indian start-ups through India-specific venture funds.

Meanwhile, the networking and mentoring group TiE has begun spreading its wings in India. It opened its first Indian chapter in the winter of 1999. Now it has chapters in six Indian cities: Mumbai, Bangalore, Delhi, Hyderabad, Chennai, and Calcutta. The opening of these chapters in India made the national newspapers, and people like Rekhi and Bhatia have become celebrities.

A New Business Model for Start-ups: One Leg in Each Country

The last year has also seen the emergence of a new business model for young Indian start-ups: firms that hope to marry Indian technical skills with U.S. marketing savvy to create intellectual property rather than simply execute contracts. In the tech world, the distinction is between products and services. A typical example of a product is Windows 95. Products are scalable, which means potentially larger profits without

---

24. Sadanand Dhume, "Expatriates: Bringing It Home," *FEER*, February 2, 2000.
25. Don Clark, "South Asian 'Angels' Reap Riches, Spread Wealth in Silicon Valley," *Wall Street Journal*, May 2, 2000.

significant fresh investment. For example, Microsoft does not need to invest much more to sell a hundred copies of Windows 95 than it does to sell ten. Services, by contrast, are not scalable. Infosys, for example, makes more money by throwing more engineers into projects or by charging more per engineer.

An example of this new kind of Bangalore start-up is Ishoni Networks. Ishoni was founded by Prakash Bhalerao, a Silicon Valley Indian American. Sathish T.S., Ishoni's managing director, says that "the idea is to use the best of both worlds." By this he means hardwiring Indian engineering skills with marketing in the United States. Ishoni's engineers in Bangalore have helped design a semiconductor that could help lower the cost of Internet access by as much as 40 percent, but the company's market, as well as its marketing team, is based in Silicon Valley.

Ishoni is not the only firm started with Bhalerao's help. It shares its Bangalore offices with two others: optical networking company Amber Networks and broadband firm Alopa Networks. Bhalerao's investment in the firms is only about $7 million, but he has used his contacts in the United States to invest a total of about $200 million. In a sense, Ishoni neatly illustrates the importance of Indian Americans as a bridge between the U.S. market and Indian scientific skills and between U.S. investors and Indian companies.

Indian Americans and Software Services

While Indian Americans are helping establish a new generation of ambitious young product start-ups in Bangalore and Hyderabad, they are also influencing the relatively mature software service industry. To put it simply, thus far software service companies such as Infosys have grown in two ways: by adding rapidly to their total workforce and by making more profits per engineer. In 1998, each engineer employed by Infosys made about $42,000 per year for the company. By 2000, this number was up to $68,000. This was possible because clients who had first come to Infosys for cheap coding work, such as fixes for the Y2K bug, often stayed on and offered the company more complex tasks such as programming for e-commerce. E-commerce–related work had soared to nearly 30 percent of the company's profits by October 2000, compared with just 2 percent in March 1998.[26]

---

26. Sadanand Dhume, "Grand Ambition," *FEER*, October 5, 2000.

The current recession has slowed the dramatic growth of technology companies in the United States and will likely affect the piggyback success of India. But, ironically, a slowdown may well lead to a temporary increase in the two-way flow between the countries as laid-off tech workers move back to India while they wait for the U.S. economy to pick up again.

Moreover, the United States remains by far the most important market for Indian software exports. Both established Indian software firms and start-ups see a greater presence in the United States as critical to their success. For software firms such as Infosys, the ambition is to transform themselves into information technology consulting powerhouses, to be thinkers rather than mere implementers. This will require greater proximity to their U.S. clients. As in the case of fledgling product firms, common cultures and ethnic networks will likely lead Indian software service firms, too, toward using Indian Americans as a bridge to the United States. According to the COO of a Bangalore software service start-up, one reason for this is a better "cultural fit."[27]

Other Parts of the Economy

Their location and networks put Indian Americans in a unique position with regard to India's technology industries. But their sheer wealth also means that they contribute in more traditional ways. K.V. Kamath, the chairman of India's ICICI, a leading financial company, estimates that overseas Indians in the United States have deposited about $10 billion in India, a whopping 40 percent of all overseas Indian deposits. In addition, he estimates that their remittances, which total about $4.5 billion, account for about a third of all overseas remittances to India.

The Government of India has long seen the diaspora as a source of foreign exchange. In 1998, the Indian government mopped up $4.2 billion and blunted the effect of economic sanctions by issuing so-called Resurgent India bonds. The upside for India was that it allowed the government to raise money at lower interest rates than it would have been able to get on the international market. But experience shows that there are limits to the benefits of such "patriotic" funds. Drawn by attractive interest rates, overseas Indian money poured into the country in the 1980s.

---

27. Subroto Bagchi, MindTree Consulting, interview by the author, September 15, 2000.

But at the first hint of trouble in the early 1990s, depositors panicked and withdrew their cash.

Perhaps more interesting is the indirect or tangential impact of Indian Americans on India's economy. For instance, the importance of India's technology sector, influenced like no other sector of the economy by the diaspora, goes far beyond the dollars it has earned. Infosys, for example, went to the U.S. capital market for cash, brand building, and the shares with which to buy U.S. companies and draw and keep international talent. Since then, its performance on Nasdaq has drawn U.S. analysts' attention to India's technology sector.

The range of industries now represented by the Indian companies listed on U.S. stock exchanges shows how the ripple effect from software has spread. Nine companies have followed Infosys to list on either the New York Stock Exchange (NYSE) or Nasdaq. On NYSE, these are ICICI (financial services), ICICI Bank (banking), Silverline Technologies (software), VSNL (telecommunications), Wipro (software), Dr. Reddy's Laboratories (pharmaceuticals), and Satyam Computer Services (software). On Nasdaq, Infosys Technologies was followed by two Internet companies, Satyam Infoway and Rediff.com, neither of which are traded in India.

This is beneficial to India because the Securities and Exchange Commission requires foreign firms that list on a U.S. exchange to comply with U.S. accounting and disclosure standards, which tend to be more rigorous than those in Asia and Europe. James Shapiro, NYSE's senior managing director for the Asia-Pacific region, reckons that there are about twenty Indian firms that have adopted the United States' generally accepted accounting principles ahead of a possible listing and that India is ahead of China in terms of a willingness to embrace U.S. standards of transparency and good corporate governance.

An additional tangential effect of the Indian American community is that it provides a ready-made pool of retail investors for Indian companies that list on U.S. stock exchanges. Trading long-distance in India is not easy, and, like other investors, Indian Americans often feel more secure investing in stocks listed closer to where they live. Moreover, Indian blue chips that list in the United States have brand recognition among many recent Indian immigrants. Kamath estimates that a sixth of the interest in ICICI's limited offering of U.S. depositary shares in September 1999 was from retail investors, "a significant part" of which was from overseas Indians. He says the presence of this demand makes it easier for Indian companies to list in the United States.[28]

So the United States is much more than a source of capital. It is also a source of higher standards of corporate governance and disclosure to shareholders. While it is not possible to isolate the Indian American role in this, Indian companies are certainly helped by a pool of investors in the United States with an interest in India but an unwillingness to plunge directly into the Bombay Stock Exchange.

The Impact on Philanthropy

Another spillover effect of Indian American economic success has been a surge in big-ticket philanthropy for India—or, since many projects are still in the planning stage, a surge in promises of big-ticket philanthropy. The wealth created among the Indian community in the United States by the tech boom in the late 1990s has ratcheted up the size and scope of charitable projects. The reasons for giving back to India are varied. Some of those who have gone to the United States and succeeded beyond anybody's wildest imagination feel a responsibility toward those less fortunate than themselves in India and toward the educational system that helped them. Giving also confers prestige within the Indian American community. Vanity, or the fact that a couple of million dollars can ensure that a school in a prominent Indian university is named after you, doesn't hurt either. Whatever the reasons, Indian American giving is now on India's radar screen. At least half a dozen big-ticket projects promise to have more effect on India than any previous philanthropic efforts.

The biggest beneficiaries so far have been universities—both brand-new ones, such as the Indian School of Business, and established schools, especially the IITs. But educational endowments are only part of the story. Indians in the United States are giving more to charities in India and are mobilizing for disaster relief. Others hope to contribute by helping build a world-class Internet backbone or by using the Internet to help India bridge the so-called digital divide between it and rich countries.

Overseas Indians' contributing to charities at home is nothing new. Each year, Indian Americans send hundreds of thousands of dollars to religious trusts such as the Shri Satya Sai Trust and Gospel for Asia.[29] Nor is giving back to India a preserve of the rich, as Om Dutta Sharma,

---

28. K.V. Kamath, e-mail interview by the author, May 29, 2001.
29. Priya Viswanath, *Diaspora Philanthropy and Non-Resident Indians in the U.S.* (New Delhi: Charities Aid Foundation, 2000).

a New York taxi driver who funds a school for girls in a small village in Uttar Pradesh, can testify.[30]

Not surprisingly, the Indian Institutes of Technology have drawn the most support from Indian Americans. Many of those who have made good—such as Kanwal Rekhi, Vinod Gupta of InfoUSA, and Gururaj Deshpande of Sycamore Networks—are IIT graduates. The IITs offer two attributes not entirely common in India: a world-class education and a system of meritocracy that is seen as untainted by the corruption that characterizes many areas of public life. Moreover, as funding from India's cash-strapped central government has come under strain, the IITs themselves have opened up to finding resources elsewhere.

The amounts involved may seem small compared with the massive endowments of large U.S. universities. But in India, where it costs the government an estimated Rs. 125,000 (less than $2,700) per year per IIT student, a million dollars goes a long, long way. A group of IIT alumni in the United States is trying to raise $1 billion for the institutes. But the money has already started pouring in. The IIT Bombay Heritage Fund, established in 1996 and registered as a nonprofit organization in the United States, has already raised millions of dollars from alumni. Kanwal Rekhi is helping pay for a brand-new school of information technology at IIT Bombay to be named after him. Vinod Gupta has given $2 million to set up a management school at IIT Kharagpur. Rakesh Mathur, who founded Jungle, has donated $1 million to IIT Bombay. Gururaj Deshpande has pledged $100 million over twenty years to his alma mater, IIT Madras.

The IITs aren't the only beneficiaries of this philanthropic boom. A group that includes Purnendu Chatterjee, Gururaj Deshpande, Vinod Khosla, and Vinod Gupta has announced plans to open a Global Institute of Science and Technology (GIST) in collaboration with the University of California at Berkeley. The first GIST is supposed to begin accepting students by 2003, and the plans call for the school to expand to six campuses and eventually to enroll 20,000 students. Chatterjee has spoken of turning India into the "Saudi Arabia of the new economy."

Vinod Gupta is among the most prolific Indian American donors, both to philanthropy and to politics. He says he went to the United States with $58 and a suitcase of clothes. Apart from funding the management

---

30. Celia Dugger, "In New York, Just a Cabby: In India, a School's Hero," *New York Times*, January 23, 2000.

school at IIT Kharagpur, he has dished out $1 million for a women's polytechnic in Rampur, Uttar Pradesh, named after his mother. It will be affiliated with a community college in his state of residence, Nebraska, and will allow local women to take classes in textile designing, nursery training, fashion designing, and, of course, information technology.

The George Foundation, set up by New Jersey–based Abraham George, has helped establish a journalism school in Bangalore with a curriculum and logo based on Columbia University's Graduate School of Journalism. The George Foundation also helps school more than 300 poor children and has set up clinics to investigate lead poisoning.[31]

Others have adopted lower profiles or different styles of giving. The Nurul Hasan Foundation has poured $1 million into education. B.V. Jagadeesh, another cofounder of Exodus Communications, has donated $1 million to improve government-run schools in Bangalore. Indian Americans have also spearheaded the Sankhya Vahini project, an effort to build an Internet backbone in southern India. Digital Partners, a Seattle-based group that includes several current and former employees of Microsoft, has chosen India as the first country in which it hopes to use the Internet and technology to close the so-called digital divide.

An earthquake in January 2001 showed how networks developed for entirely different purposes can be mobilized for charity. On January 26, an earthquake measuring 7.9 on the Richter scale ripped through the western Indian state of Gujarat, flattening entire towns and villages and killing upwards of 20,000. Half a world away, Indian networks in the United States joined a massive Indian and international relief effort. Within weeks, TiE had managed to raise $25 million for earthquake relief. It also spearheaded the United Community Appeal for India, a nonprofit organization supported by more than two dozen business, cultural, religious, and charitable organizations. Indian Americans at Cisco Systems raised $400,000 for the victims, which was matched by the company.

The Gujarat earthquake also led to the creation of another group— the American India Foundation (AIF), which has a long-term commitment to providing financial, technological, and managerial resources toward helping the people of India realize their full potential and strengthening the bonds between the United States and India. AIF's honorary chairman is Bill Clinton, who traveled to Gujarat with the foundation.

---

31. Viswanath, *Diaspora Philanthropy.*

Not surprisingly, several Indian Americans already prominent in philanthropy are associated with AIF: these include Rajat Gupta of McKinsey; Victor Menezes, the chairman and CEO of Citibank; Kanwal Rekhi; Vinod Gupta; Gururaj Deshpande of Sycamore Networks; Sabeer Bhatia; and Purnendu Chatterjee. On May 23, 2001, the American India Foundation raised about $800,000 for the quake victims at a single dinner in New York. Meanwhile, over the last eight years, CRY, Inc., an established Indian charity, has seen its annual collections from the United States rise more than fortyfold, from $19,200 in 1992 to $800,000 in 2000.[32]

The Impact on Policy in India

For most of the fifty-four years since India's independence, policy has been the preserve of politicians and a British-style permanent civil service. Until recently, the outstanding example of a member of the Indian diaspora who had an impact on policy in India was Sam Pitroda, who returned to India in the 1980s to help run telecommunications policy for then prime minister Rajiv Gandhi. Going further back, the Indian American demographer S. Chandrashekhar spearheaded the revamp of India's family-planning program in the 1960s.

Pitroda's and Chandrashekhar's efforts may have been laudable. But they were also ad hoc and had more to do with personal commitment than with any institutional mechanism meant to tap the talent of overseas Indians. Only recently has the Government of India institutionalized reaching out to the Indian diaspora for policy advice. Partly, this shows the tremendous psychological impact and larger-than-life image that successful Indian Silicon Valley entrepreneurs have in India, but it is also a function of domestic Indian politics.

The rise to prominence of Indians in Silicon Valley has coincided with the coming to power in India of a government sympathetic to overseas Indians. Ideologically, the Bharatiya Janata Party (BJP), which heads the ruling coalition in New Delhi, and its parent body, the Rashtriya Swayamsevak Sangh (RSS), or national volunteer corps, have long embraced "ethnic" rather than "civic" nationalism—the idea that Indians, or at any rate Hindus, are bound together by blood ties.

In a nutshell, the RSS's ideas on citizenship are based on kinship and ethnicity, akin to the German ideal. In contrast, the Indian National Con-

---

32. Ibid.

gress, which has ruled India for most of the five decades since independence, has always subscribed to a civic ideal of nationalism, whereby allegiance to the Constitution and other symbols of the Indian state, not blood or ethnicity, define Indian citizenship. Hence, whereas the Overseas Friends of the BJP (OFBJP) has a rationale for its existence based on ideology, groups that represent other Indian political parties in the United States do not. Similarly, though other Indian groups have also subscribed to long-distance nationalism—noticeably Sikhs, who have campaigned for the creation of a separate Sikh homeland called Khalistan—their demands have never been given a sympathetic hearing in India's corridors of power.

In the United States, members of groups such as the OFBJP have campaigned in Indian elections, have helped raise funds for the party, and have donated to controversial Indian causes such as the program to build a temple at a disputed site occupied by a mosque in the northern Indian town of Ayodhya.[33] For its part, the BJP, a party that has long championed the cause of dual citizenship, has historically sought, and in some measure won, support from overseas Indians, particularly those in the United States and to a lesser extent in the United Kingdom. In January 2001, Prime Minister Vajpayee, speaking at a convention of overseas Indians in New Delhi, called for a partnership among "all children of Mother India" and asked overseas Indians to help make India a "knowledge superpower."[34]

Ever since coming to power in March 1998, the BJP has only reinforced its links with the overseas Indian community. At a trivial level, Prime Minister Vajpayee has had both his knees operated upon by a New York–based Indian American surgeon, Dr. Chittaranjan Ranawat, who was duly honored the same year with a government award. More seriously, senior Indian government officials such as National Security Advisor Brajesh Mishra have used the offices of well-connected ethnic Indians abroad. After India's nuclear tests in May 1998, Mishra is reported to have used the Hinduja brothers to arrange a meeting with British prime minister Tony Blair. Indian Americans were well represented at official banquets during Vajpayee's state visit to the United States in 2000.

A trip by Mishra to Washington, D.C., in July 2001 illustrates that Indian government officials from the BJP make it a point to cultivate

---

33. Sadanand Dhume, "No Place Like Home: Hindu Nationalism Draws Strength from US Supporters," *FEER*, February 25, 1999.

34. "PM to NRIs: Make India Knowledge Superpower," *Economic Times*, January 7, 2001.

influential overseas Indians. Apart from meeting with Vice President Cheney, National Security Advisor Rice, and the director of the CIA, Mishra found time to breakfast with one R. Vijayanagar, a Florida heart surgeon and fund-raiser for the Bush brothers.[35]

Broadly speaking, the impact of Indian Americans on policy in India has been confined to two areas: technology policy and policies toward the diaspora itself. That Indian American technology entrepreneurs are now being asked to help the Government of India formulate policy reflects the BJP-led government's high degree of comfort with foreign citizens, as long as they happen to have Indian (or better still, Hindu) blood, as well as the headline grabbing and resultant celebrity in India of people like Rekhi and Bhatia. The impact on India's policies toward its diaspora reflects not only the ideological shift at the very top of the Indian government but also the government's belated recognition of the economic and political potential of overseas Indians.

Technology Policy

In August 1999, the Securities and Exchange Board of India (SEBI)— India's equivalent of the SEC—established a committee including K.B. Chandrasekhar and Sabeer Bhatia to advise it on ways to attract more venture capital to India. In January 2000, SEBI's initiative was followed by the Government of India. The newly created Ministry of Information Technology set up a "Select Group with Overseas Indians" to advise it.[36] Those included, apart from the minister of information technology, the secretary of information technology, and another government official, were Kanwal Rekhi, Vinod Khosla, Suhas Patil, K.B. Chandrasekhar, and Sabeer Bhatia.

The Chandrasekhar committee's recommendations were credited with the liberalization of Indian venture capital laws in March 2000.[37] Indian American lobbying is also supposed to have helped nudge the Indian government toward embracing a more business-friendly telecommunications policy after being persuaded that poor telecom infrastructure was an obstacle to the growth of the technology sector.

Of course, it would be a mistake to overstate the importance of over-

---

35. K.P. Nayar, "A Washington Itinerary," *Telegraph*, July 11, 2001.

36. Ministry of Information Technology, document no. Secy (IT)/2000/275.

37. "Sinha Sheds Inhibition, Seduces VCFs by Sloughing Off Red Tape," *Economic Times*, March 1, 2000.

seas Indians in terms of driving Indian policy. For example, domestic and foreign telecommunications firms also lobbied hard for a new policy. But that overseas Indians have a voice at all in Indian policy making is significant, and that the Government of India has sought to institutionalize that voice is even more so.

Policies Toward the Diaspora

Dual citizenship has long been at the forefront of Indian diaspora groups' wish list from the Government of India. When out of power, the BJP has talked about granting Indians this right, but more than three years into Vajpayee's prime ministership it remains an unfulfilled promise. Instead, economic self-interest and an appeal to ethnic sentimentalism have delivered what is supposedly an alternative of sorts: the Government of India's person of Indian origin (PIO) card. A government brochure promoting the card asks applicants to "renew ties with the land of your origin" and promises "a passport to visa-free travel to India and other attractive privileges." Inside, it proclaims, "The scheme is broad-based, covers up to four generations and also foreign spouse of a citizen of India or a PIO."

Those eligible for a PIO card include any person who has at any time held an Indian passport; anyone either of whose parents, grandparents, or great-grandparents was born in and permanently resident in India as defined in the Government of India Act, 1935, or in other territories that became part of India thereafter, provided that the relative was not at any time a citizen of a country specified by the central government; and anyone who is a spouse of a citizen of India or a person of Indian origin as described above. In effect, the PIO card is little more than a twenty-year visa, though it does promise, among other things, "parity with non-resident Indians in respect of facilities available to the latter in economic financial and educational fields" and "all facilities in the matter of acquisition, holding, transfer and disposal of immovable properties in India except in matters relating to the acquisition of agricultural/plantation properties."[38] The relatively high cost of a PIO card, $1,000, shows that it is targeted for the most part at Indians in wealthy countries such as the United States, though the Government of India has recently spoken of reducing this fee.

In August 2000, the Government of India appointed the High-Level

---

38. Government of India brochure on the PIO program.

Committee on the Indian Diaspora.[39] Its chairman, L.M. Singhvi, a member of Parliament and a former Indian high commissioner to the United Kingdom, was given cabinet rank, indicating the measure of importance attached to the five-member committee. Its terms of reference include reviewing "the status of Persons of Indian Origin (PIOs) and Non-Resident Indians (NRIs) in the context of constitutional provisions, Laws and rules applicable to them both in India and the countries of their residence"; studying "the characteristics, aspirations, attitudes, requirements, strengths and weaknesses of Indian Diaspora and their expectations from India"; and taking note of "the role that the PIOs and NRIs may play in the economic and social and technological development of India." In addition, the committee has been asked to recommend a policy framework for "forging a mutually beneficial relationship with the region or PIOs and NRIs and for facilitating their interaction with India and their participation in India's economic development."

A background paper prepared for the committee by the Ministry of External Affairs is more specific about the importance India attaches to ethnic Indians in the United States:

> Persons of Indian Origin (PIOs) are also an important resource in presenting India in proper perspective to the opinion-builders and decision-makers in their respective countries. In recent years, we have seen an increasingly important role being played by the Indian community in mobilizing political support for issues of vital concern to India in USA, Canada and UK. The community in US lent valuable support in projecting India's point of view to opinion makers particularly the Congressmen, Senate members and media. . . .
>
> The policy of economic liberalization and reforms since 1991 has opened vast opportunities for business and investments in India. The PIOs are naturally keen to make use of these opportunities. The 1990s have witnessed the emergence of the new generation Indian entrepreneurs particularly in the Silicon Valley. It is, therefore, evident that a vast potential exists for the PIOs to play an important and meaningful role in India. The time is, therefore, most opportune to launch a concerted effort for developing a strong and mutually beneficial relationship with the Indian Diaspora, which has an estimated income of US$300 billion. A coherent policy and single-contact-point organization are absolutely necessary for this purpose.[40]

---

39. Foreign Secretary's Office, Ministry of External Affairs, order dated August 18, 2000.
40. Ministry of External Affairs, "Committee for Indian Diaspora: A Background Paper," undated.

More specifically, the paper shows that India's Foreign Ministry is eager to use overseas Indians to fuel both its foreign policy interests and its economic ambitions:

> There is a sizeable Indian community in the US, Canada and UK. PIOs in North America are a class apart because of their affluence and high positions they occupy in industry and academia. They are becoming politically active. They, therefore, can be expected to play an increasing important role in the political field. As witnessed in the aftermath of nuclear tests and the Kargil crisis, they proved to be valuable for articulating India's concerns in the media and to opinion-makers. Some of the specific areas in which the PIOs can play a major role are Science & Technology (IT, Biotechnology, Agriculture, Space, Energy, Environment, Healthcare and Medical Research), Management and Finance, Exports, Tourism, Investments, Education etc. The presence of Indian professionals in large numbers in the finance and insurance sector could be particularly useful in attracting investment to India.

The appointment of the Singhvi committee coincided with the creation of a new division within the Ministry of External Affairs, India's Foreign Ministry. The NRI division is headed by an additional secretary, a high-ranking official in the Indian civil service. In addition, the Ministry of External Affairs, which is headed by Jaswant Singh, one of the most powerful members of India's cabinet, provides secretarial and other inputs to the committee. But with the BJP's promise of granting dual citizenship unfulfilled after more than three years in office, there is a good chance that the ardor of Indian superpatriots living in the United States toward the party may cool.

The Impact on U.S. Policy Toward India

On September 23, 2000, U.S. president Bill Clinton attended a fundraiser at the Mountain View, California, home of an Indian American doctor and Democratic Party activist. The president praised the Indian community for its industriousness and enterprise and credited it with playing a major role in reversing almost forty years of distrust in India-U.S. relations.[41] An hour and a half later, Clinton had managed to raise

---

41. Richard Springer, "Hi-Tech Tycoons Raise $1M for Democrats," *India-West*, September 29, 2000.

$1 million for the Democratic National Committee. Another Indian American event the same day raised $400,000 for congressional candidate Mike Honda.

The U.S. presidential election of 2000 marked a political coming of age for the Indian American community. Never before had members of the community raised as much money. Wealth, numbers, and networks linking Indians across the United States and with India—in short, the same factors that allow Indian Americans to have their voices heard in New Delhi—have also raised the profile of the community in U.S. politics. Not surprisingly, some of the names mentioned in Indian American political circles are the same as those connected with technology companies or philanthropy in India. Vinod Gupta has donated several thousand dollars to Hillary Clinton's Senate campaign, and Kanwal Rekhi says he regularly holds political fund-raisers at his home.

Having grown up in a democratic and intensely political culture, Indian Americans are generally quick to grasp the nuances of politics, though often this means boasting about having a picture taken with Tipper Gore rather than making a substantial impact on policy. Even so, there's no doubt that Indian Americans are better organized than ever before and have ambitions of emulating the success of other ethnic groups that play a role in U.S. foreign policy, such as Jewish Americans and Irish Americans.

Perhaps the best-known symbol of the growing Indian American clout in U.S. politics is the Congressional Caucus on India and Indian Americans. With approximately 120 members, the India Caucus is the largest ethnic political grouping on Capitol Hill. When the caucus was founded in 1993, it had only four members. The India Caucus was not able to prevent the imposition of economic sanctions on India following its test of nuclear weapons in the summer of 1998. But it has given India a loud voice on the Hill and has contributed to what the group's former chairman, Representative Gary Ackerman of New York, has called the United States' "clear pro-India tilt."[42]

In the summer of 1999, as India and Pakistan fought a bitter eight-week miniwar in the mountains of Kashmir, members of the House International Relations Committee threw weight behind India, calling on the Clinton administration to oppose Pakistan's support for the in-

---

42. Murray Hiebert, "Patriot Games: Indian-Americans Are Using Their Growing Political and Economic Clout to Influence U.S. Policy on South Asia," *FEER*, March 23, 2000.

cursion into Kashmir and to block loans from international financial institutions until Islamabad withdrew its forces from the Kargil, Drass, and Batalik areas.[43] The resolution did not come to the full House for a vote because Pakistan's prime minister, Nawaz Sharif, rushed to Washington and agreed to withdraw Pakistani troops from Kargil. Within the House committee, though, it passed with twenty-two votes in favor, five opposed, and one abstention. A proposed amendment calling for a plebiscite in Kashmir, opposed fiercely by India, was easily beaten back by twenty votes to seven.[44]

The existence of the India Caucus reflects at least three trends in the Indian American community: growing numbers, increased economic clout, and increased political awareness. These are also reflected in the emergence of a clutch of Indian American political organizations and professional organizations. Though most of these groups are not explicitly set up to influence U.S. policy toward South Asia, their networks and contacts allow them, or individuals associated with them, to articulate an Indian viewpoint to U.S. lawmakers—especially on emotionally charged issues such as Kashmir, alleged Pakistani support for terrorist groups operating in India, and the lifting of economic sanctions on India.

Among the oldest of these organizations is the Indian American Forum for Political Education (IAFPE). Established in 1982, IAFPE describes itself as "the only political voice of 1.5 million Indian Americans in the United States."[45] IAFPE has twenty-eight chapters across the United States. It describes its main objectives as promoting political awareness and developing civic consciousness among Indian Americans and educating members about issues affecting the lives of "persons of Indian origin residing in the United States." The group encourages Indian Americans to vote and assists those who run for public office. Indeed, most of IAFPE's concerns are domestic: immigration, affirmative action quotas (which it feels discriminate against Indian American students), and getting second-generation Indian Americans involved in politics by helping them intern with congresspersons and senators.

"Improving US-Indo relations and the image of India in US media by providing unbiased facts about India" is last among the five major issues the group is concerned with. The first four involve barriers to equal

---

43. Kargil Crisis House International Relations Committee, www.indiatogether.org/us/record/kargil.htm (accessed May 5, 2001).
44. Ibid.
45. www.iafpe.org/info.htm#Objectives (accessed May 5, 2001).

opportunity: quotas restraining Indian American students in university admissions and professional training, Indian American representation in government at all levels, U.S. government agencies' support of Indian American small businesses, and legal immigration issues such as spouse reunification, green cards, and support for new immigrants from India.[46]

Yet, despite its emphasis on local issues, IAFPE remains engaged with U.S. policy toward India. Indian diplomats and high-ranking government officials from India are invited to speak at the group's annual conference. U.S. officials who formulate policy toward India, such as the assistant secretary of state for South Asia, are also invited and often attend. Many of the questions put to them by the audience are about the need for Pakistan to be declared a terrorist state rather than the need for, say, more streamlined family-reunification procedures. In addition, individual members of IAFPE have lobbied their congresspersons and senators on behalf of India. Swadesh Chatterjee, the president of the forum, was among those awarded a Padma Bhushan, India's third highest civilian honor, by the Indian government in 2001. In Indian American circles, Chatterjee, who runs an industrial instruments company in North Carolina, is widely credited with helping soften Senator Jesse Helms's stand toward India.

Another influential overseas Indian body is the Association of American Physicians from India (AAPI). AAPI claims to represent about 35,000 Indian doctors in the United States. Though it runs about a dozen charitable clinics in India, most of the group's work is focused on lobbying for issues concerning so-called international medical graduates.[47] (The vast majority of Indian doctors in the United States graduated from Indian medical schools, another aspect of the Nehruvian legacy of focusing on tertiary education.) The group wants Medicare to continue to fund residency positions at current levels and supports the waiver of J-1 visas, which usually require students to return to their country of origin, for doctors.

Despite its avowedly domestic political agenda, AAPI also acts as a voice for India. It takes some credit for the existence of the India Caucus. Thanks to its sheer size and the wealth of its members, AAPI has managed to attract political heavyweights to its annual convention, in-

---

46. Ibid.
47. www.aapiusa.org (accessed May 6, 2001).

cluding President Bill Clinton, who addressed the convention in 1995, Hillary Clinton in 2000, and numerous congresspersons.

A newer group is the Indian American Political Advocacy Council (IAPAC), established by a group of Seattle-area Indians in 1994. IAPAC takes a more overtly pro-India position than IAFPE. Its home page says that "over one million Indian Americans are invisible to the American political process."[48] It goes on to elaborate,

> Despite being the most highly educated ethnic community in the country, Indian-Americans do not occupy important political positions in the US government or participate in the political process. It is no surprise that US policies frequently ignore or go against the interests of the community. These are manifested, for example, in the sale of arms to unstable governments of the Indian subcontinent, changes to immigration laws detrimental to family reunification and the potential for trade disruption by the threat of sanctions. Policies such as these will continue unless a strong coalition of Indian-Americans exerts its presence in the political process.

IAPAC's website links to another site that aims more overtly to influence U.S. policy toward India. Indiatogether.org includes a section on lobbying Congress.[49] Apart from providing form letters to members of Congress, the site also allows users to track how their congressperson has voted on India-related issues such as the Burton Amendment, which sought to limit U.S. development assistance to India, and the House International Relations Committee resolution on Kargil.

It is difficult to tell whether Indian American groups will become less and less concerned with India as the community becomes older and better integrated into mainstream America. For now at least, these groups have emerged as a powerful factor, though by no means the most important factor, in tilting the United States' South Asia policy away from its traditional ally Pakistan and toward India.

Conclusion

Though India has long had a large diaspora scattered across the world, until recently the flow of emigrants, ideas, and capital was largely one

---

48. www.iapac.com/index.htm (accessed May 6, 2001).
49. www.indiatogether.org/us/lobby.htm (accessed May 6, 2001).

way. The rise of a large community of wealthy Indians in the United States, many of them successful entrepreneurs in globalized new-economy technology industries, has the potential to change this dramatically. These Indians, unlike their counterparts who left India at a different time or who emigrated to different lands, have an outsize voice in shaping India.

Anecdotally, this can be seen in the emergence of the NRI as a character in popular Hindi cinema. For example, both the male leads in the 1997 hit *Pardes* live in the United States—but they fall in love with an Indian girl.[50] Though overseas Indians are often portrayed negatively in Hindi films, as rich, spoiled, and sexually depraved, the image portrayed by the Indian press is quite different. India's English-language newspapers lavish attention on Indians who have done well for themselves outside the country, particularly those who have made it in the United States. Indian websites such as Rediff.com, which caters largely to an overseas Indian audience, mix Indian news with news about the diaspora in the United States.

More concretely, Indian Americans, especially the new breed of wealthy technology entrepreneurs, have begun to make their presence felt in India's own nascent technology sector. Indian Americans also continue to affect the Indian economy by subscribing to government bonds and by holding foreign currency deposits in India. More tangentially, they have helped create a retail market for Indian companies that list in the United States, thereby contributing to a growing trend toward more transparency and better corporate governance. Some Indian American wealth has spilled over into philanthropy, where the most obvious benefits will be to those who graduate from a slew of universities and departments that are either planned or already up and running.

Meanwhile, reflecting political changes in India and its increasing integration with the global economy, the Indian government has begun to look to successful Indian Americans for advice and to address some of their concerns. It is also much more willing than in the past to take the help of Indian Americans in pursuing its foreign policy goals. If the next ten years are anything like the past ten, then chances are that Indian Americans will build upon their early inroads into Indian business, policy, and philanthropy and will continue to make themselves heard in debates shaping U.S. policy toward South Asia.

---

50. Shubada Deshpande, "Hollywood Woos the NRI," *Little India*, October 1999.

The Subordinate Caste Revolution

Christophe Jaffrelot

India claims to be a democracy—indeed, the world's largest democracy
—and there are serious reasons to accept that claim. It is certainly one
of the few countries in the South to have established a stable parliamentary system with regular free and fair elections. One may object that
India's democracy lacks substance, since the institutional mechanisms
of the state are superimposed on a social system that is dominated by
the logic of castes, which seems incompatible with the values of democracy. A normative commitment to equality, after all, would seem necessary for a "real" democracy. This essay explores the explicit and growing
role of caste-based political parties in India and how their commitment
to affirmative action fits with the evolving Indian democratic polity.

   In the classic Sanskrit literature dealing with castes, Hindu society is
divided into four *varnas*: the brahmins (priests and literati), the Kshatriyas
(warriors), the Vaishyas (crafts- and tradespeople), and the Shudras (servants of the other *varnas*).[1] The "untouchables," who are now officially
designated as Scheduled Castes (SCs), are not part of the *varna* system
but exist beneath it. Their name reflects the fact that they not only occupy the bottom of society but suffer from the most pronounced stigma
of impurity. Ritual purity is a key element of the system of *jatis*, which
are the real castes, in contrast to the *varnas*, which ignore the untouchables. The word *jati* derives from *jan*, "to be born," and the endogamous
nature of the *jati* system indeed reflects the name: one is born into the
caste one's parents belong to. The *jatis* are organized in a hierarchical
way based on their status, defined in terms of ritual purity along a con-
tinuum ranging from the brahmins to the untouchables.[2] This hierarchy

---

1. Brahmins, Kshatriyas, and Vaishyas are all considered "twice born," or *dvija*.
2. However, qualitative leaps exist in this gradation since the *varna* system gives structure to the profusion of *jatis*. Each *jati* belongs to a specific *varna*. The *jatis* of the twice-
born *varnas* naturally enjoy a higher status than those of the Shudras, and those of the
untouchables are the lowest of all.

of inherited statuses goes with economic activities. For instance, brahmins avoid manual work as much as possible, especially if it implies forms of violence (as does agriculture, which destroys microorganisms); nonviolence is a brahminical ideal that also manifests itself in a vegetarian diet. On the contrary, the Chamars, one of the main untouchable *jatis*, are leather workers who are particularly impure because they not only treat organic matter but also work with cattle skin, and the cow is a sacred animal par excellence in Hinduism.

The rationale of caste does not lend itself to the egalitarian values of democracy but to the persistent domination of a small, ascriptive elite. Certainly, representative democracy does not imply that the assemblies reflect the composition of society like a mirror, but the exclusion of entire large groups over a long period of time is an insuperable impediment simply because the interests of large sections of the population are not defended efficiently. For decades in India, politicians coming from the upper layers of society and representing their interests have competed through different parties or factions and alternated in power in a kind of closed circuit. The large number of parties in competition in the political arena has masked a great social homogeneity: representatives of the social elite have always dominated the mainstream parties. India may therefore be a case of political democracy without any social democracy, because the plebeians have never been able to get access to political responsibilities, at least not in North India.

One needs to distinguish, indeed, the situation prevailing in the North from that of the South. The first sections of this chapter will highlight this contrast between the South and the North, with a focus on the conservative overtone of the system institutionalized by the Congress Party, for many years the dominant party in India. Then the chapter will examine the impact of affirmative action programs in order to show that, while they were implemented in North India much later than in the South, they played a major role in the political mobilization of the lower castes there, especially after the Mandal affair of 1990. In this context, the chapter will scrutinize the rise of the low-caste-dominated political parties in Uttar Pradesh and Bihar, their two main strongholds. The last section will qualify this phenomenon by arguing that, though all the political parties pay some lip service to the lower castes, they are not promoting their cause in the same way.

The Progressive South: The Ethnicization of Caste and Affirmative Action

The overrepresentation of the social elite in the political sphere has always been more pronounced in the Hindi-speaking states than anywhere else. In the South, the upper castes lost ground early. There was an element of class in this diverging trajectory. The kinds of land settlement that the British introduced in India were not the same in these two areas. While the *zamindari* system (and its variants such as the *taluqdari*, *malguzari*, and *jagirdari* systems) prevailed in North India, the *raiyatwari* system was more systematically implemented in the South. In the North, when the colonizers went to levy estate taxes, they often used *zamindars* who had been established under the Mughal Empire; these intermediaries of the central authority, who were often upper-caste Rajputs or Muslims of aristocratic descent, were allowed to levy taxes the peasants owed against payment of a tribute. They were recognized as landowners by the British in exchange for the privilege of collecting taxes in the rural area. In the South, where the Mughal administration had not been as powerful, the British did not find such a dense network of *zamindars* (or the equivalent). They tended to select individual farmers as landproprietors and direct taxpayers. This *raiyatwari* system (from *raiyat*, "cultivator") was more conducive to the formation of a relatively egalitarian peasantry than the *zamindari* system.

For another thing, these two megaregions have always had different caste profiles. In the Hindi belt, the caste system has traditionally been the closest to the *varna* model, with its four orders and its untouchables. In the South, the twice born are seldom "complete," since the warrior and merchant castes are often absent or poorly represented. Correlatively, members of the upper *varnas* are fewer in the South than in the North: according to the 1931 census, they represented about 20 percent of the population—including 10 percent brahmins—in the United Provinces (today Uttar Pradesh) and 24.2 percent in Rajputana (today Rajasthan), whereas in the South, the proportion of the brahmins and even of the other twice born was and still is low. In Tamil Nadu and Andhra Pradesh, for instance, the brahmins represented about 3 percent of the population according to the 1931 census, and the other upper castes were marginal, which is still the case.

In addition, the caste system underwent an earlier and more significant change in South India. The caste system has often been analyzed by anthropologists as one based on the typically Hindu notion of ritual purity, which explains the domination by the custodians of this value system, the brahmins, who occupy the most prestigious position in the social order. This hierarchical arrangement explains the central role played by Sanskritization, a practice that M.N. Srinivas has defined as "the process in which a 'low' Hindu caste, or tribal or other group, changes its customs, ritual, ideology and way of life in the direction of a high, and frequently, 'twice-born caste' that is the Brahmins, but also the Kshatriyas or even the Vaishyas."[3] By adopting the most prestigious features of the upper castes' ethos, the lower castes explicitly acknowledge their social inferiority.

Things changed early in the South, primarily in reaction to the census operations organized by the British and their decision to establish the rankings of the castes (*jatis*) within the *varnas*. Caste associations were created to put pressure on the administration in order to improve the castes' rank in the census tables. This move was in keeping with the logic of Sanskritization, since the objective was not to opt out of the system but to rise within it according to its own rules and values. However, caste associations became secularized when the British started to classify castes on, for instance, the basis of the concept of martial races in order to recruit these groups into the colonial army. The associations also claimed new advantages from the state through quotas in the education system and in the administration. Caste associations therefore became interest groups.[4] In terms of social transformation, the most remarkable achievement of these associations concerns the unity of the caste groups. They have successfully incited the subcastes to adopt the same name in the census and to break the barriers of endogamy, a process that was especially successful in the South.[5] S. Barnett has convincingly argued that this kind of fusion tended to transform castes into

---

3. M.N. Srinivas, *Social Change in Modern India*, 3rd ed. (Hyderabad: Orient Longman, 1995), 6.

4. Susanne Hoeber Rudolph and Lloyd I. Rudolph have underlined the modern character of caste associations in "The Political Role of India's Caste Associations," in *Social Change: The Colonial Situation*, ed. Immanuel Wallerstein (New York: J. Wiley, 1966), 448.

5. This has been observed by Robert Hardgrave in the case of the Nadars of Tamil Nadu. Their caste association, the Nadar Mahajana Sangam, was founded in 1910, and it promoted what he calls "caste fusion" as "the unit of endogamy expanded" (Robert L. Hardgrave Jr., "Caste: Fission and Fusion," *Economic and Political Weekly* (July 1968): 1065–70. See also Robert L. Hardgrave, *The Nadars of Tamilnad* (Berkeley and Los Angeles: University of California Press, 1969).

ethnic groups.[6] This evolution was consummated with the claim by the lower castes of South India that they were Dravidians, a community with a distinctive language and common racial bonds.

The primary implication of this ethnicization of caste lies in its provision of alternative, nonhierarchical social imaginaries with a remarkable emancipatory potential. During the Madras Presidency, the low-caste leaders launched a nonbrahmin movement that portrayed the lower castes as the original inhabitants of India.[7] The movement obviously drew its inspiration from British Orientalism, since Reverend Caldwell (1819–91) had already suggested that brahmins were colonizers whereas the original inhabitants had been Dravidians who spoke Tamil, Telugu, and so forth.[8] This identity-building process crystallized with Ramaswami Naicker, alias Periyar, who founded the self-respect movement in the 1920s and the Dravidar Kazhagam in 1944. These organizations attracted low-caste people as well as untouchables into a kind of Dravidian front.

Affirmative action programs played a key role in the making of the Dravidian movement. The British implemented their first affirmative action measures during the Madras Presidency in the 1870s in order to promote the education of what they called the Backward Classes. While the list of Backward Classes increased and widened from 39 to 131 communities in the 1920s, the untouchables claimed the right to be treated as a distinct class, which led to the 1925 decision to parse out the "backward" designation between Depressed Classes (untouchables and tribals) and Castes Other than Depressed Classes.[9] In addition to establishing quotas in the education system that favored the Backward Classes, the British reserved a large number of seats (twenty-eight out of sixty-five) for the much larger "nonbrahmin" category in the framework of the 1919 constitutional reform. This measure helped the Justice Party—an explicitly antibrahmin party—to win the 1920 elections. The new government immediately developed a third area of affirmative action, the establishment of quotas in the administration. The First Communal Government Order,

---

6. S. Barnett, "Identity Choice and Caste Ideology in Contemporary South India," in *The New Wind: Changing Identities in South India*, ed. K. David (The Hague: Mouton, 1977), 401.

7. V. Geetha and S.V. Rajadurai, *Towards a Non-Brahmin Millennium: From Iyothee Thass to Periyar* (Calcutta: Samya, 1998), 43.

8. N. Ram, "Dravidian Movement in Its Pre-Independence Phases," *Economic and Political Weekly* (February 1979): 377–402.

9. P. Radhakrishnan, "Backward Classes in Tamil Nadu: 1872–1988," *Economic and Political Weekly* (March 10, 1990): 509–17.

in 1921, asked the chiefs of all administrative services, the collectors, and the district judges to issue every six months a list of their recruits classified into six categories: brahmins, nonbrahmin Hindus, Christian Indians, Muslims, Europeans and Anglo-Indians, and others.[10] From the second half of 1921, a readjustment took place as the administration recruited 22 percent of its staff from brahmins, 48 percent from nonbrahmin Hindus, 10 percent from Christian Indians, 15 percent from Muslims, 2 percent from Europeans and Anglo-Indians, and 3 percent from other groups. This move by the Justice Party's government confirmed that the quest for empowerment was one of the driving forces sustaining the nonbrahmin movement in Madras. The movement exemplifies the way affirmative action helped forge a coalition of a wide array of castes. The scope of this coalition, however, must not be exaggerated. The Panchamas (an untouchable caste), for instance, were left out by the Justice Party as soon as it gained power; the other, higher-level nonbrahmins had used them for electoral power gain only to drop them soon after.[11]

The rise to power of the Dravidian/nonbrahmin movement challenged the Congress Party to democratize itself to retain power. As everywhere else, the party had been dominated by brahmins. In the 1930s, however, Congress leaders began to realize that the Justice Party and the self-respect movement were forces to reckon with. They made "attempts to incorporate even the lowliest groups under their leadership."[12] They focused first on the lowest castes, the untouchables, but they were also able to attract other low castes such as the Nadars. The rise to power of Kamaraj Nadar epitomized this new, accommodating attitude of the Congress Party. C. Rajagopalachari, a brahmin, was then the towering figure of the Congress in Tamil Nadu. He became chief minister in 1937 and again in 1947, but Kamaraj succeeded him in 1954. At that time, the brahmins represented only 5 percent of the members of the legislative assembly (MLAs), compared with 17.2 percent in 1937,[13] which means that by the early 1950s the representation of the brahmins in the assembly was almost proportionate to their population share.

---

10. For the complete text, see Eugene F. Irschick, *Politics and Social Conflict: The Non-Brahmin Movement and Tamil Separatism, 1916–1929* (Bombay: Oxford University Press, 1969), 368.

11. Ibid., 188, 192.

12. Ibid., 145.

13. See S. Saraswati, *Minority Politics in Madras State* (Delhi: Impex, 1974); and C. Baker, "The Congress and the 1937 Elections in Madras," *Modern Asian Studies* (October 1976): 586.

North India: The Resilience of Sanskritization and Conservative Democracy Under the Congress Raj

In this chapter, North India is most often used as a synonym for the "Hindi belt." One may wonder to what extent the six states of the Hindi belt—Uttar Pradesh, Bihar, Madhya Pradesh, Rajasthan, Haryana, and Delhi—form a relevant unit. As mentioned above, these areas had a type of land settlement in common (since the *zamindari* system prevailed in most of these places) and had the same kind of caste system (since the twice born were all represented and were in large numbers). Another feature was the comparatively high proportion of princely states: two of the most important states of the Hindi belt, Rajasthan and Madhya Pradesh, were largely born from the merging of former princely states. These were all factors inhibiting the forces of social change.

In this context, the caste system did not change in the way it had in the South. Caste associations did not prepare the ground for any significant ethnicization process but instead remained within the framework of Sanskritization, partly because of the influence of the Arya Samaj. This socioreligious reform movement, for instance, canvassed for the adoption of the sacred thread by the Yadavs, cowherds who form the largest Shudra *jati* in Uttar Pradesh and Bihar. In so doing, the Arya Samaj sought to empower lower castes socially by including them in the Hindu twice-born groups, signified by the sacred thread. But the organization was still paying allegiance to the traditional caste structure. The Arya Samajists also enrolled the Yadavs in the cow protection movement. This movement, initiated in 1893 and relaunched at several points during the first two decades of the twentieth century, attracted many Yadavs who were anxious to emulate the upper castes.[14] The propensity of the Yadavs toward Sanskritization is evident from their attempt to "Aryanize" their history. The first history of the Yadavs was written by Kithal Krishna Khedekar in the late nineteenth century. This work was finalized by his son, R.V. Khedekar, and published in 1959 under the title *The Divine Heritage of the Yadavs*. The book situates the origins of the Yadavs in the Abhiras and then in the ruling dynasties mentioned as Yadavs in the *Mahabharata* and the Puranas. The caste history tries to demonstrate that the Abhiras were of Aryan

---

14. Gyanendra Pandey, "Rallying Round the Cow: Sectarian Strife in the Bhojpuri Region, c. 1888–1917," in *Subaltern Studies II*, ed. Ranajit Guha (Delhi: Oxford University Press, 1983), 104.

origin and that Rewari was the last representative of the Abhira king-doms.[15] This narrative certainly aims at giving the Yadavs an ethnic identity, but in this case the ethnicization process is embedded in the Sanskritization logic. In contrast to the lower-caste leaders of South India who tried to invent a Dravidian identity that presented the Shudras and untouchables as the original inhabitants of the country *against* the Aryans, the Yadavs claim that they *are* Aryans in order to enhance their status *within* caste society.

The untouchables of North India were also exposed to the influence of the Arya Samaj at the turn of the twentieth century. This is evident from the Jatav movement in Uttar Pradesh. The Jatavs are Chamars, untouchable leather workers, who claimed descent from the Yadu race, which allegedly entitled them to be known as Kshatriyas, like the Yadavs; once again, the Arya Samaj missions were responsible for propagating these views. They were especially successful through their schools among the sons of Agra Chamars who had become rich in the leather trade.[16] The Jatav Mahasabha, which was founded in Agra in 1917, preached moral reform, vegetarianism, teetotalism, and temperance to achieve a cleaner life and higher status. The resilience of Sanskritization helped the upper caste to maintain its social hegemony and its political domi-nation of the Congress Party.

Upper-caste notables remained the backbone of the Congress Party's network, and for decades the social deficit of democracy in North India resulted from the clientelistic politics of this party. The Congress selected its candidates from among vote-bank "owners," who were often upper-caste landlords or businesspeople who could gather the support of those who depended on them at election time.[17] Many of the landlords were former rulers (maharajas or nawabs). The typically Indian notion of vote banks is a key element in this pyramid of power. The system has been convincingly defined as depending on the votes "that can be delivered by local potentates acting as political intermediaries between the parties and the electorate, and a personalised and particularistic structure of political

---

15. L. Michelutti, "Ahirs-Yadavs Between Society and Politics" (paper presented at the Fifteenth Conference of the Association for Modern South Asian Studies, Copenhagen, September 1996), 16.

16. Owen Lynch, *The Politics of Untouchability: Social Mobility and Social Change in a City of India* (New York: Columbia University Press, 1969), 68–69.

17. See Myron Weiner, *Party Building in a New Nation: The Indian National Congress* (Chicago: Chicago University Press, 1967), 15.

Table 1

Caste and Community of the MPs Elected in the Hindi Belt, 1952–67 (in %)

Castes and Communities	1952	1957	1962	1967
Upper castes	64.00	58.60	54.90	55.50
Intermediate castes and OBCs	5.45	6.67	9.86	12.39
SCs/STs	21.18	25.00	26.76	26.15
Muslims	5.42	4.76	4.23	3.67
	N = 203	N = 210	N = 213	N = 218

Source: Database compiled by the author on the basis of interviews.
Note: This table relies on the figures concerning Uttar Pradesh, Bihar, Rajasthan, Madhya Pradesh, Delhi, Chandigarh, and the Hindi-speaking districts of Punjab (which were to form Himachal Pradesh and Haryana).

support."[18] This sociopolitical domination relied on class relations[19] but also on caste, since the "personalised" rapport in question had to do with reverence and fear vis-à-vis the superior. Class and caste largely coincided in this power structure. The clientelistic dimension of the Congress fit with the vertical arrangement of society, as is evident from the caste background of the members of Parliament (MPs) from the Hindi belt in the 1950s and 1960s. As shown in table 1, in 1952, 64 percent of the MPs belonged to upper castes, and that was still the case of 55.5 percent of them in 1967; over the same period, the intermediate and low castes rose from 5.5 percent to only 12.5 percent of the total, and the Scheduled Castes and Tribes rose from 21 percent to 26 percent because of reservations.[20] Like the SCs (the official designation for the untouchables), the Scheduled Tribes (STs; the official designation for the tribal population) benefit from quotas in proportion to their number.

In spite of these quotas, the SCs and STs were marginalized in North India after independence, preventing them from emerging as a political force, as the fate of Bhim Rao Ambedkar's political parties testifies. Ambedkar, the first pan-Indian leader of the SCs, launched three political parties: the Indian Labour Party (1936), the Scheduled Castes

18. "Voting Behaviour in a Developing Society: A Working Paper," in *Party System and Elections Studies*, ed. Centre for the Study of Developing Societies (Bombay: Allied Publishers, 1967), 280.

19. Pranab Bardhan has identified three "dominant proprietary classes" in India: industrial-capitalists, rich farmers, and white collars/professionals. See *The Political Economy of Development in India* (Oxford: Blackwell, 1984).

20. In 1952, the percentage of MPs whose caste I could not identify was 3 percent, and in 1967 it was 1.5 percent.

Federation (1942), and the Republican Party of India, whose concept he defined just before he died in 1956. None of these parties really took off. First, they did not succeed in transcending the deep cleavages that divided the SCs. Therefore, the parties remained confined to one or two groups, such as the Jatavs in North India and the Mahars—Ambedkar's caste—in Maharashtra. Second, the Congress had become adept at co-opting SC leaders who were known for their moderation, such as Jagjivan Ram in Bihar, or who toned down their militancy once they were accommodated in the power structure, such as B.P. Maurya in Uttar Pradesh. This strategy was one of the reasons the Congress succeeded in attracting SC voters who tended to cast their votes for individuals and follow their advice, irrespective of the party they belonged to. As a result, the ruling party tended to attract voters who were poles apart in the social structure and presumably in their political interests: besides a large number of members of the upper castes (especially brahmins), many SC people voted for the party. For this reason, the Congress support base has been presented as a "coalition of extremes."[21]

Naturally, the parties that were competing with the Congress indicted this approach to society and politics. Historically, in North India, two kinds of strategies have prevailed among those who have attempted to dislodge the upper-caste, urban establishment from its position of power. The first strategy concentrated on the mobilization of peasants (*kisans*). It was initiated by members of cultivating castes, such as Chhotu Ram—a Jat—in Punjab in the 1920s–1940s and Swami Sahajanand—a Bhumihar—who became a leading figure of the Bihar Kisan Sabha in the 1930s. The second strategy relied more on caste identity and was primarily articulated by socialist leaders such as Ram Manohar Lohia, who regarded caste as the main obstacle to an egalitarian society. While the "*kisan* school" endeavored to gather all those engaged in cultivation on the basis of socioeconomic demands, the caste-oriented socialists attempted to form an alliance of nonelite groups on the basis—mainly—of affirmative action techniques: they asked for caste-based quotas, especially in the administration, in favor of the Other Backward Classes (OBCs). Indeed, affirmative action played a key role in the political mobilization of the lower castes in North India.

---

21. Paul Brass, "The Politicization of the Peasantry in a North Indian State," *Journal of Peasant Studies* 8 (1980): 3–36.

The Political Impact of Affirmative Action

Under the British Raj, as the Madras Presidency played a pioneering role in the making of the policies of affirmative action, the central administration gradually moved in the same direction and eventually tried to harmonize the local classifications. The time-honored expression the central government used to designate the lower and intermediate castes had first been Depressed Classes, a group for which seats in local and national assemblies were reserved from 1919 on. However, after the 1935 Government of India Act, the untouchables were designated as SCs, and the denomination spread throughout the provinces of British India. The untouchables continued to be designated as SCs even after independence, when the lower castes were designated as OBCs. While the former received a quota of 15 percent—their share in the general population—in the education system, the assemblies, and the administration, the latter were not treated the same way. Their very definition was a problem, as evident by the use of the word *class* instead of *caste* in "Other Backward Classes," though the term was used to designate the lower castes other than the SCs. How is it that caste was the relevant criterion for identification in one case and class in the other? One must go back to the Constituent Assembly debates to understand this.

On December 13, 1946, Jawaharlal Nehru, in his first speech before the Constituent Assembly on his objectives resolution, announced that special measures were to be taken in favor of "minorities, backward and tribal areas and depressed and other backward classes."[22] He did not elaborate further, and, interestingly, senior congressmen such as K.M. Munshi resisted any effort to clarify what these OBCs were.[23] Article 340 of the Indian Constitution, voted on January 26, 1950, stated, "The President [of the Republic] can by decree nominate a Commission formed by persons he considers to be competent to investigate, within the Indian territory, on the condition of classes suffering of backwardness as well in social as in educational terms, and on the problems they meet, the way of proposing measures which could be taken by the Central or a State Government in order to eliminate difficulties and improve their condition."

The first Backward Classes Commission was appointed on January 29, 1953, under the chairmanship of a former disciple of Mohandas K.

---

22. *Constituent Assembly Debates,* vol. 1 (New Delhi: Lok Sabha Secretariat, 1989), 59.
23. Ibid., vol. 7, 697.

Gandhi, Kaka Kalelkar.[24] Its report relied heavily on the concept of caste to define the OBCs, so much so that it established a list of 2,399 castes, representing about 32 percent of the Indian population, that formed the bulk of the "socially and educationally backward classes." The OBCs were therefore defined as those castes that, in the Indian social system, are situated above the untouchables but below the upper castes and the intermediate castes that are predominantly made up of peasant-proprietors. The OBCs form the bulk of the Shudras, and their professional activity often consists of working in the field or as artisans. In order to redress the socioeconomic and educational malaise of the OBCs, the Kalelkar Commission formulated two main recommendations. First, the OBCs should benefit from a 70 percent quota in technical education institutions (including the disciplines of applied sciences, medicine, agriculture, veterinary studies, and engineering).[25] Second, quotas had to be reserved for them in the central and state administrations: 40 percent of the vacancies in classes III and IV, 33.3 percent in class II, and 25 percent in class I.[26] The Indian administration is divided into four categories—like the *varna* system—ranging from the elitist class I, where one finds the Indian Administrative Service, to the plebian class IV, where one finds sweepers, who come mostly from the SCs.

The report was rejected by Nehru's government. G.B. Pant, the home minister, objected that "with the establishment of our society on the socialist pattern . . . , social and other distinctions will disappear as we advance towards that goal."[27] He also disapproved of the use of caste as the most prominent criterion for identifying the Backward Classes. He considered that "the recognition of the specified castes as backward may serve to maintain and even perpetuate the existing distinctions on the basis of caste."[28] The report was presented before Parliament accompanied by a memorandum by Pant on September 3, 1956, but was not even discussed.[29] In May 1961, the Nehru government decided that there was no need for an all-India list of the OBCs and that consequently there

---

24. *Report of the Backward Classes Commission*, vol. 1 (Delhi: Government of India, 1955).

25. Ibid., 125.

26. Ibid., 140.

27. *Memorandum on the Report of the Backward Classes Commission* (Delhi: Ministry of Home Affairs, n.d.), 2.

28. Ibid.

29. *Report of the Backward Classes Commission: First Part*, vols. 1 and 2 (New Delhi: Government of India, 1980), 2.

would be no reservation policy for them at the center. Even though they were responsible for Article 340 of the Constitution, congresspeople were obviously reluctant to cater to the needs of the lower castes, either because of sheer conservatism or because of a deliberate negation of the role of caste as opposed to the Marxist category of class. They did support positive discrimination programs in favor of the SCs, probably because these were in the most pitiable condition and because they would not be in a position to pose a threat to the upper-caste establishment even after the implementation of such programs. In fact, this policy enabled the Congress Party to patronize SC leaders in a clientelistic manner.

The socialists—especially the followers of Lohia—remained the main proponents of affirmative action in favor of the OBCs. The adepts of *kisan* politics, including Charan Singh, were also gradually attracted to it to a lesser extent.[30] Over the last decades, these two groups have contributed to the rise of middle-caste peasants and then of the OBCs in North Indian politics. The first significant changes occurred in the 1960s when the middle castes and OBCs massively entered the Bihar and Uttar Pradesh legislative assemblies under the auspices of the socialist parties and Charan Singh. *Kisan* politics asserted itself in the 1970s and 1980s, thanks to Charan Singh and his lieutenants. The two traditions merged in 1977 in the Janata Party, a party that was to rule India until 1979 and whose government prepared the ground for the relaunching of quota politics by appointing the Mandal Commission.

On December 20, 1978, Prime Minister Morarji Desai announced the government's decision to appoint the Second Backward Classes Commission, whose terms of reference were close to those of the first one: it had to determine the criteria defining the OBCs and to recommend measures, such as reservations in the administration, that could contribute to their social uplift.[31] In contrast to the Kalelkar Commission, this commission did not include any members of the upper castes; it included only OBC members, three out of five of whom were MPs or ex-MPs. The chairman of the commission, Bindhyeshwari Prasad Mandal, was a Yadav who had been elected MP in Bihar in 1967 on a socialist ticket and who had been chief minister of this state for a month in 1968. He

---

30. For more details, see Christophe Jaffrelot, "The Rise of the Other Backward Classes in the Hindi Belt," *Journal of Asian Studies* 59 (2000): 86–108.
31. *Report of the Backward Classes Commission: First Part,* vii.

played an important part in the Janata Party, and in 1980 he became a member of the party's central election commission. Unsurprisingly, the Mandal Commission advocated the socialist approach of affirmative action: "To treat unequals as equals is to perpetuate inequality. When we allow weak and strong to compete on an equal footing, we are loading the dice in favour of the strong and holding only a mock competition in which the weaker partner is destined to failure right from the start."[32]

The Mandal Commission argued that in India the caste system was the root cause of structural inequality. It had therefore no inhibition against recognizing caste as the main factor in the backwardness of the OBCs. The members of the commission considered that this social category was made up of castes—mostly of low ritual status[33]—that represented 52 percent of the Indian population. After identifying the OBCs, the Mandal Commission investigated their needs and recommended in its report that 27 percent of the posts in the central administration and in public sector undertakings should be reserved for them. This recommendation reflected an Ambedkarite and socialist-like approach of compensatory discrimination, since the objective was to give the OBCs access to power, not to give them jobs. The report read, for instance, "By increasing the representation of OBCs in government services, we *give them an immediate feeling of participation in the governance of this country.*"[34]

The report was submitted to Indira Gandhi's government in December 1980, but it was not laid on the table of the Lok Sabha until April 30, 1982, and then there was barely a quorum in the house, a clear indication of the ruling party's priority. The most vehement speakers were MPs from the Lok Dal, the party Charan Singh had created some time after the breakup of the Janata Party. One of them, Chandrajit Yadav, emphasized that the main finding of the Mandal Commission report was that "the other backward classes constituted 52% of our population."[35] OBC leaders were obviously realizing that the "community" was in a majority and could form an unbeatable constituency. The senior most representative then in the house, Defense Minister R. Venkataraman, considered that the Mandal Commission report, which had identified

32. Ibid., 21.
33. Brahmin and Rajput subcastes that suffered from economic deprivation were classified as OBCs, too.
34. *Report of the Backward Classes Commission: First Part,* 57. Emphasis added.
35. *Lok Sabha Debates,* vol. 31 (New Delhi: Lok Sabha Secretariat, 1982), col. 359.

3,743 castes, contradicted the findings of the Kalelkar Commission, which "identified somewhere 2,000 and odds" such castes. A few days after the Lok Sabha debate, the home minister, Giani Zail Singh, gravely declared that "the Central Government have forwarded the Report of the Commission to the various State Governments for obtaining their views."[36] That was the only action taken by the Congress.

The presentation of the Mandal Commission report before the Lok Sabha marked the partial conversion of Charan Singh to the notion of quota politics. In 1982 he held a meeting outside the Lok Sabha to put pressure on the MPs for the adoption of the report's recommendations. However, the Lok Dal was not in a position to continue its fight for the implementation of the Mandal report. There were many reasons for this: First, *kisan* leaders were not interested in demanding the implementation of the Mandal Commission report when they did not belong to an OBC caste. The Jats, for instance, were in this situation. Second, the party was increasingly suffering from caste-based differences. In 1987, the split of the Lok Dal into two parties—Lok Dal (A) and Lok Dal (B)—resulted partly from the desire of Yadav leaders, such as Mulayam Singh Yadav, who joined Lok Dal (B), to emancipate themselves from Jat tutelage. The tension remained prevalent within the Janata Dal, but this party's policy consummated the triumph of quota politics, not only within the party but at an all-India level. In fact, what was at stake was North India: in the South, the upper castes had already been displaced from their seat of power, while in the North this process really began in the late 1980s within the framework of affirmative action policies.

The Janata Dal and the Empowerment of the OBCs in the Hindi Belt

Twenty years after the first Janata experiment, a second one started with the rise to power of the Janata Dal in 1989. Once again, this success was due to North Indian voters: 101 of the 143 seats won by the Janata Dal came from the four largest states of the Hindi belt. It was a significant achievement for a party that had been founded one year before, on October 11, 1988. But the Janata Dal had not been developed from scratch. In North India, it relied on the local network of the Janata Party, the Lok Dal (A) of Ajit Singh, and the Lok Dal (B) of Devi Lal—another Jat

36. *Memorandum Explaining Action Taken on the Report of the Second Backward Classes Commission* (New Delhi: Government of India, Ministry of Home Affairs, 1982), 5–6.

leader who had taken over the party and become chief minister of Haryana. All these parties merged in the Janata Dal. While the Janata Party had been a heterogeneous coalition-like party whose followers ranged from socialists to Hindu nationalists, the Janata Dal primarily amalgamated only two currents of Indian politics, that of the socialists and that of Charan Singh.

The discourse of the party chief, V.P. Singh, was heavily loaded with socialist references. The 1989 National Front election manifesto promised that "implementation of reservation policy will be made effective in government, public and private sector industrial undertakings, banking institutions, etc., by resorting to special recruitment drives so as to fulfill their quotas within the shortest possible time"[37] and that "the recommendations of the Mandal Commission will be implemented expeditiously."[38] V.P. Singh became prime minister in December 1989, and he announced this decision in a one-and-a-half-page *suo moto* statement in both houses of Parliament on August 7, 1990. He justified it in his Independence Day address on August 15 by the need to give "a share to the poor in running the Government."[39] As the Mandal Commission had, he looked at the administration as a power institution: "Bureaucracy is an important organ of the power structure. It has a decisive role in decision-making. We want to give an effective here [*sic*] in the power structure and running of the country to the depressed, down-trodden and backward people."[40]

This approach could not please the proponents of *kisan* politics. All the Jat ministers strongly objected to the notion that their caste should be included on the list of OBCs.[41] A signature campaign was organized among the MPs, and 107 signatures were collected from Jat and Muslim leaders who also wanted some of their coreligionists to be recognized as OBCs.[42] V.P. Singh made a vague promise but refused to dilute the Mandal scheme. He announced the implementation of the Mandal Commission report only a few days after Devi Lal resigned from his government.

The new quota of 27 percent did not represent many jobs. Of the

---

37. *National Front: Lok Sabha Elections 1989 Manifesto* (New Delhi: V.P. Singh, Convenor, National Front, 1989), 26.

38. Ibid., 27.

39. "Justice for the Poor," in *Evolution of Socialist Policy in India*, ed. Surendro Mohan, Hari Dev Sharma, Vinod Prasad Singh, and Sunilam (New Delhi: Bapu Kaldate, 1997), 360.

40. Ibid., 361.

41. Satpal Malik claims that he was the first minister to ask for the inclusion of the Jats (interview by the author, New Delhi, October 25, 1998).

42. Rachid Masood, interview by the author, New Delhi, October 28, 1998.

204,288 recruitments that had been made in 1988, 55,158 jobs would have been given to members of OBCs according to the new reservation policy. In fact, the number of posts was declining (from 226,781 in 1985 to 204,288 in 1988) whereas the candidates were more and more numerous (from 2.4 million in 1985 to 2.9 million in 1988).[43] But the quota was for that very reason even more strongly resented by the upper-caste people who regarded administration as their—already shrinking—monopoly. In 1980, the OBCs represented 12.55 percent of the central services and the SCs and STs 18.72 percent (the OBCs represented less than 5 percent in class I services, as against the high castes' 90 percent).[44] Besides, quotas for the SCs and STs often remained unfilled.

Soon after V.P. Singh announced the implementation of the Mandal Commission report, upper-caste students set up organizations such as the Anti-Mandal Commission Forum, based at Delhi University. The agitation started in Delhi, where students burned degrees, carried away the corpse of "merit," and damaged about sixty buses on August 24, 1990.[45] Generally speaking, North India was the epicenter of this agitation not only because of the upper-caste students' mobilization but also because of the behind-the-scenes activities of the Bharatiya Janata Party (BJP), or Indian People Party—the Hindu nationalist party whose strongholds are in the Hindi belt—the Congress Party, and Devi Lal in Haryana. Immediately after the first anti-Mandal demonstrations, leaders from the Janata Dal organized a countermobilization. V.P. Singh went to Patna for a rally at which slogans such as "Brahmin saala desh chhado!" (Bastard brahmin, get out of the country!) were shouted. Thus, 1990 was marked by an exacerbation of the cleavage between upper and lower castes, an atmosphere that explains the emotional value of the OBCs as a social category at that time. The main achievement of V.P. Singh was therefore to make a broad range of castes coalesce under the OBC label and, consequently, to contest the elite groups' domination more effectively than before. "Other Backward Classes" had become a relevant category for the lower castes because they had a vested interest in it, namely, the quotas promised by the Mandal Commission report. Many

---

43. *India Today*, September 15, 1990, 36–37.

44. These figures are based on replies furnished by thirty central ministries and departments and thirty-one attached and subordinate offices and public sector undertakings under the administrative control of fourteen ministries (for the complete statistical figures, see *Report of the Backward Classes Commission*, 42).

45. Anirudh Prasad, *Reservational Justice* (New Delhi: Deep and Deep, 1997), 58–59.

Table 2

Caste and Community of the MPs Elected in the Hindi Belt, 1980–99 (in %)

Castes and Communities	1984	1989	1991	1996	1998	1999
Upper castes	46.90	38.20	37.11	35.30	34.67	30.90
Intermediate castes	5.31	8.00	5.43	7.53	8.89	6.40
OBCs	11.10	20.87	22.60	24.80	23.56	22.20
SCs	17.26	17.78	18.10	18.14	18.22	17.80
STs	7.52	7.56	8.14	7.52	7.56	7.30
Muslims	9.73	5.78	4.52	3.54	5.33	5.00
	N = 226	N = 225	N = 221	N = 226	N = 225	N = 221

Source: Database compiled by the author on the basis of interviews.

of those who had been known as Shudras had internalized this administrative definition of their identity in the early 1990s simply because they
thought they could derive benefits from it. However, the category also
crystallized because of the attitude of the upper castes that had rejected
reservations in the administration. The cleavage between upper and lower
castes had suddenly been reinforced by a collective, open hostility on
the part of the former and even by the unleashing of violence. The low
castes began to share a political identity that was expressed in terms of
the OBCs versus the upper castes: caste had become the building block
of a larger social coalition.

The OBC phenomenon helped the low castes to organize themselves as
an interest group outside the vertical, clientelistic Congress-like pattern.
This enabled the low castes to benefit from their main asset, their massive
numbers, at the time of elections. A similar process had already taken
place in the South. In states such as Tamil Nadu, Andhra Pradesh, and
Karnataka, the upper castes had been dislodged from power in the 1960s
and 1970s. Their demographic weakness had been largely responsible for
their decline, whose main beneficiaries had been "upper Shudras," such
as the Kammas and the Reddys in Andhra Pradesh. In this state, the percentage of brahmin MLAs declined from 7.6 percent in 1957 to 4 percent
in 1978, while that of the upper Shudras rose from 36 percent to 39 percent and that of the OBCs from 13 percent to 19 percent.[46] The transition
in the Hindi belt began only in the late 1990s, as table 2 shows. Indeed,

---

46. Adapted from G. Ram Reddy, "The Politics of Accommodation: Caste, Class and
Dominance in Andhra Pradesh," in *Dominance and State Power in Modern India,* ed.
Francine Frankel and M.S.A. Rao, vol. 1 (Delhi: Oxford University Press, 1987), 305.

the percentage of OBC MPs from North India increased in the late 1980s and early 1990s because low-caste people had become more aware of their common interests and had decided not to vote any longer for upper-caste candidates but instead to cast their ballots for those from their own social milieu. Now, the OBCs represent 52 percent of society and form in many constituencies an unbeatable majority.

The percentage of OBC MPs from North India doubled from 11.1 percent in 1984 to 20.9 percent in 1989, largely because the Janata Dal, the winner of the ninth general elections, had offered a larger number of candidacies within the party to OBC candidates. The proportion of upper-caste MPs fell below 40 percent for the first time. Interestingly, the percentage of OBCs among the MPs continued to grow in 1991, in spite of the Congress Party's comeback, and in 1996, when the BJP became the largest party in the Lok Sabha. This evolution took place at the expense of the upper castes, because all the political parties were now giving larger numbers of tickets to OBC candidates. That was precisely the goal V.P. Singh had been pursuing. He was to declare in a lecture at Harvard University, "Now that every party is wooing the deprived classes, with every round of elections more and more representatives of the deprived sections will be elected. This will ultimately be reflected in the social composition of the local bodies, state governments, and the central government. A silent transfer of power is taking place in social terms."[47]

This approach of social change eventually prevailed at the expense of *kisan* politics: Jats reacted strongly to Singh's policy and deserted the Janata Dal. But lower castes rallied around the party and its regional offshoots in North India, especially in key states such as Uttar Pradesh and Bihar. In these states, two Janata Dal leaders from the caste of the Yadavs, Mulayam Singh Yadav and Laloo Prasad Yadav, took over in 1989–90 and promoted the interests of their own group by implementing new affirmative action programs.

Uttar Pradesh and Bihar: The Key States

Uttar Pradesh and Bihar deserve special mention not only because they are the two largest Indian states in terms of population (and, therefore, in terms of Lok Sabha seats—85 and 54 out of 542, respectively) but also because the rise to power of the lowest castes has been more dra-

---

47. Vishwanath Prasad Singh, "Power and Equality: Changing Grammar of Indian Politics," reproduced in Prasad, *Reservational Justice*, 316–17.

matic in these states than anywhere else in North India. Bihar has been governed by an OBC chief minister since 1990. In Uttar Pradesh, Mulayam Singh Yadav occupied the post twice—in 1989–91 and in 1993–95—and an SC-dominated party, the Bahujan Samaj Party, has achieved unprecedented electoral performances. The root cause of this socio-political change is well known since it unfolded in the post-Mandal context. But what are the main consequences of this silent revolution, and how has it materialized?

As chief minister of Uttar Pradesh in 1989–91, Mulayam Singh Yadav issued an amending ordinance giving the OBCs of the state the same reservations—27 percent—as the Mandal Commission report had recommended. After he formed the government once again on December 4, 1993, as the leader of a coalition with the Bahujan Samaj Party, his first decision was to implement the 27 percent quota. Then the government voted in the Uttar Pradesh Public Services (Reservation for Scheduled Castes, Scheduled Tribes and Other Backward Classes) Act on March 22, 1994. This new law reserved 21 percent of the posts for the SCs, 2 percent for the STs, and 27 percent for the OBCs.

Reservations were introduced in the *panchayati raj* institutions along the same pattern as in the administration. While the Seventy-Third Amendment to the Indian Constitution, in 1993, made the reservation of seats for SCs (in proportion to their demographic weight) and for women (33 percent) mandatory at all levels of the *panchayati raj* system, in June 1994, the Mulayam Singh Yadav government amended the Uttar Pradesh Panchayat Act of 1947 to include these changes and added one more modification: it granted a 27 percent quota to the OBCs.[48]

In addition to the administration and local body reservations, Mulayam Singh Yadav made provisions for 27 percent reservation for OBCs in medical colleges and educational institutions teaching engineering and management.[49] This decision was strongly resented in Uttarakhand, where the OBCs made up only 2 percent of the population.[50] The agitation there was judged illegitimate and politically motivated by Mulayam Singh

---

48. George K. Lieten and Ravi Srivastava, *Unequal Partners: Power Relations, Devolution and Development in Uttar Pradesh* (New Delhi: Sage, 1999), 250.

49. In 1994 his government had also passed another reservation scheme, the Uttar Pradesh State Universities Reservation in Admission for Scheduled Castes, Scheduled Tribes and Other Backward Classes, which provided a 21 percent quota for the SCs, a 2 percent quota for the STs, and a 27 percent quota for the OBCs.

50. On the Uttarakhand issue, see E. Mawdsley, "Uttarakhand Agitation and Other Backward Classes," *Economic and Political Weekly* (January 27, 1996): 205–10.

Yadav, who decided to repress it and launched a countermobilization. He emphasized that he was fighting for the 95 percent deprived people against the 5 percent privileged ones.

In order to strengthen his image as a low-caste leader, he transferred upper-caste bureaucrats to nonessential posts. The number of district-level bureaucrats from the upper castes decreased dramatically. These decisions—which were intentionally publicized—were made partly because of pressure from the Bahujan Samaj Party, but they were in tune with Mulayam Singh Yadav's strategy. Mulayam Singh "pampered" his fellow caste members in the administration. Out of 900 teachers appointed under his second government, 720 were Yadavs. In the police forces, out of 3,151 newly selected candidates, 1,223 also belonged to this caste.[51] This policy alienated the Kurmis, the second-largest OBC caste of the state.[52]

However, the performance of Mulayam Singh's party in the general elections of the 1990s in Uttar Pradesh suggests that he has succeeded in broadening his base. From about 13 percent of the valid votes in 1991, Mulayam's party reached about 21 percent in 1996–98 and then 24 percent in 1999, only 3.6 percentage points fewer than the "winner," the BJP.

As in Uttar Pradesh, the rise of the OBCs in Bihar is primarily the rise of the Yadavs. The Yadavs represented the largest caste group among the Bihar MPs in 1991, after the Mandal affair (17.3 percent as against 7.7 percent for the Rajputs). In 1996, they represented twice the percentage of the second-largest group, the Rajputs, at 22.2 percent as against 11.1 percent. Laloo Prasad Yadav, a Janata Dal leader who became chief minister of Bihar in March 1990, deliberately introduced a new style of politics highlighting the rustic qualities of the low-caste people of Bihar. For instance, he made a point of speaking the Bhojpuri dialect. Once voted into power, he increased the quota for the OBCs from 20 percent to 27 percent, and this was voted into law in 1992. In August 1993, the Patna University and Bihar University Amendment Bill was passed, according to which there would be 50 percent reservation of seats for the OBCs in the senates and syndicates of these universities.[53] Most of the

---

51. *India Today*, October 15, 1994, 37.
52. On the divisions within the OBCs, see Jaffrelot, "The Rise of the Other Backward Classes."
53. This and the information in the two following paragraphs is from S.N. Chaudhary, *Power-Dependence Relations: Struggle for Hegemony in Rural Bihar* (New Delhi: Har-Anand, 1999).

vice-chancellors and directors of these educational institutions have since been selected from among the OBCs. Still, in 1993, a member of the Indian Administrative Service from the SCs replaced a brahmin as chief secretary, and a member of the OBCs took over the charge of director general of police from another brahmin. Three years after Laloo Prasad Yadav took over, seventy upper-caste officials had sought—and obtained—transfer to the center because of the humiliation and ill treatment they suffered in Bihar. In addition to these voluntary shifts, the state government has transferred twelve out of thirteen divisional commissioners and 250 of the 324 returning officers in order to have more lower-caste people at the helm at the local level.

The government has also given jobs to a larger number of members of the OBCs. In 1996, the University Service Commission of Bihar recruited 1,427 lecturers for the universities and their constituent colleges in the state. Protests were immediately lodged because most of the candidates were OBC members, and more precisely Yadavs. In 1993, the Bihar Vidhan Sabha passed the Panchayati Raj Bill, according to which "the Panchayats with majority of people belonging to backward classes will be reserved for them only and in these Panchayats upper castes will be debarred from even contesting elections."

The fact that the lower castes have partly taken over power in Bihar is evident from the social profile of the governments of Laloo Prasad and his wife, Rabri Devi, who succeeded him in 1997 after he had to resign because of a charge of corruption registered against him. The percentage of ministers from the OBCs increased from an already high 46.5 percent in 1990–95 to 64.47 percent in 1995–2000. Significantly, this empowerment went almost exclusively to the upper OBCs—including the Yadavs—whose share rose from 35.2 percent to 57.89 percent, whereas the percentage of the lower OBCs decreased from 11.3 percent to 6.58 percent.

Similar to the case in Uttar Pradesh, the Kurmis resented the bias of Laloo Prasad Yadav in favor of his caste fellows when he appointed Yadavs as heads of important boards such as the Bihar Public Service Commission, the Bihar Secondary Education Service Commission, the Bihar State Electricity Board, and the Bihar Industrial Development Corporation.[54] Kurmi leaders felt sidelined, and one of the most prominent of them, Nitish Kumar, left the Janata Dal in 1994 to sponsor the creation of the Samata

---

54. Ibid., 242.

Dal with George Fernandes. This party made an alliance with the BJP in the mid-1990s. In spite of the division of the OBCs, the Rashtriya Janata Dal (RJD) of Laloo Prasad Yadav retained power thanks to the support of the Muslims and a large section of the SC voters. In Bihar, the party rose from an already high 27 percent of the valid vote in 1998 to 28 percent in the 1999 general elections and the 2000 assembly elections.

The OBCs, and more specifically the Yadavs, have thus benefited more than any other low-caste groups from the policies followed by Mulayam Singh and Laloo Prasad in Uttar Pradesh and Bihar, two states in which the Yadavs form the largest component of the OBCs. The OBCs, however, are not the only ones to have benefited from the post-Mandal mobilization. The *dalits*, or "broken men"—to use the name that people of the SCs tend to apply to themselves nowadays—have also profited by it.

A New Party of the Dalits: *The Bahujan Samaj Party*

The main political party advocating the cause of the *dalits*, the Bahujan Samaj Party (BSP), which was officially founded on April 14, 1984, has made rapid progress on the electoral front. Its growth from 2.07 percent of the valid vote in 1989 to 3.64 percent in 1996 enabled the party to obtain from the Election Commission the status of a national party after the 1996 elections, and it went on to get 4.7 percent of the valid vote in 1998. This growth chiefly resulted from the organizational efforts of the party's founder, Kanshi Ram, who had first launched trade unions of low-caste civil servants.[55] But it was also due to the electoral strategy of the BSP and the post-Mandal context, especially in Uttar Pradesh. While the BSP has reached double digits in another state—Punjab—Uttar Pradesh is the only state in which it has made real inroads in the last ten years, going from 9.93 percent of the valid vote in the 1989 general elections to 20.9 percent in 1998.

According to the Centre for the Study of Developing Societies (CSDS) opinion polls of 1996 and 1999,[56] most of the supporters of the BSP come from the SCs, and more precisely from the Chamars (the largest caste of Uttar Pradesh, with about 13 percent of the population of that

---

55. For more details, see Christophe Jaffrelot, "The Bahujan Samaj Party in North India: No Longer Just a Dalit Party?" *Comparative Studies of South Asia, Africa and the Middle East* 18 (1998).

56. The main results of these surveys have been published in *India Today*, August 31, 1996; P. Kumar, "Dalit and the BSP in Uttar Pradesh: Issues and Challenges," *Economic and Political Weekly* (April 3, 1999); and *Frontline*, November 19, 1999, 41.

state). In the 1990s, three-fourths of the Chamars voted for the BSP, according to the surveys.

The leap forward that the BSP achieved between 1993 and 1996 in Uttar Pradesh enabled the party to reach power through coalitions. The mobilization of the upper castes against the implementation of the Mandal Commission report had triggered a countermobilization that cut across low-caste cleavages. Not only did the OBCs discover the need for more solidarity and more activism, but the *dalits* felt the same, especially when the very notion of reservations—including for the SCs—started to be questioned by some upper-caste movements. The BSP was even more clearly a potential ally of the OBCs because Kanshi Ram acknowledged their need for quotas in the administration. The context created by the Mandal affair was therefore conducive to the alliance between the new party of Mulayam Singh Yadav, the Samajwadi Party (SP), and the BSP in 1993. However, this alliance also responded to tactical considerations fully in keeping with the pragmatic nature of Indian electoral politics. Kanshi Ram explicitly admitted, "The reason why I concluded alliances with Mulayam Singh Yadav is that if we join our votes in U[ttar] P[radesh] we will be able to form the government."[57]

In the 1993 assembly elections, the Samajwadi Party won 109 seats out of 425, and the BSP won 67. The two parties formed the government thanks to the Congress Party's support. Mulayam Singh Yadav became chief minister, and the BSP obtained eleven ministerial portfolios in a government of twenty-seven. Relations between the two partners, however, soon deteriorated. First, the BSP was becoming worried about the "Yadavization" of the state. Second, the OBCs, who were anxious to improve their social status and to keep the SCs in their place, reacted violently to the *dalits'* efforts to achieve social mobility. The OBCs' and the *dalits'* class interests are clearly antagonistic in Uttar Pradesh since the latter are often landless laborers or cultivators with very small plots who work for the former. Conflicts over the wages of the agricultural laborers and disputes regarding landownership have always been acute, but they have become even more frequent since the *dalits* and the OBCs grew more assertive following the 1993 elections. These bones of contention partly explain the increasing number of atrocities against the *dalits*.[58]

The breakup of the SP-BSP coalition showed how difficult it was to

57. Interview, *Sunday,* May 16, 1993, 10–11.
58. A. Mishra, "Challenge to the SP-BSP Government," *Economic and Political Weekly* (February 19, 1994), 409.

associate OBCs and SCs. It had been possible in 1993 because of the Mandal affair, but ties between the two parties began to weaken once the battle for quotas had been won. The 1993 assembly elections had been the culminating point of the anti–high caste mobilization. Yet the divorce between the SP and the BSP did not bring the latter back to square one. In fact, the BSP put an end to the coalition with the SP only to become actively involved in another alliance, in an even more favorable position. On June 3, 1995, Mayawati, Kanshi Ram's closest associate in Uttar Pradesh, became chief minister of the state with the BJP's support. This alliance was primarily directed against Mulayam Singh Yadav, whom the BSP and the BJP wanted to keep in check because of his increasing political influence that reflected the growing assertiveness of the OBCs, and especially the Yadavs. The alliance of the BSP with the BJP epitomized the convergence of the *dalit* and upper-caste leaders against the OBCs.

With Mayawati as chief minister, the largest state of India was for the first time governed by a member of the SCs, a Chamar.[59] For many members of the SCs, she became a source of pride. Mayawati's accession to Uttar Pradesh's top post therefore played a major part in the consolidation of the BSP's main vote bank. This consolidation also resulted from the benefits Mayawati granted to members of the lower castes. For example, the Ambedkar Villages Scheme, which had been started by Mulayam Singh Yadav to allot special funds for socioeconomic development for two years to villages whose populations were at least 50 percent *dalit*, was revised to include villages with at least 30 percent *dalit* (and even 22 percent in certain areas). Mayawati gave special treatment to the *dalits* of these villages since "all the roads, handpumps, houses, etc., have been largely built in their bastees [neighborhoods]."[60] Grants were created for *dalit* children attending classes between levels one and eight. As for the OBCs, Mayawati announced that they were to benefit from 27 percent of the state budget and that the quotas introduced by Mulayam Singh Yadav would be implemented as soon as possible.

Mayawati also altered the composition of the bureaucracy. She appointed supporters to key positions. More than 1,500 transfers took place in Uttar Pradesh during the 136 days of her government. This allowed

---

59. Before Mayawati, there had been only three *dalit* chief ministers, and none of them had been a woman: D. Sanjiviah in Andhra Pradesh, Ram Sunder Das in Bihar, and Jagannath Pahadiya in Rajasthan.

60. Sudha Pai, "Dalit Assertion in UP: Implications for Politics," *Economic and Political Weekly* (September 13, 1997): 2314.

her to post an SC district magistrate at the helm of almost half of the districts.[61] Her empowerment policy went much further than the Mandal scheme had. The BJP became worried because the BSP was reinforcing its local implantation, and the party withdrew its support from Mayawati on October 18, 1995.

The BSP decided to stand alone six months later, in the 1996 Lok Sabha elections. Yet the party doubled its share of valid votes in Uttar Pradesh, from about 10 percent in the 1989, 1991, and 1993 elections to 20.6 percent (9,483,739 votes, 50 more than the SP received). The Mayawati government had obviously enabled the party to broaden its base among the lower castes by showing that *dalits* could occupy the seat of power (in itself a very strong symbol) and exercise it to the profit of the downtrodden. The BSP was especially successful in consolidating the SCs behind its candidates. According to the aforementioned CSDS survey, during the 1996 assembly elections, 63.4 percent of the SCs voted for the party, as against 26 percent of the non-Yadav OBCs, 4.3 percent of the Yadavs, 4.7 percent of the Muslims, and less than 1 percent of the upper castes.[62]

Immediately after the 1996 elections in Uttar Pradesh, the BSP leaders announced that they would form a coalition with any political force willing and able to allocate the chief ministership to Mayawati. After six months of President's Rule, the BJP accepted their conditions. This decision can once again be explained by the apprehensions that Mulayam Singh Yadav generated in the BJP and the BSP.[63] According to the BJP-BSP agreement, Mayawati would be chief minister for six months, followed by a BJP leader, and the two would then function in rotation. As for the government, it would be made up half by BJP and half by BSP ministers. The BSP therefore came back to power thanks to a new reversal of alliances.

During her six-month tenure, Mayawati transferred 1,350 civil and police officials.[64] Only two days after taking power, she announced that 250 constable-clerks would soon be recruited from among the SCs and STs.[65] She also revived the Ambedkar Villages Scheme under her direct

---

61. *Frontline*, December 1, 1995, 31.

62. Kanchan Chandra and Chandrika Parmar, "Party Strategies in the Uttar Pradesh Assembly Elections," *Economic and Political Weekly* (February 1, 1997): 215.

63. As a cabinet minister in the Deve Gowda government, Mulayam Singh had indeed acquired a strong influence over the governor of Uttar Pradesh, Romesh Bhandari.

64. *Times of India*, September 18, 1997.

65. Ibid., March 23, 1997.

supervision and stated that she was focusing her political tenure "on one section of society," the *dalits*.[66] The Rs. 3.5 billion (350 crore) scheme covered 11,000 villages. Mayawati also implemented the Scheduled Castes and Scheduled Tribes (Prevention of Atrocities) Act of 1989 in a more drastic way than any of her predecessors.

After six months in office, Mayawati turned the post of chief minister over to Kalyan Singh from the BJP, but the BSP immediately criticized the government order he issued stating that the act mentioned above should not be misused and withdrew its support from him. However, contrary to Kanshi Ram's expectations, the Kalyan Singh government did not fall, because the BJP had attracted a sufficient number of defectors from the Congress Party and the BSP to stay in power. The breakaway group from the BSP consisted of twelve MLAs, all of whom were rewarded with ministerial berths in Kalyan Singh's cabinet.[67] The BSP contested the 1998 Lok Sabha elections on its own in Uttar Pradesh, and it polled almost the same number of votes as in 1996.

While the BSP has consolidated its base in Uttar Pradesh, it is on the decline everywhere else, largely because of organizational difficulties, including factionalism: as Ambedkar had, Kanshi Ram tends to concentrate power in his own hands, depriving his party of a strong structure and causing much jealousy. The BSP is also affected by the reaction of upper-caste-dominated political parties, as is evident from the co-option of some of its MLAs by the BJP in Uttar Pradesh and by the Congress in Madhya Pradesh.

The rise of the OBCs and *dalits* to power in North India, in conjunction with the rising electoral participation of the low castes, has led Yogendra Yadav to consider that India has experienced a "second democratic upsurge" in the 1990s.[68] A transfer of power is certainly taking place, but this analysis needs to be qualified from three points of view. First, this phenomenon has not spread evenly across the Hindi belt; states such as Rajasthan, for instance, lag behind. Second, the OBCs and the *dalits* are still very much divided, with those benefiting from the ongoing social democratization of Indian political democracy forming a new

66. Interview, *India Today*, August 11, 1997, 33.
67. The BSP petitioned the speaker, K.N. Tripathi, since this breakaway group represented less than one-third of the BSP legislative group and its members, therefore, should have been disqualified. But Tripathi—a senior BJP leader—argued in his 148-page report that the breakaway group had initially had twenty-six members.
68. Yogendra Yadav, "Reconfiguration in Indian Politics: State Assembly Elections 1993–95," *Economic and Political Weekly* (January 13, 1996): 96.

elite that comes from only a few castes, as is evident from the quasi-hegemonic role of the Yadavs and Chamars. Finally, the main political parties, the Congress and the BJP, have undertaken to counter this "silent revolution." As the first two issues have been dealt with elsewhere,[69] this essay will now turn to the third one.

The Congress, the BJP, and Mandal

In the late 1990s, for a brief period, three of the four largest states of the Hindi belt were governed by OBC chief ministers: Kalyan Singh in Uttar Pradesh, Rabri Devi in Bihar, and Asok Gehlot in Rajasthan. Madhya Pradesh alone had an upper-caste chief minister, Digvijay Singh. Interestingly, the three OBC chief ministers belonged to three different parties: the Bharatiya Janata Party, the Rashtriya Janata Dal, and the Congress Party. Certainly, this is an indication of the rise to power of the lower castes in North India, but while the RJD is naturally committed to the cause of the OBCs, the other two parties may be more eager to defuse the mobilization of the lower castes than anything else.

The way the Janata Dal and its offshoots—the Samajwadi Party and the RJD—on the one hand and the Bahujan Samaj Party on the other hand consolidated their bases among the OBCs and the SCs, respectively, in the 1990s posed a threat to the Congress and the BJP in North India. Until then, the former had owed most of its success to its catchall party profile, while the latter, like its earlier incarnation, the Jana Sangh, not only had upper-caste members at its helm but primarily represented the urban middle class of North India, which could hardly compete with the OBCs in terms of numbers. Both parties had to adjust to the Mandal challenge.

The Congress Party's Nostalgia for the "Coalition of Extremes"

The implementation of the Mandal Commission report generated a debate within the Congress. Low-caste leaders of the party—such as then treasurer of the Congress Sitaram Kesri, a Banya from Bihar, where his caste is classified with the OBCs—were favorably inclined toward the report.[70] But these leaders were rather isolated. V.P. Singh's decision to

---

69. See Jaffrelot, "The Rise of the Other Backward Classes."
70. K.C. Yadav, *India's Unequal Citizens: A Study of Other Backward Classes* (Delhi: Manohar, 1994), 91.

implement the recommendations of the Mandal report was strongly criticized in the Lok Sabha by Rajiv Gandhi, then Congress president and leader of the opposition, on September 6, 1990. He considered that a "national consensus" had to be evolved[71] and that caste-based reservations could only divide Indian society.[72] Alternatively, he suggested, the quotas should be based on economic criteria and "assistance should be given to the truly poor, to the landless, to the people falling in the poorest category."[73] Obviously, the Congress tried to maintain its "coalition of extremes" by indirectly promising quotas to the poor brahmins and new concessions to the SCs. The party, therefore, continued to display indifference toward the OBCs, at the risk of further alienating this group.

The Congress regained power, though without securing a clear-cut majority, after the May–June 1991 general elections. Soon after, on September 25, Prime Minister Narasimha Rao issued an office memorandum that amended that of V.P. Singh by reserving 10 percent of the posts in the government services to "economically backward sections of the people" who were not covered by the existing quotas; the poor from the upper castes were to benefit from this scheme. The Congress was still attempting to blur the cleavage between the upper castes and the lower castes and to recapture the allegiance of the former. The change in reservations was declared invalid by the Supreme Court in a November 1992 judgment in which the judges emphasized that economic criteria could not be used in the definition of "backwardness" under Articles 15 and 16 of the Constitution. The Congress had to resign itself to the centrality of caste in the identification of OBCs, and it began to adjust to their rise.

This was evident from the way the government negotiated the "creamy layer" issue. This issue crystallized when the Supreme Court asked the government to exclude from the list of OBCs eligible for quotas those who did not need any help from the state—the "creamy layer" of the OBCs. The Prasad committee appointed by Rao to do this considered that the progeny of farmers who owned irrigated land that represented more than 65 percent of the statutory area fit this category. The Janata Dal protested that the criterion was too strict. Subsequently, the welfare minister, Sitaram Kesri, displayed a conciliatory attitude during an all-

---

71. See the debate reproduced as Appendix 1 of Seema Mustafa, *The Lonely Prophet: V.P. Singh, a Political Biography* (New Delhi: New Age International, 1995), 206.

72. On the following day, Rajiv Gandhi accused V.P. Singh of conducting "the country to the edge of caste war" (*Indian Express*, September 8, 1990).

73. Ibid.

party meeting he organized himself, and the proportion of land was increased to 85 percent in August 1993. Later, he even invited private sector enterprises to establish quotas for the OBCs.[74] During the 1996 election campaign, the Congress tried to project itself as the spokesperson of the OBCs. Its manifesto argued,

> Reservations for the Backward Classes was an idea of the Congress. Jawaharlal Nehru made this into a Constitutional Principle in 1952. . . . In 1990, due to its ham handed and opportunistic approach, the Janata Dal Government triggered a virtual caste war in several parts of India.
>
> The election of a Congress Government in 1991 brought peace to a society that was threatened with disruption by caste strife.
>
> Quietly but firmly, Shri P.V. Narasimha Rao's Government implemented the recommendations of the Mandal Commission.[75]

The Congress was still trying to appear to be a consensus party and, at the same time, was attempting to project itself as the defender of the OBCs. However, the party was not able to attract more than about one-fifth of the OBC vote in 1996 and 1998. It had to wait until 1999 for a significant improvement in its electoral presence among the OBCs (35 percent) and the SCs (40 percent).[76] The Congress is still an upper-caste party in North India, and this regional characterization reflects a more general reality, as is evident from the social profile of the Congress Working Committee, shown in table 3.

Until the late 1980s, the upper castes represented more than 50 percent of the Congress Working Committee members. Ten years later, their percentage had substantially declined, so much so that they formed slightly more than one-third of the total. However, the OBCs did not profit by this dramatic erosion; their share remained around one-tenth of the total. Its main beneficiaries were the SCs and STs, an indication of the persistent coalition of extremes pattern.

The BJP's Efforts to Defuse the "Shudra Revolution"

The situation is somewhat different in the case of the BJP. The Hindu nationalist movement has always been known for its upper-caste, even

---

74. See the interviews with Sitaram Kesri in *Sunday*, October 2, 1994, and *Times of India*, July 4, 1995.

75. Indian National Congress (I), *Election Manifesto: General Election 1996* (New Delhi: AICC[I], 1996), 11–12.

76. Yogendra Yadav, Sanjay Kumar, and Oliver Heath, "The BJP's New Social Bloc," *Frontline*, November 19, 1999, 40.

Table 3

Caste and Community of the Members of the Congress Working Committee

Castes and Communities	1981	1987	1998
Upper castes	11	11	10
Intermediate castes	1	0	3
OBCs	3	3	3
SCs/STs	1	0	5
Muslims	2	2	3
Christians	1	1	2
Sikhs	1	1	0
Unidentified	2	1	2
Total	22	19	28

Source: Fieldwork at the AICC office, New Delhi.

brahminical, character. This specificity stems from the content of *hindutva*, or the Hindu nationalist ideology, itself: shaped by brahmins, it relies on an organic view in which castes are seen as the harmonious components of society.[77] Since its creation in 1925, the Rashtriya Swayamsevak Sangh (RSS), or National Volunteer Association, has grown by attracting to its local branches (the *shakhas*) Hindus who value this ethos, either because they belong to the upper castes or because they want to emulate them. Therefore, the technique of "conversion" of low-caste people to *hindutva* relies on the logic of Sanskritization.

The RSS immediately criticized the announcement by V.P. Singh on August 7, 1990, that the recommendations of the Mandal Commission report would be implemented. Reacting to the "Rajah's caste-war," the *Organiser* (the RSS's mouthpiece) attacked not only the politics of quotas favoring the OBCs, denounced as the pampering of vote banks, but also the policy of affirmative action itself from the RSS's traditional organicist angle: "The havoc the politics of reservation is playing with the social fabric is unimaginable. It provides a premium for mediocrity, encourages brain-drain and sharpens caste-divide."[78] On the implicit assumption that it was virtually harmonious, the "social fabric" was regarded in this case as in need of preservation from state intervention.

---

77. For details, see Christophe Jaffrelot, *The Hindu Nationalist Movement and Indian Politics: 1925 to the 1990s*, 2nd ed. (Delhi: Penguin, 1999), chap. 1.

78. *Organiser*, August 26, 1990, 15.

The *Organiser* came to embrace the cause of the upper castes publicly when one of its columnists wrote, "There is today an urgent need to build up moral and spiritual forces to counter any fall-out from an expected Shudra revolution."[79] The RSS high command followed more or less the same line as the *Organiser*. Rajendra Singh, then the chief of the RSS, considered that "there should be a gradual reduction in the job quotas."[80] In response to the new caste-based politics, the RSS launched a new program in January 1996 called *samarasya sangama*, "confluence for harmony," which provided that each RSS worker should adopt one village to contribute to its development in order, in the words of Rajendra Singh, to promote "social harmony between various sections of the society and social assimilation."[81]

The BJP, however, did not react to the Mandal affair and the rise of the low castes in the same way. The party leaders did not dare openly attack V.P. Singh's decision regarding the implementation of the Mandal Commission report because they were apprehensive of alienating OBC voters. They instead fostered the students' anti-Mandal agitation behind the scenes. When one of the party's Rajya Sabha members, J.K. Jain, began a fast against the implementation of the Mandal report, he was criticized by the high command and had to fall into line.[82] The BJP was cautious about projecting its views. The upper-caste character of Hindu nationalism had become a greater handicap for the BJP in the 1990s because of the growing political consciousness of the low castes, as the 1993 elections testified.

Those election results, when the BJP lost both Uttar Pradesh and Madhya Pradesh at least partly because of OBC and *dalit* voters, led the party leaders to promote a larger number of low-caste people in the party apparatus. In January 1994, Hukumdev Narain Yadav was appointed as special invitee to the party's national executive board, and Uma Bharati, a Lodhi, became chief of the Bharatiya Janata Yuva Morcha (the youth wing of the BJP). The main advocate of the inclusion of an increasing number of low-caste members at all the levels of the party apparatus was K.N. Govindacharya, himself a brahmin and then one of the BJP general secretaries. He called this policy "social engineering." However, this strategy was opposed by some of his colleagues and by RSS leaders,

---

79. M.V. Kamath, "Is Shudra Revolution in the Offing?" *Organiser*, May 1, 1994, 6.
80. *Organiser*, December 18, 1994, 20.
81. *Organiser*, January 14, 1996, 7.
82. For more details, see Jaffrelot, *The Hindu Nationalist Movement*, 431.

who objected on principle to any artificial transformation of the so-called social equilibrium and did not want to give a new importance to caste as a result of pressures from the Mandal affair. Murli Manohar Joshi, a former president of the BJP, opposed the move and even implicitly questioned the notion of social engineering in general by asking, "What social justice has been brought in the name of social engineering? Rural poverty has increased and most of the rural poor continue to be Dalits."[83]

In a way, the BJP fell into line with the mother organization, the RSS, during the all-party meeting on reservations that was held in 1995 under the auspices of the then union welfare minister, Sitaram Kesri. At that meeting, the BJP representative, Atal Bihari Vajpayee, alone opposed the extension of reservations for SCs and STs and refused to express a willingness to increase the ceiling of 50 percent reservation for these two categories and the OBCs.[84] However, as the eleventh general elections approached, the BJP amended its earlier position on the reservation issue. Before the 1991 elections, the BJP had expressed very general views: "Reservation should . . . be made for other backward classes broadly on the basis of the Mandal Commission Report, with preference to be given to the poor amongst these very classes and . . . [a]s poverty is an important contributory factor for backwardness, reservation should also be provided for members of the other castes on the basis of their economic condition."[85]

In 1996, the BJP retained the social harmony discourse[86] but made precise promises to the OBCs:

> 1. Continuation of reservations for the Other Backward Classes till they are socially and educational [sic] integrated with the rest of society;

---

83. Interview, *Sunday,* January 26, 1997, 13.

84. Kesri consulted the political parties before bringing before Parliament a constitutional amendment bill designed to nullify the 50 percent ceiling imposed by the Supreme Court on reservations and a bill seeking the extension of reservations for the SCs and STs in government jobs beyond 1997. Addressing a convention of SC and ST MLAs, ministers, mayors, deputy mayors, members of municipal corporations, and *panchayat* office bearers in Bhopal, he denounced the BJP as the biggest enemy of the SCs, STs, and OBCs on the basis of Vajpayee's stand (*National Mail* [Bhopal], May 19, 1995).

85. *Towards Ram Rajya: Mid-Term Poll to Lok Sabha, May 1991—Our Commitments* (New Delhi: Bharatiya Janata Party, 1991), 27.

86. The manifesto also said, "The task is nothing short of rekindling the lamp of our eternal 'Dharma,' that *Sanatan* thought which our sages bequeathed to mankind—a social system based on compassion, cooperation, justice, freedom, equality and tolerance." *For a Strong and Prosperous India: Election Manifesto 1996* (New Delhi: Bharatiya Janata Party, 1996), 5.

2. A uniform criteria [*sic*] for demarcating the "creamy layer";

3. Flow of reservation benefits in an ascending order so that the most backward sections of the OBCs get them first;

4. Ten per cent reservation on the basis of economic criteria to all economically weaker sections of society, apart from the Scheduled Castes/ Scheduled Tribes and the Other Backward Classes.[87]

The BJP had admitted the inevitability of quotas for the OBCs but tried to combine the criterion of caste with socioeconomic criteria. This compromise reflects the debate within the BJP between the advocates of "social engineering" in favor of the low castes and those who want to abstain from acknowledging caste conflicts and amending the supposedly harmonious structure of society.

Another dimension of this compromise was the BJP's strategy of indirect "Mandalization": the party did not promote low-caste people (either as election candidates or office bearers) but made alliances with parties having a base among the OBCs, such as the Samata Party, a Kurmi-dominated breakaway of the Janata Dal in Bihar. While the BJP had received only 16 percent of the vote in 1991, largely because it remained identified with the upper castes and the tribal belt of the South, its alliance with the Samata Party enabled it to make inroads in northern and central districts thanks to that party's base among the Kurmis and the Koeris (another OBC caste). In several constituencies, these low castes were allied with upper castes (brahmins, Rajputs, Bhumihars, and Kayasths), which helped the BJP a great deal. The party won eighteen seats, as opposed to five in 1991. The BJP admitted the need to become more rural and even to "Mandalize" itself, but only indirectly.

After the 1998 elections, the BJP formed a coalition, the National Democratic Alliance (NDA), that enabled Vajpayee to become prime minister. This alliance was formalized before the 1999 elections to such an extent that the party did not prepare an election manifesto for itself; there was only one manifesto for the entire NDA. As it was now the pivotal force of a larger coalition whose components were often less upper caste oriented than the BJP itself, the party tended to dilute its stand further regarding the reservation issue. In the NDA election manifesto, one could read, "If required, the Constitution will be amended to maintain the system of reservation. . . . We are committed to extending

---

87. Ibid., 62.

Table 4

Caste and Community of the BJP MPs Returned in the Hindi Belt (in %)

Castes and Communities	1989	1991	1996	1998	1999
Upper castes	53.13	52.33	46.28	43.40	37.96
Intermediate castes	1.56	4.65	4.96	6.61	7.41
OBCs	15.62	15.10	17.40	20.50	16.67
SCs	17.20	18.60	21.50	18.80	19.40
STs	7.80	5.80	7.40	6.73	8.34
Muslims	1.56			0.83	0.93
Sikhs	1.56	1.16	0.83	0.83	
Sadhus		2.33			1.85
Unidentified			1.65	2.48	7.41
	$N = 64$	$N = 86$	$N = 121$	$N = 122$	$N = 108$

Source: Fieldwork by the author.

the SC/ST reservation for another 10 years. Reservation percentages above 50%, as followed by certain states, shall be sanctified through necessary legislation measures."[88]

Vajpayee himself, while campaigning in Rajasthan, declared that his government "would implement the reservation policy in right earnest."[89] Obviously, the BJP leaders had become more responsive to the OBCs' demands not only because of their coalition partners but also in order to attract more OBC voters. However, the BJP remains an upper-caste party, as is evident from the social profile of its MPs and office bearers, shown in table 4.

The last five elections have shown a steady erosion of the percentage of members of the upper castes among the BJP MPs of the Hindi belt, from 53 percent in 1989 to 43 percent in 1998 and 38 percent in 1999. However, those who benefit from this trend are less the OBCs than the dominant castes (mainly the Jats) and even the *dalit* candidates, who are often elected with the support of upper-caste BJP voters. Indeed, the decrease in upper-caste MPs does not coincide with diminishing attractiveness of the party to the upper-caste voters or with growing attractiveness to the OBCs and the SCs and STs. Besides, the efforts of the party to woo the OBCs are real but limited; the rise in OBC MPs

88. National Democratic Alliance, *For a Proud, Prosperous India: An Agenda. Election Manifesto, Lok Sabha Election, 1999* (New Delhi: Printed and published at the Bharatiya Janata Party, for and oh behalf of the National Democratic Alliance, 1999), 8.

89. Cited in the *Hindu,* August 25, 1999.

probably reflects the increasing number of OBC candidates fielded by the party, but by and large the OBCs' share remains around 20 percent. (Incidentally, this is also the percentage of OBC voters who support the BJP, according to the 1999 CSDS survey.) Moreover, while the party is steadily giving more tickets to OBCs election after election, it does not make much room for this group in the party apparatus. In 2000, the removal of Kalyan Singh from the post of Uttar Pradesh chief minister under pressure from the upper-caste lobby and the appointment of Bangaru Laxman as party president even suggests that the BJP may follow the Congress Party strategy of building a coalition of extremes.[90]

Conclusion

India has come a long way since the early days of its conservative democracy. The political system of the 1950s and 1960s was characterized by the domination of elite groups (the upper-caste intelligentsia, the business community, and the landowners) that maintained the clientelistic arrangement of the "Congress system." This system was democratic in the sense that there were frequent, competitive elections, the press was free, and the judiciary was independent, but its beneficiaries all came from the same upper-caste groups. Paradoxically, Indian democracy has acquired a social dimension through caste—an institution based on hierarchy but undergoing transformation. South India led the way from the late nineteenth century, when low-caste groups began to emancipate themselves from the rigid hierarchy of Indian society through an ethnicization process and affirmative action policies. In North India, attempts at ethnicizing caste were hindered by the pervasive ethos of Sanskritization, but the policies of affirmative action led to the same result as in the South several decades later.

Indeed, the main landmark in the low castes' ascendancy to power in North India in the late 1980s and early 1990s was the implementation of the recommendations of the Mandal report. The lower castes mobilized throughout North India and formed a front against the upper castes' vocal hostility to the new scheme of reservations. As a result, OBC leaders were elected in large numbers to Parliament and took over in Uttar Pradesh and Bihar. In the wake of this mobilization, the *dalits* deserted

---

90. For more details, see the afterword to Thomas B. Hansen and Christophe Jaffrelot, eds., *The BJP and the Compulsions of Politics in India*, 2nd ed. (Delhi: Oxford University Press, 2001).

the Congress for a new party, the Bahujan Samaj Party, which aggressively fought upper-caste domination in North India. In 1997, growing recognition of the SCs in the Indian political system found expression in the election of K.R. Narayanan, a *dalit* from Kerala, as president of the country.

India is therefore experimenting with a silent revolution. Power is being transferred from an upper-caste elite to plebeian groups without much violence. Certainly, riots took place during the Mandal affair, but violence remained limited. The relative quiescence is primarily due to the fact that the whole process is incremental: the upper castes are still in command, with people of the OBCs forming a second line of leadership, a new generation in waiting. The educational and social limitations of the lower castes are such that they will probably not be in a position to generate a full-fledged new elite for years. Second, the rise to power of the lower castes has been very uneven. They have taken over in Bihar, but they remain in a subaltern position in Rajasthan, for instance. Third, the conflict is not based on clear-cut political opposition, since upper-caste-dominated parties have low-caste people among their ranks and vice versa (even the BSP has upper-caste office bearers). Fourth, the upper castes are losing ground in the political sphere and in the administration, but the liberalization of the economy—which, like the Mandalization process, began in the early 1990s—has opened new opportunities to them in the private sector; they may not regret losing their traditional monopoly over the bureaucracy so much when they see these greener pastures.

Fifth, and more important, the rise to power of the lower castes is not irreversible and linear. There is clearly a trend, but there are also several handicaps to overcome. The lower castes suffer from a structural lack of unity. The divorce between the Samajwadi Party and the Bahujan Samaj Party in 1995 showed that an alliance between the OBCs and the *dalits* is very difficult to maintain, partly because these two groups have conflicting class interests. Besides, the SCs and the OBCs themselves do not really form social categories.

Finally, the rise to power of the lower castes is also hindered by the response of the upper castes to their new assertiveness and ambitions. Mainstream political parties are resorting to old techniques in this regard. The traditional Gandhian discourse on the organic unity of society is still articulated by the RSS in order to weaken *dalit* militancy, and the Congress Party is still using its old strategy of co-option to build a "coalition of extremes." The BJP has adopted the latter to a certain extent. It also endeavors to defuse the mobilization of the OBCs by diluting the social cohesiveness of this already not so homogeneous social grouping. In the late 1990s, BJP politicians successfully advocated the inclusion of the Jats on the list of OBCs toward this very end.

The extension of the social groups benefiting from quotas may well be the favorite tactic of the BJP for making "quota politics" nonoperational. This tactic may take on an even larger dimension with the introduction of quotas for women in the elected assemblies: if 33 percent of the seats are reserved for women, the upper castes may well be the first beneficiaries of the reservations—a rather ironical conclusion that brings to mind that in Europe the conservatives were responsible for enlarging the franchise in order to exploit their influence over "their" peasant voters. However, the peasants in question eventually emancipated themselves from their patrons, and in India, too, this tactical move may only slow down the silent revolution in the making.

The Challenges of India's Health and Health Care Transitions

Mark Nichter and David Van Sickle

India has made considerable progress in improving the health and welfare of many of its citizens, but the country still faces major public health challenges. These challenges range from undernutrition and infectious disease to chronic diseases associated with aging, and from environmental and occupational health problems to afflictions of modernization associated with tobacco consumption, changes in diet, and new sources of stress. Today, India is experiencing an increase in chronic disease among the better-off coupled with a continued high prevalence of infectious disease among the impoverished.[1] Many scholars credit this health transition to an interplay of modernizing social forces and medical interventions. This argument is based on the premise that, as a result of modernization, Western allopathic medicine is increasingly accessible to people in the developing world, that it is efficacious in these settings, and that people make use of health resources in ways that result in prolonged life and improved health.[2]

These explanations, however, overlook the impact of changes in the availability of medicines and use of health care services on patterns of

---

1. This shift from infectious to chronic disease is known as the epidemiological transition. We maintain reservations about juxtaposing acute and chronic disease when describing the health transition in India. First, for a significant proportion of India's population, acute diseases are experienced so often and with such consistency that it may be more accurate to describe them as chronic afflictions of poverty. Second, it is essential to consider the potential ramifications of childhood malnutrition and acute illness throughout the life cycle and to recognize that chronic diseases often associated with modernity may also occur as a result of poverty. There is mounting evidence, some of the most compelling coming from India, that low birth weight and early life malnutrition—not to mention untreated childhood infections—may be associated with an increased risk of chronic health problems, including adult hypertension, coronary heart disease, non-insulin-dependent diabetes, and autoimmune thyroid disease. See Nevin Scrimshaw, "Editorial: The Relation Between Fetal Malnutrition and Chronic Disease in Later Life," *British Medical Journal* 13 (1998): 1102–3.

2. For a critical overview of the concepts of health and health care transition, see

health. A paradoxical feature of the health transition is that, as rates of mortality fall, rates of morbidity (real and perceived) tend to rise, increasing demand for health services. This, in turn, initiates a set of market dynamics that contributes to rising levels of awareness about health and health care costs. Moreover, sociopolitical and market forces contribute to ill health through factors such as defective modernization, capitalist expansion, and environmental degradation. Understanding the factors that affect the environments in which Indians live and work and those that influence their ability to maintain health and respond to illness is critical to understanding the health and health care transitions in the country. With that in mind, we examine long-standing, emergent, and reemerging health challenges facing India under the headings of demographic change, maternal and child mortality, infectious diseases, diseases of modernity, and environmental health. We then highlight an accompanying set of factors that influence patterns of health service and pharmaceutical use. Finally, we examine the relationship between the transitions in health and health care using information from the Indian state of Kerala.

The Health Transition

The Population Picture

In the last thirty years, the number of Indians has doubled, and in the last decade, the country has added some 170 million people, reaching an official population of one billion last year. Today, the country is home to an enormous, and steadily rising, population of young children, as well as an increasing proportion of elderly persons, presenting unique challenges to the health care system. The past fifty years of population growth have been accompanied by significant, but uneven, improvements in basic health and economic indicators, levels of literacy and educational attainment, and the relative status of women. Infant mortality, for example, has fallen by more than half overall, and life expectancy has risen in step, though large regional differences remain. The proportion of poor people in the population has declined significantly in the same

Emily Zielinski Gutierrex and Carl Kendall, "The Globalization of Health and Disease: The Health Transition and Global Change," in *Handbook of Social Studies in Health and Medicine,* ed. Gary Albrecht, Ray Fitzpatrick, and Susan Scrimshaw (London: Sage, 2000).

period, though the actual number has doubled.[3] At the same time, India's middle class has grown dramatically. As a result, India has experienced a sharp increase in the demand for consumer goods as well as a burgeoning advertising industry. While increasing levels of literacy are contributing to better health and lower levels of fertility, half the population completes four years of education or less.[4] Notably, women are much more likely to be illiterate than men, but they play a much larger role in providing for the well-being of their children. The persistence of additional gender-based disparities in rates of morbidity and mortality further illustrates the need for greater commitment to female literacy, education, and health.

Since India launched the Family Welfare Program in the 1950s, average fertility has dropped from more than six children per woman to just over three, moving the country about two-thirds of the way toward its goal of replacement-level fertility.[5] Overall, almost half of eligible couples now use some form of contraception;[6] however, the prevalence of contraceptive use varies widely among states. Since abortion was legalized in 1971, the reported number of legal procedures has reached about 600,000 annually, although estimates suggest that up to ten times as many illegal abortions take place because of the limited availability of providers and facilities that offer legal abortions.[7] Rates of complications after abortion are high and constitute a significant cause of infertility. Sterilization continues to account for a high proportion of modern contraceptive use, with female sterilization accounting for an estimated nine of every ten procedures. The lack of alternatives routinely offered at government health centers (aside from the provision of condoms) and the poor quality of care following procedures are strong arguments for increasing the variety and availability of family-planning methods.

Historically, there have been significant differences in fertility rates between North and South India. Although these rates now appear to be converging, social perceptions of the regional differences have engaged

3. Robert Cassen and Pravin Visaria, "India: Looking Ahead to One and a Half Billion People," *British Medical Journal* 319 (1999): 995–97.

4. Ibid.

5. UNICEF, "Information: Country Statistics—India," www.unicef.org/statis/Country_1 Page 78.html (accessed July 14, 2001); Cassen and Visaria, "India: Looking Ahead."

6. USAID, "India: Introduction—India Overview," www.usaid.gov/country/ane/in (accessed July 14, 2001).

7. According to the World Bank, only about 10 percent of eligible facilities actually have a trained provider and the necessary equipment.

Indian politics, focusing attention on the significance of Hindu-Muslim differences. The Bharatiya Janata Party (the Hindu Right's most powerful political party) has propagated the myth that Indian Muslims are in league to render Hindus a minority in their "own country." For political purposes, Muslims are stereotyped as being sexually aggressive and seeking to have as many children by as many wives as possible. At the aggregate level, Muslim fertility rates are somewhat higher than those of Hindus, with Muslims making up almost 10 percent of India's total population in 1951 and more than 12 percent in 1991. But, as noted by scholars such as the Jeffreys, the Hindu Right's interpretation of Muslim demographic behavior falsifies and simplifies complex demographic processes.[8] Far from constituting an Islamic strategy for gaining power, higher rates of fertility among India's Muslims reflect their lack of power. These rates are best understood through an examination of such factors as women's literacy, rates of infant and child mortality, the social status of women and the marriage age of girls, levels of poverty, and access to health services. Finally, it may be noted that the vast majority of government primary health care workers are Hindu. A common complaint among Muslims is that they receive poorer-quality health services than Hindus. Whether or not this is the case, communal distrust and fears of sterilization may undermine Muslims' confidence in the government health sector in northern states.

Overall, the demographic changes altering the composition of the Indian population have added to the complexity of health and health care in the country. Next, we present a review of the health challenges facing India and its diverse and rapidly changing populace.

Maternal, Child, and Infant Mortality

There are a number of indicators that suggest a country occupies an early stage of health transition. Two of the most important are rates of maternal and infant/child mortality. In India, these rates, though declining, remain unacceptably high. A recent assessment suggests that the decline in child mortality noted in the 1980s and 1990s is slowing.[9] Several conditions contribute to the high rates, including young age of childbearing and its subsequent health risks, maternal malnutrition, and

8. Roger Jeffrey and Patricia Jeffrey, "Religion and Fertility in India," *Economic and Political Weekly* (September 2, 2000): 3253–59.

9. Mariam Claeson, Eduard Bos, Tazim Mawji, and Indra Pathmanathan, "Reducing Child Mortality in India in the New Millennium," *Bulletin of the World Health Organization* 78, no. 10 (2000): 1192–99.

a high prevalence of anemia. Mothers also tend to give birth in rapid succession: in one-third of the cases, the birth interval is less than twenty-four months.[10] As many as two-thirds of births are assisted by traditional midwives or family members. Some of these midwives are highly skilled, while others do little more than assist a woman in dealing with the "impurity" of the birthing event. Although the Government of India has initiated several training courses for birth attendants, most have been didactic rather than apprenticeship based. The practices of midwives often remain little changed, although they do seem more likely to refer cases of difficult delivery to hospitals. Only about half of all pregnant women receive any prenatal care in India.

The national infant mortality rate for India is estimated to be 60–72 deaths per 1,000 live births, with more impoverished states having rates significantly higher than the national average. Approximately 40 percent of infant mortality occurs in the first twenty-eight days of life, owing to causes such as low birth weight and poor management of childbirth.

Another important indicator of early stage health transition is the survival of children. Every year, 2.5 million Indian children, approximately one of every nine who live past infancy, die before reaching the age of five. Even with notable declines in rates of child mortality in many states, malnutrition, diarrheal diseases, acute respiratory infections, and immunizable diseases present persistent challenges to child survival.[11]

Malnutrition and Nutritional Deficiencies

The growth of more than half of Indian children younger than four is moderately or severely stunted, and almost one-fifth can be classified as moderately or severely wasting.[12] To address this problem, the Government of India initiated a feeding program for children, pregnant women, and lactating mothers through the Integrated Child Development Services (ICDS) scheme. Begun in 1975, ICDS has reached about three-quarters of its target population of 63 million children under six years of age as well as 13.6 million pregnant and lactating women through activities at a network of

10. K. Srinivasan, *India: Towards Population and Development Goals* (New Delhi: Vedams Books, 1997).

11. While rates of child mortality are still high, notable declines have occurred. For example, between 1992 and 1998, rates in Madhya Pradesh, Bihar, and Orissa fell from 128–31 to 103–5 and in Uttar Pradesh from 141 to 113.

12. UNICEF, "India 1999 Annual Report: Country Office Annual Reports," www.intranet.unicef.org/PD/PDC.nsf.

Anganwadi centers. Evaluations of the effectiveness of the ICDS program in reducing malnutrition have been disappointing when compared with secular trends in areas not covered by ICDS schemes. One reason is that the ICDS program largely caters to children aged three to six, when the priority group for malnutrition is children aged six months to two years.[13]

Efforts to address protein-calorie and micronutrient deficiencies have a long history in India, but they face significant challenges associated with the acquisition and distribution of appropriate resources to those who need them the most. For example, UNICEF has estimated that 200 million Indians are at risk of iodine deficiency disorders and that 70 million have goiter. In recent years, the Indian government has made considerable progress in reducing iodine deficiency by making iodized salt widely and cheaply available and by prohibiting the sale of noniodized salt. These advances may now be in jeopardy because of the recent decision by the prime minister and the Health Ministry to lift the two-year-old ban on the sale of noniodized salt. India's scientific and medical community has criticized the decision as a shortsighted bow to a campaign by Hindu nationalists and small-scale salt producers in the state of Gujarat. These groups assert that iodized salt is unnecessary for much of the population, that its promotion is part of a conspiracy by international companies to capture the salt market, and even that iodized salt renders people more vulnerable to tuberculosis, diabetes, and cancer. Nationalists have also complained that iodization has added unnecessarily to the cost of salt. In reality, it adds only a fraction of a penny to the cost of a pound of salt.

Diarrhea

Nearly one-fourth of all childhood deaths in India (some 600,000 per year) result from diarrhea, and the vast majority of those deaths could be prevented by oral rehydration therapy (ORT), which makes use of prepackaged oral rehydration salts, homemade sugar and salt solutions, or food-based preparations, all of which are cheap and easy

---

13. The ICDS program has been successful in improving the immunization status of pregnant women and children, increasing health checkups and managing morbidity, and creating awareness about child nutrition. See B.N. Tandon, "Nutrition Intervention Through Primary Health Care: Impact of the ICDS Projects in India," *Bulletin of the World Health Organization* 67 (1989): 77–80; *Integrated Child Development Services Status Appraisal in Five States* (Hyderabad: National Institute of Nutrition, 1992); and Shanti Gosh, "Integrated Child Development Services Programme: Need for Reappraisal," *Indian Pediatrics* 34 (1997): 911–18.

to prepare in the home. Deaths due to diarrhea-related dehydration have declined in recent years, but this has only highlighted the remaining health problems associated with persistent diarrhea and dysentery and the threat they pose to children who are already malnourished. Invasive forms of bloody diarrhea, especially infection by the bacteria *Shigella*, are also important contributors to child mortality.

A recent nationwide survey reported that rates of use of ORT were increasing, particularly in critical cases of severe diarrhea; however, many people remain unfamiliar with ORT, and others often give it in the wrong quantities. Primary health workers need to clarify that these preparations are a treatment for dehydration and not a medicine for diarrhea in order to ensure that people will not consider them ineffective and abandon their use. Diarrheal treatments and medications available over the counter or from the private sector are largely ineffective in curing diarrhea and often make the illness worse. Raising rates of ORT use among the public and lowering rates of use of unnecessary antibiotics, antidiarrheals, and IV fluids requires that private practitioners and chemist shop attendants advise their patients about ORT and adhere to government recommendations even when doing so may undermine their business. The pharmaceutical industry's marketing practices also need to be monitored. In the case of *Shigella* infection, aggressive marketing of medications for amoebic dysentery by pharmaceutical companies has increased the likelihood that the disease will be mistaken for amoebic dysentery and subsequently mistreated. Finally, short courses of vitamin A and zinc, which compensate for nutritional deficiencies and appear to reduce diarrheal severity and duration, need to be promoted.[14]

In India's urban slums, diarrhea attack rates are often three times higher than in rural areas, despite better access to safe drinking water. The primary reasons for this include an inadequate supply of water and latrines, poor household water storage and handling, and poor food hygiene. Slum dwellers themselves add poisoning by pesticides and food adulteration to this list. Clearly, the control of diarrhea requires renovation of Indian infrastructure, including the water supply and sanitation and sewerage systems, in addition to investment in technical fixes and educational programs.

---

14. M.K. Bhan, "Control of Diarrhoeal Diseases," *Lancet* 351 (April 25, 1998): 1269–71.

Acute Respiratory Infection

Acute respiratory infection (ARI) is the most common cause of death in children under five years of age in developing countries. Acute lower respiratory infections (ALRIs)—which, in contrast to upper respiratory infections, rapidly become life threatening—account for 13 percent of all deaths in India and an estimated 25 percent of all mortality in children under five. At any given time, approximately 15–20 percent of children under age five in India have some type of ARI. The large number of cases of ARI places great strain on the health care system, accounting for more than one-fourth of consultations and about one-fourth of hospital admissions.

Death due to ALRI can be averted by early recognition of key signs (rapid breathing and chest retractions) and prompt treatment with antibiotics. Early diagnosis and antimicrobial treatment by primary health care (PHC) workers—using a simple algorithm developed and promoted by the World Health Organization (WHO)—are important parts of the Indian strategy for reducing ALRI mortality, particularly in rural areas. In some states, the government has trained up to 80 percent of PHC staff in the use of the algorithm, which has been proven to reduce mortality significantly in pilot projects. Among private practitioners, however, management of ARI is often inadequate and may well be contributing to rising rates of antimicrobial resistance to the major antibiotic (cotrimoxazole) recommended by WHO for first-line treatment. Given the erratic patterns of drug use in India and the speed at which resistant organisms may develop and spread, regional surveillance and monitoring of drug sensitivity is a priority for health care planning. Controlling indoor air pollution through the promotion of better cooking hearths and stoves would also be a major step toward limiting ARI-related morbidity and mortality. Some researchers estimate that between 30 and 45 percent of ARI deaths are attributable to indoor smoke exposure and that its health consequences are comparable to those of tobacco use.[15]

Immunizable Diseases and the Status of Immunization Programs

Since the launch of the government's universal immunization program in 1985, there has been significant progress in reducing cases of and

---

15. Kirk R. Smith, "National Burden of Disease in India from Indoor Air Pollution," *Proceedings of the National Academy of Sciences of the United States* 97, no. 24 (2000): 13286–93; Nigel Bruce, Rogelio Perez-Padilla, and Rachel Albalak, "Indoor Air Pollution in Developing Countries: A Major Environmental and Public Health Challenge," *Bulletin of the World Health Organization* 78, no. 9 (2000): 1078–92.

deaths from immunizable diseases. Nevertheless, several such diseases continue to threaten child survival in India. Among these, tetanus, pertussis, and measles continue to be fairly prevalent, and polio is the focus of a major eradication effort. A primary obstacle to controlling these diseases is the difficulty of sustaining community interest in immunizations. Critics argue against investing scarce resources in special immunization campaigns and technical solutions to child survival rather than in community-based programs that enhance participation in local problem solving.

Supporters of vertical disease control and eradication programs in India point to the polio eradication program to illustrate what is possible given political and community support, international assistance, and hard work. Since 1988, when the World Health Assembly passed a resolution to eradicate polio by the year 2000, the number of polio cases has fallen by more than 95 percent around the world. This progress toward eradication of poliovirus has been made possible by practical diagnostic tools and the availability of an effective intervention (vaccination) and delivery strategy.[16]

In India, significant progress in eliminating polio has occurred as the result of a better surveillance system and the Pulse Polio immunization program. Previously, poliomyelitis surveillance in India involved only the passive reporting of clinically suspected cases. However, in 1997 a national coordinating center and infrastructure was established to collect, analyze, and distribute reports of suspected cases of polio by PHC workers and specially trained surveillance officers. Identification of potential cases or outbreaks in an area sets in motion intensified immunization activities. Immunization activities at the national level were also intensified and continue today in the form of the Pulse Polio campaign, best known for its periodic mass immunization efforts. Pulse Polio activities also involve community and house-to-house vaccination efforts, during which all children under age five are given oral polio vaccine regardless of their previous immunization status. Together these efforts have led to a sharp reduction in the number of reported cases of polio, which is down from 24,257 in 1988 to 134 cases as of September 9, 2000.

---

16. Circulation of the wild virus now appears to be confined to a handful of countries, of which India is home to the largest remaining pool of polio transmission in the world. Thus, progress toward the eradication of poliovirus in India has been critical for the success of the global initiative.

Despite this promising decline, the success of the program has not gone uncriticized. Opponents point to the costs of mounting the Pulse Polio effort, calling attention to the neglect of other public health programs. Some have drawn attention to recent evidence that oral polio vaccine viruses can persist in human populations and maintain the potential to revert to virulence, requiring long-term eradication efforts.

Nevertheless, India's success with polio has piqued interest in other life-saving vaccinations that might be administered through the primary health care infrastructure, such as those for organisms associated with pneumonia and for the hepatitis B virus (HBV). It is estimated that 3–4 percent of the Indian population is infected with HBV. Most of these individuals become infected as infants or young children, and many cases progress to hepatocellular carcinoma or cirrhosis of the liver. Despite its cost—approximately twenty times that of the DPT vaccine—the HBV vaccine is cost effective, given the high prevalence of the disease and the prohibitive cost of treatment, and there is growing support for making HBV vaccination a part of India's national immunization program.[17]

Infectious Diseases: The Lessons of Tuberculosis, HIV/AIDS, and Sexually Transmitted Infections

Tuberculosis: The Continuing Challenge

Tuberculosis (TB) is one of the most sensitive barometers of poverty, overcrowding, and undernutrition. India has more active cases of TB than any other country in the world. Despite a long tradition of TB research in India and the existence of a national TB program since 1962, it remains the leading cause of death in the country. Each year, two million Indians develop active TB, and, despite the presence of effective therapies, half a million die from the disease. More women die from TB than from all causes of maternal mortality combined. Because most TB cases occur in economically active individuals, the impact of the infection is far greater than is conveyed by epidemiological statistics alone.

---

17. Before a national HBV vaccination program can be pursued, however, more information is required to decide the appropriate timing of the vaccination. At issue is when the first dose of HBV vaccine should be given to achieve optimum efficacy. This question can only be answered by determining the relative magnitudes of horizontal and perinatal transmission. If the main mode of transmission is perinatal, it is important that the first dose be given as early as possible after birth. If HBV is acquired later in childhood, HBV vaccination might be integrated into the routine childhood immunization schedule.

TB management in India presents a formidable challenge because of its long incubation period, the occurrence of both clinical and subclinical cases, and the poor effectiveness of BCG vaccine in preventing TB. Reinfection and reactivation of latent infections are other causes of concern, as immunity is unstable and may be lowered by viral infections, certain medications, and metabolic disorders such as diabetes.[18] Control of TB also requires significant efforts, including systematic screening, prompt identification of likely cases, laboratory confirmation of infected individuals, an ample supply of the right medications given in the right doses, compliance by the patient with a six-month course of four medications (designed to prevent drug resistance as well as cure the disease), and investigation of sputum-positive cases (indicating possible drug resistance) following three to four months of therapy.

The early symptoms of pulmonary TB (cough, chest pain, and fever) resemble those of other diseases common in India and are found in 5–10 percent of the population at any given time. This makes community-based screening a frustrating activity, as many people meet TB screening criteria but test negative for infection. On the other hand, TB is often mistaken for pneumonia in clinical practice and is treated with antibiotics that may temporarily reduce symptoms.

Confusion about symptoms complicates health care seeking and treatment for patients as well. Most poor to lower-middle-class Indians afflicted with TB seek symptomatic care for several months from three to six private practitioners until their health worsens and they find it difficult to work. Delays in seeking care are longer for women than men as they have fewer resources available to them and more domestic duties. Government hospitals are rarely visited first because of long waiting times and their reputation for administering poor-quality drugs or not having drugs in stock. Private practitioners—many of whom do not inform poor patients that free, good-quality treatment is available from government clinics and nongovernmental organizations (NGOs)—play up this stereotype in order to secure more clientele.

Studies carried out between the 1970s and the 1990s have repeatedly identified private practitioners as the biggest barriers to TB control in

---

18. T. Ramakrishnan and P. Chandrasekhar, "The Control of Tuberculosis: A Continuous Game of Snakes and Ladders," *Journal of Bioscience* 24, no. 2 (1999): 143–52.

India.[19] Many of these practitioners have little or no formal training in biomedicine and yet administer and prescribe allopathic drugs. Private doctors with M.B.B.S. degrees often violate tuberculosis treatment guidelines by giving their patients wrong combinations and inappropriate doses of medication, contributing to the rise of multidrug-resistant strains of the disease.[20] One study found 71 faulty prescriptions among a set of 100 issued by private doctors.[21] Others substitute single drugs (like one of the fluoroquinolones popular in India) for TB regimens that appear to be ineffective or cause the patient to complain of side effects, an ill-advised strategy that increases the chance of resistance to yet another drug. Private practitioners also widely prefer x-rays to sputum examination for initial diagnosis, for treatment monitoring, and as a criterion for stopping treatment, despite the fact that sputum testing yields much more specific results and important information about infectiousness. Finally, while government doctors are required to pursue "defaulters"—patients who fail to show up for their medicine—private doctors rarely track these individuals, and they frequently do not report cases to health authorities, jeopardizing the ability to collect accurate epidemiological data.

The poor pay dearly for TB treatment at the hands of private doctors. The out-of-pocket costs for TB diagnosis and treatment in India are estimated at between $100 and $150, half the annual income of many daily wage laborers. Over time, many TB patients seeing private providers switch to government services as their funds become depleted. As a result, long-duration patients tend to accumulate in government-run services.

Following a review of the national TB program in 1992, a new pro-

---

19. Klass W. van der Veen, "Private Practitioners and the National Tuberculosis Programme in India," *Journal of Research and Education in Indian Medicine* 6, nos. 3–4 (1987): 59–66; Dinesh M. Nair, Annie George, and K.T. Chacko, "Tuberculosis in Bombay: New Insights from Poor Urban Patients," *Health Policy and Planning* 12, no. 1 (1997): 77–85; Vikram Pathania, Joel Almeida, and Arata Kochi, "TB Patients and Private For-Profit Health Care Providers in India," *TB Research* (a report of the Global TB Programme of the World Health Organization, 1997); Vikram Pathania, "Why the Indian TB Control Programme Must Stop Ignoring Private Practitioners," *International Journal of Tuberculosis and Lung Disease* 5, no. 2 (2001): 201–3; M.W. Uplekar and D.S. Shepard, "Treatment of Tuberculosis by Private General Practitioners in India," *Tubercle*, 72, no. 4 (1991): 284–90; S. Rangan and M.W. Uplekar, "Socio-Cultural Dimensions in Tuberculosis Control," in *Tuberculosis: An Interdisciplinary Perspective*, ed. J.D. Porter and J.M. Grange (Singapore: Imperial College Press, 1999).

20. Ganapati Mudur, "News: Private Doctors in India Prescribe Wrong Tuberculosis Drugs," *British Medical Journal* 317 (1998): 904.

21. *Indian Journal of TB* 45 (1998): 141–43.

gram, based on Directly Observed Treatment, Short Course (DOTS), was introduced in 1993 as the revised national tuberculosis program. It ensures that a ready supply of medication is available to each patient who agrees to a care plan in which health staff or a designated DOTS provider in the community directly supervises the patient's medication taking. According to Indian government accounts, the program is a huge success, with reported cure rates of over 80 percent. The challenge will be to go to scale, as less than 15 percent of India's population is presently covered by the program. Medicine supplies will need to be carefully managed and in some cases discreetly distributed, because TB is a stigmatized disease, especially for unmarried women. Logistics and cultural sensitivity will demand that alternative patient observers be identified for different population sectors. A notable success of the DOTS program is that medicines are now administered in blister packs, which has bolstered patients' confidence in the quality of government TB medications, a former problem that drew patients to the private sector.

The need for improved and expanded coverage of TB control programs cannot be overstated, but DOTS is not a panacea. It is likely that many patients will still seek care from private practitioners, and achieving a cure rate above 80 percent will require attention to the needs of special populations, including the destitute. A final challenge is the likelihood of the expansion of drug-resistant strains of the disease. Thomas Frieden of WHO has commented that 2–3 percent of people in India with TB have the multidrug- resistant type.[22] Two percent (40,000 cases per year) is a significant number in India, especially given a growing HIV problem that is closely associated with the rise in TB.

Sexually Transmitted Diseases

In the Hindi-speaking belt of North India, venereal disease is aptly referred to as *gupt roga*, or "the hidden disease," not because it is often asymptomatic but because it is stigmatized. Existing epidemiological data on sexually transmitted diseases (STDs) in India are poor; nevertheless, available reports suggest that rates of STDs in India are alarmingly high and on the increase. Some prominent public health officials have gone so far as to identify STDs as the third most important category of communicable disease in India, after malaria and tuberculo-

---

22. Sanjay Kumar, "Plans to Expand India's 'Astounding' DOTS Programme," *Lancet* 355, no. 9205 (2000): 731.

sis. The number of cases reported at the 350 government STD clinics doubled between 1981 and 1987, with most cases diagnosed as gonorrhea.[23] Moreover, the cases of STDs seen at government clinics may represent only a fraction of the total number, as men commonly consult private practitioners or counter attendants at chemist shops. Studies from Tamil Nadu indicate that only half of those in need of medical attention for a symptomatic STD seek care from qualified medical practitioners,[24] and ethnographic observations in South India suggest that few young men consult doctors at a government clinic when they first suspect they have an STD.[25]

Recent accounts suggest an increase in adolescent sexuality and STDs, particularly troubling given the rapid escalation of HIV infection in India. Among STD patients attending government clinics, the prevalence of HIV is already high. It is estimated that the control of STDs would reduce the prevalence of HIV by 40 percent. To achieve this goal, it is important to educate the population, especially youth, about the dangers of risky sex, STD symptoms and trajectories, and what to do (as well as what not to do) following risky sex as a means of harm reduction. However, the cultural and social mores of India complicate forthright discussion of sexual activity, particularly among the young and unmarried. A recent educational intervention in the slums of Lucknow, however, found that culturally sensitive sexual health programs introduced through established community networks are accepted.[26] Finally, it is essential to make STD services more easily accessible and to improve the quality— and confidentiality—of these services. The popularity of private practitioners who advertise themselves as sex-disease specialists but provide care of questionable quality must also be addressed.

HIV/AIDS

Although prevalence rates of HIV/AIDS in the Indian population are still low, the country is reported to have the largest HIV-positive popula-

---

23. S. Lal, "Sexually Transmitted Diseases Control Programme in India: A Public Health Approach," *Indian Journal of Public Health* 37, no. 2 (1992): 33–36.

24. USAID, "U.S. Fiscal Year 1999 Congressional Presentation," www.usaid.gov/pubs/cp99/ane/in.htm (accessed July 14, 2001).

25. Shally Awasthi, Mark Nichter, and V.K. Pande, "An Interactive STD-Prevention Program for Youth in a North Indian Slum," *Studies in Family Planning* 31, no. 2 (June 2000): 138–50.

26. Ibid.

tion in the world.[27] Over 98,000 laboratory-confirmed cases of HIV have been identified, and estimates suggest that as many as 4 to 5 million Indians may already be infected.[28] Deaths due to AIDS are expected to rise to half a million annually.[29]

Rates of HIV infection are growing particularly rapidly among commercial sex workers in cities such as Mumbai, Chennai, and Calcutta and among intravenous drug users in the northeastern states of India. The epidemic has also spread rapidly in the areas adjoining these epicenters. The states of Maharashtra, Tamil Nadu, and Manipur account for over three-fourths of AIDS cases and over two-thirds of HIV infections in India, with Maharashtra reporting almost half the total number of cases in the country in 1997. Although HIV was previously believed to be primarily an urban disease, surveillance data now indicate that it is fast spreading into rural areas. According to UNAIDS, in Tamil Nadu the infection rate is three times higher in villages than in cities, possibly a result of labor migration patterns, with disease transmission mapping onto transportation routes.[30]

There is considerable debate in India about the amount of money being spent on HIV/AIDS, which critics argue diverts funds and attention from other public health programs of equal importance. Many also argue that by pouring a large amount of money into HIV/AIDS, international organizations have redirected the activities of NGOs away from community-based health activities and toward vertical programs. In the wake of such criticism, activists note that the government is not equipped to handle the AIDS crisis and that the private sector has not stepped in and offered assistance. In fact, it is commonplace for HIV-positive patients to be turned away by both government and private sector doctors, especially when they are in need of surgery.

---

27. World Bank, "India Country Brief, 2000. Regions and Countries: South Asia," www.wbln1018.worldbank.org/sar/sa.nsf (accessed July 14, 2001).

28. Much larger estimates of HIV prevalence exist. However, one must exercise caution with statistics on AIDS in India because many are based on spurious data cooked up in the wake of huge international AIDS funding initiatives that have turned scientists and NGO groups into stakeholders. Recently, the National AIDS Control Organization, India's top agency responsible for tracking HIV infection, admitted that it has been publishing inaccurate figures of new HIV cases detected in the country for the past three years.

29. Cassen and Visaria, "India: Looking Ahead."

30. Sanjay Kumar, "India Has the Largest Number of People Infected with HIV," *Lancet* 353, no. 9146 (1999): 48.

The Midstage Health Transition: Diseases of Modernity

Two interrelated and often co-occurring chronic diseases exemplify the complexity of India's health transition: heart disease and diabetes. Each of these diseases presents a comparable epidemiological profile: rising prevalence, particularly among the urban population, and a similar basic set of risk factors associated with poverty and stress as well as with modernization and the rise of the middle class. Each is, in addition, a risk factor for the other, and the management of each requires routine monitoring, dietary changes, and often medications. Together, they illustrate health care challenges that are not about to be solved by technical fixes and lead us to think more broadly about the primary health care needs of adults and elders who are chronically ill.

Epidemiological studies show a steadily increasing trend in the prevalence of hypertension across India over the last forty years, in contrast to the developed countries, where a significant decrease has occurred. The prevalence of heart disease in urban areas in India is now between 15 and 30 percent—fourfold higher than in the United States, though the rates were similar in 1968.[31] A doubling of mortality attributable to circulatory factors is predicted to occur in India by 2015, by which time coronary heart disease will likely have become the most common cause of death. A rapid increase in stroke mortality has already occurred. A similar rise in the prevalence of diabetes has taken place. By 2025, the diabetic population, already the largest in the world, will double, reaching more than 57 million. Most of these cases are type 2, or non-insulin-dependent diabetes mellitus (NIDDM); the prevalence of type 1, or insulin-dependent diabetes, remains much lower in India than throughout the Western world. The costs of treating diabetes are high, and it is predicted that diabetes will be one of the chief health problems contributing to rising health care costs in India over the next two decades. Hypertension and stroke occur at a relatively younger age in Indians than in other populations. Indians develop coronary artery disease five to ten years earlier than people in the United States, and the occurrence

---

31. Hypertension Study Group, "Prevalence, Awareness, Treatment and Control of Hypertension Among the Elderly in Bangladesh and India: A Multi Centre Study," *Bulletin of the World Health Organization* 79, no. 6 (2001): 490–500.

of first myocardial infarction under the age of forty is five to ten times higher in Indians.[32]

Within India, consistently higher rates of both hypertension and diabetes are reported among urban populations.[33] In general, diabetes is approximately four times more common in urban than rural populations. The reported prevalence of hypertension is typically two to three times lower in rural than in urban populations, though this disparity is less significant in the southern part of the country.

High blood pressure is adequately controlled with medication in only one-fifth of Indian patients.[34] In some areas, fewer than 10 percent of patients are aware of their hypertension. Similarly, community-based prevalence studies have found that only a fraction of Indian diabetics are diagnosed and managed at an early stage and suggest that the majority are presently suffering from diabetes-related complications, including other illnesses. For example, diabetics in India are four times more likely to be hypertensive than the general population, twice the relationship typically reported in other countries.[35]

Higher socioeconomic groups have a greater incidence of hypertension and coronary heart disease in India, in contrast to developed countries such as Australia and Japan, where lower social class is a risk factor for hypertension and stroke. It is likely that newly achieved affluence and rapid changes in diet and lifestyle, in association with environmental pollution and stress, predispose middle-class urban Indians to hypertension. The poor, though, also suffer from heightened rates, as a result of fetal malnutrition and low birth weight as well as rheumatic heart disease.[36] The increasing prevalence of tobacco use among rural and urban populations constitutes another important risk factor.

An examination of the epidemiological profile and distribution of

---

32. E.A. Enas and J.L. Mehta, "Malignant Coronary Artery Disease in Young Asian Indians: Thoughts on Pathogenesis, Prevention and Treatment," *Clinical Cardiology* 18 (1995): 131–35.

33. S.L. Chadha, N. Gopinath, and S. Shekhawat, "Urban-Rural Differences in the Prevalence of Coronary Heart Disease and Its Risk Factors in Delhi," *Bulletin of the World Health Organization* 75, no. 1 (1997): 31–38.

34. Urmila Thatte, "Drug Therapy of Hypertension: In Search of an Optimal Regimen," *Journal of the Association of Physicians in India* 47, no. 2 (1999): 169–76.

35. R.B. Singh, S. Bajaj, M.A. Niaz, S.S. Rastogi, and M. Moshiri, "Prevalence of Type 2 Diabetes Mellitus and Risk of Hypertension and Coronary Artery Disease in Rural and Urban Population with Low Rates of Obesity," *International Journal of Cardiology* 66, no. 1 (1998): 65–72.

36. K.S. Reddy, "Cardiovascular Disease in India," *World Health Statistics Quarterly* 46 (1993): 101–7.

NIDDM in India suggests that malnutrition and migration as well as lifestyle changes associated with westernization are significant factors in its increasing prevalence. Malnutrition-related diabetes may constitute a significant proportion (10–20 percent) of people diagnosed before age thirty. An analysis of data from a multicenter study of diabetic subjects between the ages of fifteen and thirty revealed significantly higher rates in rural than in urban areas, possibly a result of the effects of a higher rural prevalence of malnutrition and early deprivation. In addition, rates of diabetes are higher among migrant workers, likely a consequence of exposure to high levels of stress and fewer social resources. In urban areas, rising affluence and changing behaviors are strongly associated with risk factors for diabetes, including sedentary lifestyles, energy-dense diets high in saturated fat and refined sugar carbohydrates, excess body weight, and higher levels of hypertension.

The emerging epidemic of cardiovascular disease in developing countries may have its roots in childhood. One study of middle-class and upper-middle-class adolescent children from western India revealed a high prevalence of metabolic and dietetic coronary risk factors, such as hypertension and hypercholesterolemia.[37] In addition, a study in Mysore provided the first confirmatory evidence that low birth weight and low maternal body weight are associated with heightened rates of coronary heart disease later in life.[38] This suggests that fetal and maternal malnutrition lead to changes in utero that permanently increase susceptibility to chronic disease.

Lifestyle-Related Health Challenges: The Case of Tobacco

Modernization has also produced a number of lifestyle-related health challenges such as tobacco consumption, which exemplifies the relationship between health and political economy. In India, the increasing popularity of tobacco products is clearly the result of efforts on the part of the tobacco industry (both global and national) to foster a behavior that results in massive health problems.

---

37. R. Gupta, A. Goyle, et al., "Prevalence of Atherosclerosis Risk Factors in Adolescent School Children," *Indian Heart Journal* 50, no. 5 (1998): 511–15.

38. C.E. Stein, C.H. Fall, et al., "Fetal Growth and Coronary Heart Disease in South India," Lancet 348, no. 9037 (1996): 1269–73; C.H. Fall, C.E. Stein, et al., "Size at Birth, Maternal Weight, and Type 2 Diabetes in South India," *Diabetic Medicine* 15, no. 3 (1998): 220–27.

An assortment of cheap tobacco products is readily available on any street corner in India and in most small shops in city and countryside. Popular indigenous tobacco products include cured leaf tobacco smoked in a hookah; hand-rolled *bidi* smoking sticks; chewing tobacco, which is commonly added to the traditional *paan* (betel leaf with areca nut, lime paste, and, sometimes, aromatic spices); tobacco powder to be placed inside the lip; and snuff. In addition to a variety of cigarettes (almost all locally produced), several other new tobacco products have entered the market, including prepackaged forms of chewing tobacco mixed with lime; *gutkhar*, or cachets of aromatic spices, areca nut, and tobacco; and creamy snuff dental creams.

By present estimates, there are 185 million tobacco consumers in India.[39] The prevalence of tobacco use varies widely by region, from 33 to 80 percent among men and 7 to 67 percent among women.[40] Traditionally, the use of tobacco among females has been confined to chewing and to taking snuff. Although the prevalence of smoking among females remains low, it is rising among middle-class to upper-class urban women as a result of advertising and product placement in the (international as well as national) media that has established the image of women smokers as modern, independent, and outspoken.[41]

The health consequences of tobacco use are dire. WHO estimates that nearly half a million Indians die each year as a result of tobacco use and predicts that by 2020 the number will reach 1.5 million annually. By then, it is estimated, tobacco will be solely responsible for 13.3 percent of all deaths in India.[42] The Indian Council on Medical Research estimates that nearly 160,000 people develop cancer in India each year as a result of tobacco consumption, the most common form being oral cancer, of which India has one of the highest incidence rates in the world. It is also estimated that 25 percent of smokers over forty have chronic bronchitis.[43]

Despite some claims to the contrary, India's tobacco industry is enjoy-

---

39. Roughly 20 percent consume cigarettes, 40 percent smoke *bidis,* and the remaining 40 percent use chewing tobacco and tobacco-containing products. See Sanjay Kumar, "India Steps Up Anti-Tobacco Measures," *Lancet* 356, no. 9235 (2000): 1089.

40. Prakash C. Gupta, "Survey of Sociodemographic Characteristics of Tobacco Use Among 99,598 Individuals in Bombay, India, Using Handheld Computers," *Tobacco Control* 5, no. 2 (summer 1996): 114–20.

41. V. Ernester, N. Kaufman, Mimi Nichter, J. Somet, and S. Yoon, "Women and Tobacco: Moving from Policy to Action," *Bulletin of the World Health Organization* 78, no. 7 (2000): 866–948.

42. Kumar, "India Steps Up Anti-Tobacco Measures."

43. Ibid.

ing a period of prosperity. India produces over 110 billion cigarettes each year, worth some $2 billion. Between 1990 and 1995, cigarette consumption per capita increased in India, a distinction it shares with only two other countries: China and Indonesia. During this time, the real price of cigarettes decreased by 45 percent. Even then, cigarettes are not the biggest commercial tobacco product in India: *bidis*—small, hand-rolled smoking sticks consisting of flake tobacco wrapped in leaves—account for 55 percent of tobacco consumption. *Bidis* are cheap and therefore attractive, particularly to the working class, and by some reports are smoked more frequently throughout the day than are cigarettes. Although smaller than cigarettes, *bidis* are particularly harmful: smoking them yields more than three times as much carbon monoxide and more than five times as much nicotine and tar as smoking cigarettes.

Patterns of tobacco use differ by gender, age, and class as well as region in India but are marked by important emerging trends—in particular, shifting patterns of use among middle-class youth. However, little is known about such patterns of use or other important factors such as age of initiation. While conducting research on tobacco use in coastal Karnataka, the authors observed that the smoking of *bidis* is becoming less common among young men, who associate them with the past, rural areas, and the poor. In India, cigarette consumption increases with level of education and economic status (except in the wealthy), a relationship that is the inverse of that seen in most developed countries.

Over the last two years, various government bodies have approved legislation regulating the advertising of tobacco products, the sale of tobacco to minors, the location of tobacco vendors, and smoking in public places. In September, the government finally banned the sale of cigarettes and other tobacco products to children younger than eighteen years of age. It also barred the sale of such products within 100 meters of schools. Legislation to enlarge warning labels and strengthen the ban on advertising passed the assembly in February 2001, but warning labels are still not required on all tobacco products, and no tar or nicotine information is published on them.

Environmental Health Challenges

Over the last two decades, there has been a worldwide upsurge in concern about air, food, and water pollution. This trend is certainly apparent in India, where concern for the environment is reflected in widening public support for environmental causes and the registration of more than 12,000 environmental groups, up from 600 in 1985.[44] Articles on the dangers of pesticides and "the poisoning of India" appear regularly in newspapers and popular magazines. Adulteration of food is a commonly expressed health concern, the most recent focus of which has been the possible surreptitious introduction of genetically modified food into the country. Popular concerns about pollution and adulteration are not unfounded. Indians are estimated to carry the highest body burden of DDT and other chlorinated pesticides in the world,[45] and it is now clear that large parts of the Indian population are also exposed to some of the highest pollutant levels.[46] We focus here on two problems: the detrimental effects of air pollution on respiratory health, and the rise in vector-borne diseases such as malaria and dengue fever.

Air Pollution

India's three largest metropolitan cities rank among the ten worst polluted in the world. In large Indian cities, average levels of particles in the air are five times higher than the WHO standard.[47] Two-thirds of the outdoor air pollution in Indian cities comes from vehicles, the numbers of which have been increasing several times faster than the human population. The World Bank estimates that 40,000 Indians die prematurely every year as a result of outdoor air pollution and that pollution-related health problems cost the economy $7 billion per year, or 2 percent of GDP.[48] More recent estimates of premature deaths each year from outdoor air pollution in Indian cities have ranged from 50,000 to 300,000.

Indians also suffer from high levels of indoor air pollution as a result of the widespread use of solid fuels (often biomass) for household heating and cooking, often in unventilated situations.[49] In addition, vehicular pollutants easily penetrate homes, where they remain trapped inside, mingling and reacting with other household emissions to produce a va-

---

44. Amy Louise Kazmin, "Clean Up or Shut Down," *Business Week*, international edition, no. 3546 (September 29, 1997): 24.

45. Sandhya Venkateswaran, *Environment, Development, and the Gender Gap* (New Delhi: Sage, 1995), 190–217.

46. Kirk R. Smith, "Overview of the Indian National Burden of Disease from Indoor Air Pollution" (paper presented at the Conference on Health and Environment, Center for Science and Environment, Delhi, July 7–9, 1998).

47. Smith, "National Burden of Disease in India."

48. Kazmin, "Clean Up or Shut Down."

49. Smith, "National Burden of Disease in India."

riety of dangerous gaseous chemicals. In densely populated areas of India, the net result is elevated "neighborhood" pollution. While indoor air pollution may be less visible to the public, it constitutes a significantly more serious public health threat than outdoor pollution. Conservative estimates of premature deaths in India from such indoor exposures range from 400,000 to 550,000 annually.[50]

Malaria and Dengue Fever: Diseases of Development

Malaria has reemerged as a major public health threat in India. Each year, the Indian National Malaria Eradication Programme reports between 2.5 and 3 million malaria cases and about 1,000 malaria deaths. Across the country, resurgent malaria has invaded new ecological niches created by Green Revolution agriculture and urban development. The spread of irrigation projects and the expanded farming of water-intensive crops have increased the area inhabited by mosquitoes and the months during which they pose a threat. The emergence of malaria in the Thar desert regions of Rajasthan provides an apt example of the ability of ecological change to alter the distribution of malaria drastically.

The Indira Gandhi Canal Project, funded by the World Bank, created an 8,000-kilometer canal system that changed the ecological profile of the Thar desert. The network of canals turned a significant area into marsh, providing malarial mosquitoes with an ideal habitat for breeding. The region, in which malaria was previously not endemic, experienced an epidemic in 1994. An estimated 60–70 percent of total malaria cases were identified as falciparum (the most serious and life-threatening form), a ratio approximately twice the national average and particularly unusual because Rajasthan was not previously a falciparum-predominant area. A similar outbreak followed the construction of the Upper Krishna Dam in Karnataka.

The 1990s also saw a dramatic resurgence of malaria in urban areas such as New Delhi, Mumbai, and especially Chennai, which now records the highest number of malaria cases of any urban area in South Asia. Epidemics of dengue fever and dengue hemorrhagic fever (DHF)—its more serious form—have also become increasingly common in cities across India. In 1996, Delhi had its first major outbreak of DHF, the largest outbreak ever reported from India.

---

50. Ibid.

In many Indian cities, high population concentrations promote increased rates of transmission, and the associated ecological changes and flagging investment in public health infrastructure lead to an increase in breeding habitats. Both *Anopheles stephensi*, the mosquito that transmits malaria in urban areas, and *Aedes aegypti*, the mosquito that carries dengue virus, are well adapted to these densely populated and poorly serviced areas, breeding in anything that will hold water. Both species of mosquito breed in clean water rather than in polluted or sewage-contaminated water; nevertheless, efforts to control the insects often mistakenly target poor, periurban parts of cities and overlook the real culprits, such as apartment buildings and cisterns on roofs.

For decades, the Indian malaria program has emphasized insecticide spraying to control the vector population. More sustainable and effective strategies, such as larval habitat and breeding site eradication, have been underutilized, though they were used to great success in the past.[51] Overdependence on insecticides enhances pathogenicity and increases resistance to insecticidal agents, potentially frustrating future prospects for vector control.

Diagnosing malaria has its own set of challenges, and treatment of the disease also continues to grow increasingly problematic as resistance to antimalarial drugs escalates at an alarming rate. One factor contributing to drug resistance is that many practitioners treating the poor often engage in diagnosis by treatment.[52] They commonly dole out one- or two-day doses of antimalarial drugs to impoverished patients.

The Health Care Transition

Various kinds of medical practitioners attend to the ill in India, ranging from highly qualified practitioners of allopathic (Western) and indigenous systems of medicine to a *masala* of registered and unregistered medical practitioners who have learned their trade through apprenticeships, correspondence courses, medical texts, medical catalogues, and divine inspiration. At present, there are approximately half a million trained (M.B.B.S./ M.D.) allopathic doctors, or one for every 2,000 Indians.

---

51. See Vinay Kamat, "Resurgence of Malaria in Bombay (Mumbai) in the 1990s: A Historical Perspective," *Parasitologia* 42 (2000): 135–48, for a discussion of the history of vector control strategies and the resurgence of vector-borne diseases in urban India.

52. Vinay Kamat, "Private Practitioners and Their Role in the Resurgence of Malaria in Mumbai (Bombay), India: Serving the Affected or Aiding an Epidemic?" *Social Science and Medicine* 52 (2001): 885–909.

There is an extensive network of government primary health centers, subcenters, government hospitals, and dispensaries. However, few people—including few of the poor—use government medical facilities exclusively. Instead, government care and private care are often coextensive and are sometimes provided by the same doctor. More than half of all hospitals and almost a third of hospital beds are in the private sector.[53]

Medical care is big business in India. In 2000, total expenditure on health amounted to 5.2 percent of GDP, of which 85 percent consisted of private payments.[54] Growth of the private health care sector has taken place at all levels, from the opening of small polyclinics by doctors to the rapid proliferation of small hospitals (called "nursing homes") in towns and cities to the rise of diagnostic centers to investments in large corporate hospitals and medical schools catering to the upper class.

The Public Sector

A recent review of national survey data on health care utilization in India estimated that overall only about 18 percent of rural and 23 percent of urban outpatient services are received at government hospitals, 5 percent at primary health care centers, and another 3 percent at government dispensaries.[55] However, these aggregate figures overlook important regional differences and do not indicate whether those who consult government health care providers do so exclusively. They also do not indicate who uses government services and for what complaints. Rates of outpatient consultation at PHC centers in different rural areas of India range from 1 to 40 percent. The reasons for this variation involve the accessibility of the centers, the availability of medicines and doctors, and the quality of care offered, as well as the availability of other sources of medical care. Utilization rates of government hospitals also vary significantly across states. Rural inpatient rates range from less than a third of cases in Andhra Pradesh to more than three-fourths in fourteen of India's twenty-nine states and territories. Government hospitals serve a significant percentage of India's inpatient medical needs in much of the

53. Ramesh Bhat, "Characteristics of Private Medical Practice in India: A Provider Perspective," *Health Policy and Planning* 14, no. 1 (1999): 26–37.

54. UNICEF, "Information: Country Statistics."

55. Rama V. Baru, *Private Health Care in India: Social Characteristics and Trends* (New Delhi: Sage, 1998).

country. By comparison, the vast majority of outpatient consultations occur in the private sector.

The Private Sector

A 1993 report by the Indian Market Research Bureau estimates that there is one practitioner for every 600 people, a figure that closely approximates that obtained in Nichter's longitudinal research in coastal Karnataka. A large number of these practitioners have no formal training in biomedicine and treat between five and fifteen patients per day.[56] The numbers of these local practitioners do not appear to be dwindling, and they flourish even outside the gates of prestigious medical centers such as the Christian Medical College in Vellore, Tamil Nadu. The reasons for their popularity include their willingness to cater to patients' demands for injections and their attentiveness to local medical concerns such as folk dietetics. Their fees also appear reasonable to the poor, who are charged on the basis of medicines directly received.[57]

Each year 15,000 doctors graduate from the country's 160 medical schools and enter the marketplace along with graduates from India's 200 Ayurvedic medical colleges, most of whom will practice an eclectic blend of indigenous and allopathic medicine. Approximately 80 percent of qualified allopathic doctors registered with medical councils in India work in the private sector, as do most graduates of schools of indigenous medicine. Of those physicians who work in the public sector, many establish private practices on the side to subsidize their income.

Private health care expenditure in India has grown at the rate of 12.5 percent per annum since 1960–61. It is estimated that for every 1 percent increase in per capita income, private health care expenditure has increased by 1.47 percent.[58] Health care provision has expanded dramatically over the past two decades in rural towns as well as cities. Several market factors are responsible for the increase, ranging from the growth of the middle class to more liberal economic policies involving

---

56. Recent estimates suggest that these practitioners account for up to half of total national health expenditures. See Anil Gumber and Peter Berman, "Measurement and Pattern of Morbidity and the Utilization of Health Services: Some Emerging Issues from Recent Health Interview Surveys in India," *Journal of Health and Population in Developing Countries* 1, no. 1 (1997): 16–43.

57. Mark Nichter and Mimi Nichter, *Anthropology and International Health: Asian Case Studies* (Amsterdam: Gordon and Breache, 1996).

58. Ramesh Bhat, "Regulating the Private Health Care Sector: The Case of the Indian Consumer Protection Act," *Health Policy and Planning* 11, no. 3 (1996): 265–79.

bank loans and the importation of medical technology. Large investments in the health care industry have been made by India's corporate sector and nonresident Indians, while more modest investments have been made by India's landed agricultural class (especially in the south), whose members see their children's future in this more profitable sector.

The Growth of Nursing Homes and Small Private Hospitals

It is beyond the scope of this chapter to discuss corporate hospitals, except to note that major Indian business groups such as Apollo, Goenkas, Modi, Nandas, Oberois, and Tata have built or plan to build specialty hospitals in major Indian cities to serve the middle and upper classes. Instead, we highlight the proliferation of smaller hospitals (nursing homes) throughout India in both rural and urban areas. These establishments cater not only to the growing middle class but to members of lower classes who are skeptical about the quality of care available at government health facilities.

Nursing homes offer both outpatient and inpatient services. Most are set up to handle maternity patients and minor surgical cases; larger facilities offer an assortment of specialty care services. They range in size from small establishments owned and operated by a single physician to twenty to forty-bed hospitals with operating rooms and sophisticated diagnostic equipment attended by several consulting physicians. According to available data, the number of small private treatment facilities increased threefold between 1984 and 1992 in the rural areas of India,[59] and the number of nursing homes in urban areas has also expanded rapidly. For example, in the small city of Mangalore (monitored by Nichter), the number of moderate-sized nursing homes jumped from six in 1986 to twenty in 1994 to thirty-two in 1998. Even higher rates of growth are reported for larger cities such as Hyderabad.[60] Official statistics poorly reflect the growth of these facilities, since many of them are unregistered.

The government maintains a laissez-faire attitude toward the nursing home and private hospital business sector. These establishments are unregulated by state law and unmonitored by state departments of health. Recently, however, the quality of care offered in private health

---

59. Bhat, "Characteristics of Private Medical Practice."
60. Baru, "Private Health Care."

care facilities has been scrutinized by consumer activist groups, which have also revealed shady business practices used to exploit patients even in more reputable establishments. Some nursing homes offer excellent care at a price, but many are unsanitary and staffed by unqualified nursing personnel. Profit motives favor the overuse of costly diagnostic tests, unnecessary medical procedures (such as cesarean sections), and overmedication. A number of medical complications associated with improper care received at these facilities have been featured in the press, but holding doctors and hospital administrators accountable has proven to be very difficult. In addition, little communication exists between private treatment facilities and the Health Ministry. Cases of communicable diseases such as malaria, TB, and STDs are not reported by private providers, making it nearly impossible to generate accurate regional accounts of disease patterns.

The means used to attract clientele to nursing homes has also drawn attention. Honorary consultant doctors who maintain staff privileges in public hospitals often divert patients who can afford to pay to private facilities. They then receive kickbacks for admitting and treating patients and carrying out diagnostic tests on the premises. Collusion between nursing home owners and consultant doctors in squeezing patients for all fees imaginable is alleged to be common, and yet these facilities have grown in popularity.[61] The reason lies with the alternatives. Many people believe that government facilities are much worse than private ones.

The Growth of Diagnostic Testing Centers

Another emerging phenomenon in the private sector is the proliferation of diagnostic testing centers. In the early 1980s, small private labs began springing up in towns and cities, offering blood and stool exams. With the liberalization of bank loans and reduction of import duties (from 47 percent to 29 percent), investment in high-tech diagnostic testing exploded in the early 1990s. Moderately priced diagnostic equipment was purchased by owners of nursing homes, and entrepreneurs invested heavily in "scan" centers featuring state-of-the-art equipment previously

---

61. C.A.K. Yesudian, "Behaviour of the Private Sector in the Health Market of Bombay," *Health Policy and Planning* 9, no. 1 (1994): 72–80; Sunil Nandaraj, "Beyond the Law and the Lord: Quality of Private Health Care," *Economic and Political Weekly* (July 2, 1994): 1680–86; Bhat, "Regulating the Private Health Care Sector."

found only in large hospitals.[62] To pay off loans for equipment and make a profit, scanning centers market their services and give doctors incentives for using them. Doctors commonly receive a 10–30 percent cut of the testing fees for referring cases, which encourages them to do so even when it is not warranted. In addition, prescribing tests enhances a doctor's status because it confirms the doctor's ability to interface with modern technology. This is not to say that doctors' only motivation for using tests is self-interest. There is little doubt that testing does improve the quality of doctors' diagnoses. Our intent is to draw attention to how market dynamics drive health care transition.

The function of diagnostic tests is as much to rule out as to confirm diagnoses. This means that negative test results far outnumber positive ones. What does the Indian population think about diagnostic tests, when they are so often negative? During ethnographic research in Karnataka and Kerala between 1995 and 1998, Nichter came across many patients who suspected that the tests they had been prescribed were unnecessary. But even among those who complained about the cost of tests, many stated that they were happy they had gotten them. Negative test results were often explained to the patient as an indication that the problem had not yet surfaced rather than that it could be ruled out entirely. For patients, tests had come to symbolize the best that could be done in a world where trust in medicine as an institution had eroded and familiarity with technology had increased, and besides, test results were thought to increase doctors' interest in patients' cases.

The Commodification of Health and the Rampant Use of Medicines

Another dimension of the health care transition is the growing popularity of medications. Over 60,000 drugs are manufactured in India by some 20,000 companies, and limited amounts of imported drugs are also available. Drugs are produced by a wide range of companies: small, family-run producers of indigenous medicines; production units that replicate drugs patented in the West; large multinational drug companies that produce brand-name medicines; and national companies that manufacture generic drugs for local con-

---

62. For example, in Mangalore between 1986 and 1998, the number of ultrasound machines jumped from four to twenty-six, the number of endoscopes from two to eight, and the number of EKG machines from two to six. The number of CT (computerized tomography) scans went from one in 1990 to four in 1998. In neighboring Kerala, twenty-two of the state's twenty-six CT scans were privately owned and operated by 1995.

sumption and export.[63] Two of the trends contributing to the increasing use of medicine in India are the commodification of health and pharmaceuticalization. A growing number of people in India see their environment and work as health adverse, their food as adulterated, and their lives as increasingly conflict ridden. Many turn to medicines as a solution. Pharmaceuticals have been marketed in India to respond to popular health concerns, and advertisements play on collective anxieties.[64]

Pharmaceuticalization—characterized by a "pill for every ill" mentality—fosters self-medication and influences practitioner-patient relations by increasing the expectation that medication will be prescribed. The public waits shorter periods of time both before taking medicines for symptomatic relief and before shifting to new medicines when the expected effects are not forthcoming. Practitioners are motivated to use more powerful medications and inappropriate combinations of medications to achieve fast results. They are also compelled to prescribe newer-generation drugs and drugs with new names not already being used for self-medication and to give injections.[65]

Almost all prescription drugs are available over the counter in India, including a wide variety of antibiotics. Regulations prohibiting their sale to anyone but registered medical practitioners exist on the books but are rarely enforced. Clients often consult and receive advice from chemist shop`counter attendants who have been educated on the job. Although these attendants often have impressive knowledge about the medications stocked in their shop and their uses, they know little about the

---

63. One India-based pharmaceutical company, Cipla Ltd., recently received international attention by offering to sell the Geneva-based nongovernmental organization Doctors Without Borders anti-AIDS retroviral drugs at greatly reduced prices. It also requested the registrar of patents in South Africa to grant it compulsory licensing for an entire range of anti-AIDS drugs. The World Trade Organization allows countries to manufacture generic versions of patented drugs if they are used to combat national health emergencies. Cipla was the first company to offer to sell drugs under such a provision. See Bhakti Chuganee, "License to Heal," *Business India* (May 4–27, 2001): 23.

64. Yesudian, "Behaviour of the Private Sector."

65. Injections are a very popular form of medicine in India. Unhygienic needles and syringes are also responsible for the transmission of such diseases as hepatitis B and C. See M. Lakshman and Mark Nichter, "Contamination of Medicine Injection Paraphernalia Used by Registered Medical Practitioners in South India: An Ethnographic Study," *Social Science and Medicine* 51, no. 1 (2000): 11–28; J. Singh, R. Bhatia, J.C. Gandhi, A.P. Kaswekar, S. Khare, S.B. Patel, V.B. Oza, D.C. Jain, and J. Sokhey, "Outbreak of Viral Hepatitis B in a Rural Community in India Due to Inadequately Sterilized Needles and Syringes," *Bulletin of the World Health Organization* 76, no. 1 (1998): 93–98; M. Narendranathan and M. Philip, "Reusable Needles: A Major Risk Factor for Acute Virus B Hepatitis," *Tropical Doctor* 23 (1993): 64–66; and H.V. Wyatt and S. Mahadevan, "The Double-Edged Sword: Injections," *Indian Journal of Community Medicine* 18, no. 4 (1993): 149–51.

drugs' side effects, contraindications, and synergistic effects. In addition, their advice to clients is often economically motivated. A complex set of reciprocal relationships among pharmacy owners, medicine wholesalers, and pharmaceutical sales representatives fosters a practice known as "counter-pushing."[66] The medicines suggested to clients are often the ones that net the largest profits or incentive payments.

The Revitalization of Indigenous Medications

At the same time that the Indian public has begun consuming more allopathic medications, it has come to see them as harmful if taken for too long. Indigenous drugs have been marketed to reduce the harmful effects of strong antibiotics and to correct one's digestion following long courses of allopathic medicines. While advertisements for Ayurvedic medicines have long stated that they are "free from side effects," today they are just as likely to make reference to strengthening the immune system and ridding the body of free radicals. Advertisements also target the problems of modern living: herbal products have been developed to protect the skin from harmful air pollution, improve vitality and enhance marital relations during middle age, and improve the memory power of students.

The manufacture of indigenous medications in India has become a growth industry that serves both local and foreign markets. By some estimates, there are 9,000 firms in India that manufacture "indigenous" medicines worth over $400 million a year. Notably, many of the medicines produced are new formulations, not ancient medicines specified in texts; most are packaged to look modern, and a great many have English names.[67] Advertisements for indigenous medications have recently come under government scrutiny as a result of claims of miraculous cures for AIDS and other infectious diseases.

Antibiotic Resistance: A Side Effect of the Health Care Transition

For India, with its massive number of poor citizens and limited government health resources, drug resistance is a particularly serious problem.

---

66. Vinay Kamat and Mark Nichter, "Pharmacies, Self-Medication and Pharmaceutical Marketing in Bombay, India," *Social Science and Medicine* 47, no. 6 (1998): 779–94.

67. Just as Ayurvedic practitioners commonly administer allopathic (biomedical) drugs, doctors trained in allopathic medicine commonly prescribe combinations of allopathic and Ayurvedic drugs packaged to appear modern. See Nichter and Nichter, *Anthropology and International Health.*

Each time pathogens develop resistance to an inexpensive frontline drug, the cost of primary health care increases significantly. For a long time drug resistance in India was blamed on poor patient compliance and failure to complete recommended courses of medication. Studies revealed that patients often purchased a partial supply of prescribed medication either because of its cost or to test whether the drug was effective. Other studies found that antibiotics accounted for between 10 and 20 percent of medicines purchased over the counter and that most people purchased only a one- or two-day dose. More recent research, however, has pointed to noncompliance on the part of the health care system when essential drugs are in short supply and to the misprescribing and overprescribing of antibiotics by practitioners as major contributors to drug resistance. Many upper respiratory tract infections caused by viruses are treated with antibiotics, as are cases of diarrhea requiring only ORT. STDs and TB are treated haphazardly and often with the wrong medications.

An extensive study of antimicrobial resistance among Gram-negative and Gram-positive isolates documented an alarming 73–99 percent resistance to common antibiotics such as ampicillin, chloramphenicol, cotrimoxazole, and first-generation cephalosporins. Resistance to gentamicin and ciprofloxacin ranged from 53 to 79 percent, and that to amikacin, netilmicin, and third-generation cephalosporins ranged from 30 to 73 percent.[68]

How does this translate into disease management? Following are some examples of public health red flags:

Cholera. Multiple antibiotic resistance has been found among clinical strains of *Vibrio cholerae* in Calcutta; some strains show high levels of resistance to virtually every class of antimicrobial agent.[69]

Typhoid. A decade ago in New Delhi, typhoid could be cured by three drugs. Now, these drugs are largely ineffective.[70] One study in Karnataka found that of the 226 strains of *S. typhi* isolated over three years, 57.9 percent were multidrug resistant; only 8.8 percent of the isolates were sensitive to all the drugs tested.[71]

---

68. S. Nema, P. Premchandani, et al., "Emerging Bacterial Drug Resistance in Hospital Practice," *Indian Journal of Medical Science* 51, no. 8 (1997): 275–80.

69. P. Garg, et al., "Expanding Multiple Antibiotic Resistance Among Clinical Strains of *Vibrio cholerae* Isolated from 1992–7 in Calcutta, India," *Epidemiology and Infection* 124, no. 3 (2000): 393–99.

70. WHO, "Drug Resistance Threatens to Reverse Medical Progress," *WHO Press Release* 41, www.who.int/inf-pr 2000/en/pr2000–41.htm (accessed July 14, 2001).

71. A.M. Ciraj, K.S. Seetha, B.K. Gopalkrishna, and P.G. Shivananda, "Drug Resistance Pattern and Phage Types of *Salmonella typhi* Isolates in Manipal, South Karnataka," *Indian Journal of Medical Science* 53, no. 11 (1999): 486–89.

Salmonella. An alarming increase in multidrug-resistant salmonella has been reported in Mumbai.[72] A recent study revealed that while 573 strains were sensitive to all the antibiotics commonly used, 1,351 displayed single-drug resistance, 594 were resistant to two drugs, and 704 were multidrug resistant; one strain was resistant to all the antibiotics used.[73]

Pneumococcus. Multidrug-resistant pneumococcus has been reported in Uttar Pradesh.[74]

Gonorrhea. Significant antimicrobial resistance has been documented in *Neisseria gonorrhoeae.*[75]

Given the high and rapidly rising rates of antibiotic resistance, it is of vital importance to conduct research on the organisms responsible for contagious diseases and how sensitive they are to various drugs. The IBIS network recently set up by INCLEN is a good example of a well-functioning sentinel-surveillance system.[76] Now the Indian government must determine how to convince private practitioners, chemist shops, and the pharmaceutical industry to comply with treatment guidelines.

The Kerala Good-Health-at-Low-Cost Success Story Revisited

The Rockefeller Foundation's publication *Good Health at Low Cost* presented Kerala, India, to the world as a success story of what could be accomplished by a state government with the political will to provide high-quality basic health services to its citizens.[77] The report pointed out that although Kerala had a low per capita income, it had achieved impressively low infant and child mortality rates and a life expectancy comparable to those of developed countries. Beyond the political commitment necessary to maintain an effective health care infrastructure,

72. R. Gandhi and D.D. Banker, "Multidrug-Resistant *Salmonella,*" *Indian Journal of Medical Science* 53, no. 6 (1999): 259–66.

73. R. Mahajan, Y. Dhar, P.C. John, and J. Sokhey, "Prevalence and Resistance Pattern of *Salmonella* Serotypes in India," *Journal of Communicable Diseases* 30, no. 4 (1998): 279–82.

74. V.M. Vashishta, "Emergence of Multidrug Resistant Pneumococci in India," *British Medical Journal* 321, no. 7267 (2000): 1022a.

75. K. Ray, M. Bala, J. Kumar, and R.S. Misra, "Trend of Antimicrobial Resistance in *Neisseria gonorrhoeae* at New Delhi, India," *International Journal of Sexually Transmitted Diseases and AIDS* 11, no. 2 (2000): 115–18.

76. Invasive Bacterial Infection Surveillance (IBIS) Group and International Clinical Epidemiology Network (INCLEN), "Prospective Multicentre Hospital Surveillance of *Streptococcus pneumoniae* in India," *Lancet* 353 (April 10, 1999): 1216–21.

77. Scott Halstead, Julia Warren, and Kenneth Walsh, *Good Health at Low Cost* (New York: Rockefeller Foundation, 1985).

various scholars attributed Kerala's health transition to land legislation and social reform movements, public distribution of food grains, high levels of literacy among women, greater female decision-making power in this predominantly matrilineal region of India, an indigenous medical system (Ayurveda) that contributes to a strong sense of health consciousness, the influence of Christian missionaries on the nursing and medical professions, left-wing (Communist and labor union) political activism and high political awareness among this largely literate population, a good transportation system, and an abundant water supply.

On closer inspection, another side to Kerala's "success story" surfaced. Data from the National Sample Survey and local studies such as those of the KSSP showed that Kerala had the highest rate of reported morbidity.[78] They also showed Kerala to have the highest incidence and prevalence rates of chronic illness in India.[79] This "paradox" has been the topic of much discussion and debate in India. Rising rates of morbidity have been variously attributed to such factors as (1) an increase in the population of older citizens; (2) a better-informed and more health conscious public that consults health practitioners readily; (3) heightened concern about children's illness, given the low birth rate; (4) changing definitions of health and illness associated with lower thresholds of discomfort; (5) increased density and availability of doctors, clinics, and pharmacies; and (6) improved screening programs resulting in better and earlier diagnosis of disease. This begs the question: If perceived morbidity is high and the population is predisposed to consult medical practitioners, how is it that good health costs so little?

Low cost is a relative concept. When compared with health care expenditures in developed countries, health care costs in Kerala are low, but calculated as a percentage of Kerala's GNP, the costs are substantial. For over two decades, Kerala has spent far more of its state budget on

---

78. K.P. Kannan, K.R. Thankappan, Vinay Raman Kutty, and K.P. Aravindan, "Health and Development in Rural Kerala," Kerala Sasthra Sahithya Parishad, Trivandrum (KSSP, 1987); T.P. Kunhikannan, K.P. Aravindan, and Science Centre, KSSP, Kozhikode, "Changes in the Health Status of Kerala, 1987–1997," sponsored by Kerala Research Project on Local Development, Centre for Development Studies (1999); K.P. Aravindan and T.P. Kunhikannan, eds., "Health Transition in Rural Kerala 1987–96" (KSSP, 2000).

79. B. Gopalakrishna Kumar, "Low Mortality and High Morbidity in Kerala Reconsidered," *Population and Development Review* 19, no. 1 (1993): 103–21; P.G. Panikar and C.R. Soman, *Health Status of Kerala: Paradox of Economic Backwardness and Health Development* (Trivandrum: Centre for Development Studies, 1984). Kerala also has India's highest rate of suicide. See Murphy Halliburton, "Suicide: A Paradox of Development in Kerala," *Economic and Political Weekly* (September 5, 1998): 2341–2345.

health than other states in India, maintaining its high level of expenditure even during this past decade of fiscal crises. Nevertheless, the government of Kerala has had to impose austerity measures. While revenues spent on health staff in this fiercely unionized state have remained constant, there has been a cutback on supplies and the expansion of services. The result has been a decline in the quality of government health services in a state in which early provision of good services sensitized the population to the merits of health care. This has led an increasing number of people to seek private medical services. As Kutty has noted, the growth of the private health sector cannot be looked at as a phenomenon independent from the government's role in raising the health consciousness of the people.[80]

The lion's share of medical consultations for illness take place in the private sector. Thus, the local population's out-of-pocket health expenditure is high; health expenses may consume 8–40 percent of a poor-to-lower-middle-class household's total income.[81] Notably, the literate poor in Kerala are just as health care conscious as are members of the middle class.

Demand for health services in Kerala is high, and the supply of doctors, private clinics, and private hospitals is increasing. Private hospitals now surpass government hospitals in numbers of beds and staff and in availability of high-tech diagnostic equipment. It is currently estimated that there are 1.5 private hospitals per ten square kilometers in Kerala.[82]

Good health does not come at low cost for the population of Kerala, and medical costs are rapidly escalating.[83] Residents invest more in the health of their children because they have fewer progeny and because women are better educated and more active in health care decision making. Elders are living longer and constitute a growing percentage of the population. In the cases of children and the elderly, social values and expectations lead families to pursue medical care actively. The economic impact on households is often serious. Securing expensive treatment for a husband's or father's cancer, for example, can deplete household sav-

80. V. Raman Kutty, "Historical Analysis of the Development of Health Care Facilities in Kerala State, India," *Health Policy and Planning* 15, no. 1 (2000): 103–9.

81. Aravindan and Kunhikannan, "Health Transition in Rural Kerala."

82. Kutty, "Historical Analysis of the Development of Health Care Facilities."

83. The latest KSSP survey found that the rise in per capita medical expenditure was four times the consumer price index between 1987 and 1996. Explosive rises in prices occurred for drugs, doctors' fees, and laboratory tests and were not confined to the allopathic medicinal system. The hardest hit were the poor, whose expenditures soared. See Aravindan and Kunhikannan, "Health Transition in Rural Kerala."

ings rapidly, and it has impoverished many lower-middle-class households and left widows without resources.

What role should the Kerala state government play in providing care, considering the changes associated with the health and health care transitions? There has been a call for more decentralized planning as well as a reexamination of the purpose of primary health care centers. Considering the drop in the birthrate and increase in the rate of chronic illness, some suggest that it is time to consider providing elders and the chronically ill more services through PHC centers. Recent research by Rema Devi of Trivandrum Medical School and Mark Nichter has found that the Kerala public is responsive to this idea.

Conclusion

We have highlighted several health challenges faced by India that are associated with the health transition. Some of these challenges are long-standing, and others are new or reemerging. A few health problems, such as polio and hepatitis B, appear to be manageable by fairly straightforward (albeit hard-to-implement) interventions, but the vast majority of health challenges are outcomes of poverty, poor infrastructure, crowding, and modernization. To understand the health transition in India, it is not enough to consider the epidemiological profile of diseases and the numbers of doctors and health care facilities; one must look to those social, economic, and political factors that affect the distribution of resources and of diseases, the way in which health care is provided and disease control pursued, and the "side effects" of development, modernization, and globalization. As seen in the examinations of insecticide use and malaria control as well as of pharmaceutical practice and drug resistance, solutions that are not carefully monitored can contribute to the problem.

Does India's current health policy address the complexity of the health transition in the country? It is instructive to consider current trends and the Indian government's recent Ninth Five-Year Plan. In concert with the World Bank's structural adjustment program, the government has been cutting back its funding of health care while maintaining its investment in family planning. Although health is a state mandate in India, the central Ministry of Health and Family Welfare is responsible for programs of national importance. Aside from family planning, these include primary health care services and the prevention, control, and eradication of major communicable diseases. Vertical programs such as those for TB and AIDS have received massive funding from the World Bank, WHO, and bilateral agencies, but funding for the maintenance and expansion of routine primary health care activities has dwindled. Diminished transfers of funds to the states from the central government have imposed austerity in state health budgets. Because staff must be paid before all else, shortfalls in money are most directly felt in the area of medicine supply, which compromises the quality of care.

Critics have argued that external influential institutions such as the World Bank have guided the thinking behind the Ninth Plan, which cuts back on support to PHC centers and draws heavily on external support for vertical programs.[84] They attribute the public's loss of faith and diminished use of government health services to declining investments in health infrastructure, especially since the introduction of structural adjustment programs. They point out that the great majority of India's total expenditure on health comes from the pockets of its own citizens. While WHO recommends a minimum level of public expenditure in the health sector equal to at least 5 percent of GDP, in India it hovers around 1.5 percent.[85]

Government planners, on the other hand, point to the poor record of the government health sector. They draw attention to the public's poor utilization and bypassing of government health facilities in some places and to the overcrowding of poorly maintained facilities in others. They interpret increases in the use of private practitioners and hospitals as a sign that the public is willing and often able to pay for services. This trend, they argue, supports their rationale for policies that promote the privatization of health care in India. As for the growth of vertical programs, planners note that the Ninth Plan supports their horizontal integration.

The integration of vertical programs into the PHC system is not a new idea. An integrated approach to disease control programs was the concept behind the multipurpose health worker scheme initiated in the 1980s. The past has clearly shown that successful integration depends on good management and coordination and on clear guidelines for fi-

84. See, for example, K.R. Nayar, "Public Medicare: Unhealthy Trends," *Economic and Political Weekly* (July 29, 2000); and Imrana Qadeer, "Health Care Systems in Transition III: India, Part I—The Indian Experience," *Journal of Public Health Medicine* 22, no. 1 (2000): 25–32.

85. WHO, "Health Systems: Improving Performance," *World Health Report* (Geneva, 2000).

nancing and programming. An important managerial challenge will be to sustain vertical programs at the same time as routine tasks associated with child survival. PHC workers are already spread thin; all too often they are asked to participate in high-profile programs to the detriment of other important tasks.

Considering the significant regional variations, it would appear prudent to adapt the activities of PHC facilities and staff to meet the needs of local communities. India has a tradition of decentralized planning referred to as the *panchayat raj* system, and some states are making efforts to involve local bodies in health care planning.[86] Although the idea is sound in principle, experience suggests that community leaders default to health care activities with which they are already familiar.[87] When local-level information does not exist or is not accessible, how can community members make informed decisions about emergent community needs or the social, economic, and ecological contexts that foster ill health? Local problem solving calls for community diagnosis and a process of participatory research. This requires facilitators who are able to assist local health committees to collect and analyze relevant information on child survival, chronic diseases, environmental conditions, harmful behaviors such as tobacco use, and the needs of special groups such as women, adolescents, and elders. Where is one to find such facilitators? In addition to calling on NGOs that have been active in carrying out community analysis, it is time for India to invest in schools of public health to train such individuals. A newly initiated program in Kerala supported by the Government of India and the MacArthur Foundation has made significant headway in identifying the mix of public health and social science training relevant to meet India's needs.[88]

With the complexity of India's health and health care transitions, it would be shortsighted to think that India's health problems can be man-

86. For a discussion of the difficulties of linking the health sector to the *panchayat raj* system, see Devendra B. Gupta and Anil Gumber, "Decentralisation: Some Initiatives in the Health Sector," *Economic and Political Weekly* (February 6, 1999).

87. Joy Elamon, "People's Campaign for Ninth Plan: An Analysis of Health Sector Projects Prepared by Grama Panchayats of Thiruvananthapuram District" (unpublished M.P.H. dissertation, Achutha Menon Centre for Health Science Studies, Sree Chitra Tirunal Institute for Medical Sciences and Technology, Thiruvananthapuram, Kerala, 1998); Joe Varghese, "Resource Allocation and Programme Implementation of Decentralised Local Self-Governments in Kerala, India" (unpublished M.P.H. dissertation, Achutha Menon Centre for Health Science Studies, 2001).

88. The program is the Achutha Menon Centre for Health Science Studies, Sree Chitra Tirunal Institute for Medical Sciences and Technology, Thiruvananthapuram, Kerala.

aged by the existing PHC infrastructure engaging in business as usual, the creation of more vertical health programs, or the uncontrolled expansion of the private sector. Decentralized problem solving is necessary. The question is, How can this be accomplished with the heterogeneity of India's population, the complexity of its health bureaucracy, the variety of its health problems, and the different levels that characterize the Indian health care marketplace?

Representing India:
Indian Literature on the World Stage

Alok Rai

On Discovery

India has a penchant for being discovered. I learned as a schoolboy in the 1950s that India was "discovered" in 1498 by Vasco da Gama. What the "discoverers" discovered was, of course, varied cultures, civilizations, and peoples who had hitherto, clearly, been undiscovered. It was only years later that the oddity of the claim dawned on me. After all, did we not also learn in the same school that, for several millennia before that fateful moment when a Portuguese pirate showed up on the Malabar Coast with his guns, this same landmass—India, bounded by the Himalayas in the north and by three seas in the south, as the *Vishnupurana* has it—had supported many dynasties large and small, evolved complex societies and systems of thought that were quite as complex, and developed arts and crafts that were the envy of the ancient world? That moment gave me insight into the meaning of such "discovery": the process of claiming "discovery" says much about the nature of power exercised by the "discoverers" and serves to camouflage a process of transformation affecting both the "discovered" and the "discoverers."

Something similar might be argued with respect to a later discovery: Nehru's famous *Discovery of India*, composed in a colonial prison in 1944. Nehru, of course, discovered himself, in thinking through the contradictions of his historical situation, as an aristocratic Cambridge-educated liberal socialist, cooling his heels in prison. He also discovered (invented?) a vision of India, as an ongoing multicultural civilizational experiment, that was to have profound consequences for the country that emerged from the turmoil of the freedom struggle. His was the vision that guided the framers of the Constitution—secular, democratic, multicultural. It has had an influence well beyond the boundaries of India and provided the basis for a claim of moral authority that had to be acknowledged, if contested.

But another surprising implication of this penchant for successive discovery is the propensity to be forgotten and put out of mind—and so become available, I suppose, to being rediscovered. This implies becoming the site once again for fresh insights, not only into India itself but also into the new discoverers and the new contexts of discovery. Thus, we may segue immediately into the present context of discovery: the emergence of Indian literature on the "world stage." Is it, as has been suggested, merely the vagaries of fashion that we are dealing with? Is "India" merely the flavor of the month, and the "world stage" merely a publishers' shopwindow in which the display is renewed every so often? Is the apparently new phenomenon merely, literally, a commercial setup? One recognizes many of the old properties: the guru, retailing the "wisdom of the East," if sometimes with quantum cosmetic additions; the peacocks and princesses; the fecund, promiscuous excess. . . . Or is there something new out there, as Pico Iyer argued in an influential essay, "The Empire Writes Back," in 1993—a new literature, which he called "World Fiction"?[1] This is apparently the literature of "our increasingly small . . . global village." Iyer sees the writers of this literature as "the creators and creations, of . . . a new post-imperial order in which English is the *lingua franca*, just about everywhere is a suburb of the same international youth culture, and all countries are a part of a unified CNN and MTV circuit, with a common frame of reference in McDonald's, Madonna and Magic Johnson." For reasons that aren't quite clear—hopefully, they will become clearer as we proceed—Indians feature prominently in the lists of "World Fiction." But what are we to make of this literature and, indeed, of this phenomenon? How are we to evaluate its implicit (and sometimes explicit) claim to "represent" India? The ambiguities inherent in the word *represent* will, inevitably, complicate our inquiry: does literature represent a country in the way in which an ambassador represents a country? Or is it the aesthetic sense of *represent* that we need—the sense in which a painting or a photograph may or may not be a good representation? If indeed a claim of the former kind—standing for—is sought to be made on the basis of an assumed aesthetic claim of the second kind, then the claim itself needs to be flushed out into the open.

To pursue some answers, we must begin at the beginning. The inau-

---

1. Pico Iyer, "The Empire Writes Back," *Time* 8 (February 1993): 46–56.

gural moment of this new literature identified by Iyer is, by near universal agreement, the publication of Salman Rushdie's *Midnight's Children* in 1981.[2] But our attempt to understand the whole cultural phenomenon that has crystallized around that core in the last twenty years must encompass not only Rushdie the writer but also the country and society that he described. The tide of international attention, even as it draws a flock of Rushdie-enabled writers to ride its crests, can hardly leave unaffected those "undiscovered" others minding their business and plying their trade in their palm-thatched shacks—or, less romantically, in dusty provincial backwaters—far from the glow of media attention. Our inquiry must, over the next few pages, seek to develop an account of the *emergence*, *reception*, and *consequence* of the appearance of something called "Indian literature" on something called the "world stage."

Discovering Indian Literature

India as a territory of the world imagination has a long and varied history. It was written of by a whole range of people, from early Greek historians through sundry Chinese itinerants all the way to the bedazzled (and befuddled) accounts of European visitors to the later Mughal courts. "Fabled Ind," home of the marvelous and the grotesque, of extremes of nobility and squalor, was a topos of the world imagination for as long as anyone can remember—certainly long before 1498. Some Indian literature, too, has captured the attention of the world from time to time. The German Orientalists' discovery of the glories of the Sanskrit tradition, of its philosophy and poetry, resonated widely in the literary world of its time. Goethe's discovery of the fifth-century poet and dramatist Kalidasa, and particularly of his play *Abhignana Shakuntalam*, did something to assuage the hurt pride of the colonized, still reeling from Macaulay's 1835 Minute: "I have conversed both here and at home with men distinguished by their proficiency in the Eastern tongues. . . . I have never found one among them who could deny that a single shelf of a good European library was worth the whole native literature of India and Arabia." Never again—or so one thought.

Nearer our own time, Rabindranath Tagore moved across literary Europe in the interwar years—every inch the Oriental sage, with his flowing beard and his flowing robes, instantly recognized, widely lionized. That his English translation of his cycle of poems, *Gitanjali*, seems

---

2. Salman Rushdie, *Midnight's Children* (London: Jonathan Cape, 1981).

sentimental and overblown—did so then, does so now—makes little difference. The Nobel Prize in 1913 merely confirmed, for Indians as much as for liberal Westerners, that even in the depths of colonial India there was a stirring of imaginative life, a vision of our residence on earth, that was both different and deserving of attention.

For most international readers in the period immediately prior to ours, however, the image conjured up by the phrase *Indian literature* was not likely to derive from the German Orientalists or from Tagore. More likely than not, it would have come from the literary "India" of the colonial imagination, the literature of the British Raj. This India was, as in Kipling, the India of "the white man's burden," a teeming landscape that offered the existentialist possibility of heroism (or cowardice), but it was an India that was curiously devoid of Indians—except in menial and ancillary roles. There are, obviously, liberal variants of this genre: E.M. Forster's *A Passage to India* (1924) is an example that suggests itself. It was first at the level of politics that a change occurred, and Indians moved from being merely landscape to being people—demanding freedom from colonial rule. Nehru's metaphor for the impact of Gandhi's appearance on the stage of Indian politics has great resonance for our discussion of Indian literature as well: ". . . a sea change was visible as the need for falsehood and furtive behaviour lessened. It was a psychological change, almost as if some expert in psychoanalytical methods had probed deep into the patient's past, found out the origins of his complexes, exposed them to his view, and thus rid him of that burden. . . ."[3] It will be worth asking to what extent the new "Indian literature"—the one hailed by Pico Iyer, and now playing on the "world stage"—has been able to translate this transformation, this "sea change," into adequate imaginative forms.

A Point of Origin?

Critics, skeptics, and admirers are all agreed that the origins of this phenomenon may be traced back to the appearance of Salman Rushdie's *Midnight's Children* in 1981. It is not certain whether the chorus of acclaim for *Midnight's Children* started before or after the award of the

---

3. Jawaharlal Nehru, *Discovery of India* (Calcutta: Signet Press, 1946), 359. See chapter 8, "The Last Phase: Nationalism and Imperialism." The section starting "And then Gandhi came . . ." on p. 358 describes the effect Gandhi's advent had on the nature of the nationalist struggle.

Booker Prize. But it would be ungenerous and inaccurate to treat the wave of literary acclaim and cultural consequence that followed as a simple case of media manipulation, some kind of international hoodwink. Clearly, the recognition accorded to *Midnight's Children* marked the emergence of a new cultural phenomenon, identified above as "World Fiction," or its high-profile subset, "Indian literature on the world stage." This is the main reason why our discussion must be concerned to such a large extent with fiction, and more particularly with fiction written in English. After all, earlier Indian representation on the world stage of its own time was, as we have seen, through works of drama and philosophy and poetry. And indeed, it needs to be said that there is a considerable amount of work being done in other genres. Thus, a contemporary writer, Manjula Padmanabhan, made something of an international splash when her 1998 play about the traffic in human organs, *Harvest*, was awarded a big-ticket prize named after Aristotle Onassis. Girish Karnad, currently director of the Nehru Cultural Centre in London, is an accomplished bilingual playwright whose translations of his own Kannada plays have been performed, to much critical acclaim, in India and abroad. In fact, prior to the current phase in which fiction has grabbed all the attention, it would have been fair to say that the dominant genre of Indian writing in English, certainly, was poetry. And again, some distinguished poetry continues to be written and published. The contribution of the late A.K. Ramanujan of the University of Chicago in giving visibility to Indian literature in the United States through his translations from the classical Tamil archive has been widely recognized. His own poetic reflections on his ambiguous cultural belonging played a pioneering role in crystallizing the "Indian subject" that the fiction then adopted with such panache. His was a concern with the texture of experience when one simultaneously inhabits more than one cultural universe, a concern with what Rushdie has described as the porosity, the leakiness, of identities. The resultant flickering and unstable sense of self has become characteristic of the present time in which, voluntarily or otherwise, so many people are transgressing so many boundaries, inhabiting imperfectly mapped physical and mental worlds. In fact, readers who tire of the inevitable prolixity of fiction could do worse than to turn to two fine anthologies of contemporary Indian poetry in English: *Twelve Modern Indian Poets* and *Nine Indian Women Poets*.[4]

---

4. Arvind Krishna Mehrotra, ed., *Twelve Modern Indian Poets* (Delhi: Oxford University Press, 1992); Eunice de Souza, ed., *Nine Indian Women Poets* (Delhi: Oxford University Press, 1998).

And yet, there is no getting away from the fact that it is the fiction that has grabbed international attention on the world stage—and while we will, inevitably, come back to the things that lurk in the shadows, and even the things that didn't make it past the bouncers, we must first take the measure of the phenomenon whose centerpiece is Salman Rushdie's *Midnight's Children*. Such is its centrality that the writers who followed were frequently identified as the Rushdie generation. Some years ago the *New Yorker* published a fine photograph in which Rushdie is posed as the grand old patriarch, surrounded by his talented progeny.[5]

It is important to step back a little and take a look at the patriarch's forebears. The Indian novel in English has a long history: the first novel was Bankim Chandra Chatterjee's *Rajmohan's Wife*, published in 1864. That said, however, it is a fact that the form of the novel itself was a colonial import, and the tradition of fiction that developed, in English and in other Indian languages, frequently betrays the stress of adapting English models to Indian realities. Meenakshi Mukherjee's *Realism and Reality* is a good guide to this early history.[6]

Some of Rushdie's predecessors are undoubtedly sedate. Perhaps the most distinguished of these is R.K. Narayan, who died in May 2001 at the age of ninety-four. From the 1930s on, Narayan produced a steady stream of quietly realistic novels set in an imaginary town called Malgudi. Narayan's Malgudi has the tidy, ordered charm of prelapsarian, small-town Karnataka, but it is unlikely that his aesthetic could have withstood or accommodated the chaos of boomtown Bangalore, bloating on software, or allowed entry to the harsh realities of contemporary India, riven by hostilities of caste and class, of language and region. Another venerable name is that of Raja Rao, who spent a lifetime refining his sense of India as a teacher of philosophy in distant Texas. In the preface to his major work, *Kanthapura* (1938), Raja Rao wrote sensitively about his relationship to English and of the need to adapt English to Indian rhythms and Indian usages. Mulk Raj Anand is the third in this triumvirate of clan elders. Anand was a peripheral member of the British Social-Democratic Left in the interwar years, and he sought, in his lugubrious works of fiction—*Untouchable* (1935), *Coolie* (1936), and *Two Leaves and a Bud* (1937)—to depict harsh and inhuman aspects of Indian reality: the caste system, and hard indentured labor, as in the tea plantations of northeastern India.

---

5. *New Yorker* 23 (June 30, 1997).
6. Meenakshi Mukherjee, *Realism and Reality* (Delhi: Oxford University Press, 1985).

There is, however, an anomalous fourth, a rather wild, disreputable-looking uncle, lurking on the edges of the frame. G.V. Desani's *All About H. Hatterr* was first published in 1949. It is a violently anarchic take on the totality of India. The nominal plot device is the attempt by the eponymous hero—abetted and periodically saved by his deliciously verbose Sancho Panza, Banerrji—to find a guru who can deliver him from his wife and other relatively minor travails of this netherworld. It is, by all accounts, an extraordinary work, far ahead of its time and context. It registers in its formal disorder and its glorious, uproarious "English" some of the crucial, constitutive disjunctions of Indian life. Desani is, for Rushdie and many others, an acknowledged ancestor—though there aren't many who can live up to the legacy. Many of the Rushdiesque features are here: the linguistic inventiveness, in which gobbets of Shakespeare and kindergarten gibberish exist alongside fragments of Sanskrit, and the delight in literary miscegenation, trampolining up and down the hierarchy of genres, mixing high and low, elite and popular, creating a dazzling display of concatenations that are exponentially greater than the sum of their parts. But it is also worth asking, about Desani as well as about Rushdie, whether the literary dazzle, the genius for parody, doesn't go hand in hand with a kind of emotional coldness, an inability to give voice to the pathos and terror of "ordinary life."

One further point remains apropos Desani. *Hatterr* received its due measure of critical recognition: its presence on the Penguin Modern Classics list is, after all, a kind of canonization. But when one compares the career of *Hatterr* with that of *Midnight's Children*, it becomes immediately apparent that an assessment of the cultural phenomenon that Rushdie helped to crystallize with *Midnight's Children* must encompass more than the book itself. Here was the happy, dreamed-of, but ultimately fortuitous conjunction of a book with its historic moment.

There are at least two other distinguished—and, indeed, internationally visible—writers who must be brought into the picture. For all their nominal foreignness, both Ruth Prawer Jhabvala and Anita Desai distance themselves from the traditions of colonial fiction in which India is essentially landscape—always "timeless," with peacocks and elephants, stoic peasants and sturdy warrior types, the famous "martial races," bewhiskered and brainless. Both these writers seek to capture in their works some of the tumult and confusion of contemporary India: Jhabvala's *Heat and Dust* (1975), which also won the Booker Prize, is an obvious example. However, Jhabvala and Desai are unable ultimately to overcome the fatally limited social range of English in India. Upper-class, Anglophone protagonists, or visiting foreigners, are an obvious recourse, but when Anita Desai tries, in *In Custody* (1984), to register the pathos of the death of Urdu and its glorious poetic tradition, the result is merely awkward and embarrassing for anyone who knows anything of the power of that which is being mourned. And, I suppose, merely puzzling for those who don't. After all, if that tepid romanticism is all there is to it—vapid chatter about roses and moonlight, as I recall Forster's caricature—then what is the fuss all about? The failure is, of course, emblematic. The stuff that can't or won't "translate" is forced to compete with the stuff that will, *in addition to the stuff that comes in English anyway.*

On Newness

It is a little difficult, twenty years on, to recover a full sense of the exhilaration that *Midnight's Children* produced when it was first published. Older readers remember the excitement, even when they can't quite name its constituent elements. It is indeed a measure of the success of the book that for later, younger readers, *Midnight's Children* and its attendant excitements have become part of the air they breathe, somewhat musty, already history. I used *Midnight's Children* as a text for an undergraduate class a few years back, hoping to share some of the excitement that I had felt when I first encountered it in 1981. It was a disappointing experience for all of us, students and teacher alike. This was at least partly because of the veritable industry of explanation that had sprung up around it—with notable assistance, it should be said, from the Master himself, who explicated the implications of his text in essay after lucid essay.[7] All this busy activity, however, seemed to have stripped the machinery bare, and the creative energy that older readers remembered had, sadly, fled from the exposed skeleton.

But the thing had undoubtedly been alive once. Two decades and much dissection later, it should be possible to understand a little better what it was that went to make up that experience of novelty, for Indian *and* for Western readers. It is possible, indeed, that the "novelty" derived from different sets of reasons for the two different kinds of readers. Some-

---

7. See Salman Rushdie, *Imaginary Homelands: Essays and Criticism 1981–1991* (London: Granta Books in collaboration with Penguin, 1992).

thing similar has been argued with respect to the "magic realism" that came out of Latin America somewhat earlier: Western readers favored a more "magical," depoliticized reading, while the original addressees of those marvelous fictions were responding to the painful and familiar *realities* of their historical condition that had once again been brought alive, made articulate. It is possible, again, that the Western and Indian readings of *Midnight's Children* and the literary phenomenon of which it is the center and origin have diverged over the last twenty years, so that the shared exultation in "Indian literature on the world stage"— festivities in Pico Iyer's "global village"!—has given way, on the part of some Indians, to something like anxiety and suspicion.

The blurb writers and the first English reviewers of *Midnight's Children* were quick to assert that here, in this garrulous polyphony, the teeming subcontinent had at last found its voice. This is, *prima facie*, odd, because the subcontinent had been speaking, in myriad voices, for centuries. But there was a real sense in which *Midnight's Children* was perceived to be breaking the silence. It's that discovery thing again.

To a significant extent, it was a matter of language. Of course, Indians had been writing in English, and writing novels in English for that matter, for a long time. But there was an unmistakable sense in earlier writings that they—exceptions, mainly Desani, apart—were in the thrall of some notion of *English* English. Thus, there was a curious sense that the anarchic, polycultural, multilingual realities of Indian life had to be rendered into an ultimately decorous idiom. *Midnight's Children* showed that it was possible to incorporate linguistic and cultural elements that, even when they appeared superficially English, might well not be fully comprehensible in England. These were the bastard forms produced through a few centuries of cultural promiscuity, and it was Rushdie's achievement to accord them the necessary literary legitimacy. Indian readers have become extremely sensitive to glossary-endowed renditions of Indian life, in which elements possibly unfamiliar to Western readers are laboriously explained. Indian readers suspect, often with justification, that they are merely eavesdroppers on these glossed conversations, that they aren't the ones being addressed. *Midnight's Children* seemed to change all that.

But the matter goes deeper than mere language. The beginnings of the novel in India—in all Indian languages, including English—are invariably associated with the colonial impact. Thus, one finds the diligent imposition of nineteenth-century realist forms upon intransigent

Indian realities. It is hardly surprising that the imposition never quite works, and early Indian essays in the realist mode betray the "deforming" effect of diverse indigenous traditions. Thus, one finds elements of the folktale and of the moral fable. But the cultural confidence required to declare the inadequacy of realism and to seek other modes of formal organization does not come easy. One thinks, in this context, of the coming to maturity in India of a generation that was, in a literal sense, born free. Unshackled from various kinds of bondage, English had become an Indian language, not something timid and apologetic, liable to caricature and schoolmarmish reproach, but a multiply endowed language, capable of the varied reach, the highs and lows, of literature. And the novel too, drawing now not only upon indigenous traditions of tale-telling, of *kissagoi*, and upon the national propensity to chatter and gossip with friend and stranger about matters public and private, seemed to have become, finally, an Indian thing, capable of encompassing the garrulous realities of India.

It boils down to a matter of confidence, of courage. One doesn't need heavy theory in order to assert that one of the deepest effects of the colonial relation—of being, for an extended period of time, a subject nation—is a widespread demoralization, a sapping of cultural confidence. One of the mutated symptoms of this demoralization is a grotesque *exaggeration* of the subject nation's civilizational achievements. But the predominant consequence is an obscurely apologetic stance, a feeling of being secondhand and not quite good enough, of being mere mimic men, freaks and curiosities seeking to amuse one's betters. This is something that millions of postcolonial survivors will recognize, and many people, from Frantz Fanon to V.S. Naipaul, have written about it.

In retrospect, it seems excessive to assert that it was one book, albeit one as exuberantly brilliant as *Midnight's Children*, that broke the back of a centuries-old demoralization. We have already had occasion to reflect on the impact, in the political domain, of the advent of Gandhi: a people who had been systematically devalued and treated with contempt were enabled to shed that demoralization and see themselves as fully human beings, historical actors, and not mere victims.

The Fraying of the National Myth

The achievement of *Midnight's Children* is as much individual as it is conjunctural, due as much to the author's vivacious talent as it is to the circumstances of the time, to the whole social and cultural context, both in India and, with significant differences, in the West. What is more, looking at the conjunctural factors makes it possible for us to explore aspects of the larger cultural phenomenon that remain obscure in the bedazzled acclamation of "genius!"

The 1960s were a troubled time in India, as elsewhere. After the death of Nehru in 1964, the essentially statist project of Indian nationalism came under severe stress. One can argue forever about the reasons why this happened: the euphoria of Independence, which could drown the discords of structural inequalities and regional striving, had begun to fade; the problem of poverty, starkly accentuated by the Bihar famine of 1965–67, made the promises of that statist nationalism, still capable of mobilizing popular emotion in the Bombay films of the 1950s, appear merely hypocritical; in the face of popular unrest, both in the poverty-stricken heartland and in various "regional" struggles to secure a better deal for local constituencies, the benevolent mask of the Nehruvian state, now under the guardianship of his daughter, Indira Gandhi, had slipped, revealing the reality of repression, and worse. It was a profoundly significant time, a moment of awakening for the children of the class that was the vehicle and major beneficiary of that suddenly bankrupt nationalism.

For the poor, who had always been ground under the heel of oppression, this was no great moment of revelation. Sundry "regional" elites saw the essential weakness in central control that underlay this process and made of it a crucial political opportunity. But for the children of the metropolitan, Anglophone middle class, coming to maturity around that time—the children of Midnight, in fact—it was a moment of betrayal, rendered even more painful by the fact of their being, merely by virtue of their social location, accomplices, sharers of class guilt.

The quintessential symbol of this political and cultural moment is the movement that is indicated, in India, by the name Naxalbari. This movement drew students from privileged backgrounds into the blood and rage of politics in greater numbers than at any other time since the national movement. In the light of the profound changes, the comprehensive disillusionment, the social upheavals that it initiated, the actual political part of these events appears almost insignificant: a Maoist faction, splitting away from the parent Communist Party, sought to initiate a nationwide peasant revolt, starting from an unlikely village in distant northern Bengal.

What "Naxalbari" did most importantly, however, was to flush the deep-seated, inherent injustice of the system out into the open. The political movement collapsed, both because of its internal confusions and because of the massive, brutal, flagrantly extrajudicial, extralegal repression by the state. But the lessons of the violence could hardly be forgotten, be unlearned by the young men and women who had come to maturity in the context of that violence. The fact that significant numbers of the children of the ruling classes had become involved with the movement in various ways was felt to be particularly galling by the diehard defenders of the unmasked state. But for the children of Midnight, the once-avuncular Nehruvian state could never again recover its lost innocence. Rendered forever culpable, its hypocritically avowed project of an inclusive nationalism lay in tatters. Mrs. Gandhi's blatant "suspension" of India's one major achievement—its democracy—during the "Emergency" of 1975–77 was merely a confirmation that the masks and gloves were off, that it was too late for idealism, and that it was time for the intelligentsia, particularly the Anglophone intelligentsia that had (been) identified with that patchy nationalism, to move on.

This fraying of the myths of nationalism, then, from the late 1960s onward, created the space for the emergence of Rushdie and his fecund tribe. One of the emblematic works of this moment of "liberation" is Upamanyu Chatterjee's *English, August* (1988). Chatterjee's protagonist is a young officer in the Indian Administrative Service.[8] Chatterjee's protagonist is, as it happens, concerned mainly with his supply of marijuana and with his unfulfilled sexual desires. He has little sympathy with the people among whom he finds himself, and displays little trace of the nationalist idealism that is expected from his service and his class— and indeed from the fact that the book is written in English. What we have instead is a slangy, foul-mouthed account of a candidate member of the Indian ruling elite who has just emerged from one of the highly privileged colleges of North India and is ready to take his place in the real world, in which there are few idols and ideals. This moment of disillusionment, and the hip college lingo in which it is embodied— owing little deference to received models of linguistic rectitude or propriety—is crucial for understanding this phase of Indian literature.

---

8. The IAS is the nationalist successor to the colonial civil service, the ICS, which was deemed to be the "steel frame" that served to keep a fractious nation together. It is, in fact, like the army, one of the few "all-India" institutions. For complex reasons, it is staffed to an overwhelming extent—though this might be changing now—by the English-speaking progeny of the urban and metropolitan elite.

Everything can be talked about, there are no sacred cows, it is too late for lies. And the whole concern with "authenticity" is simply set aside: this, complete with the arrogant young sahib and his obsequious inferiors, juxtaposing college slang with tired bureaucratese, is unmistakably, unapologetically, India. The hollowing out of the institutions of the state, the draining away of its legitimacy and its glamour that *English, August* enacts, is a thematic element not only in Rushdie's *Midnight's Children* and *Shame* (1983) but also in Amitav Ghosh's *The Circle of Reason* (1986) and *The Shadow Lines* (1988). It was this complex disillusionment that Shashi Tharoor signaled in his brisk redeployment of the myths of the foundational epic, the *Mahabharata*, to develop a cynical account of the contemporary political scene in his *The Great Indian Novel* (1989).

It is not, however, that the broadly secular-nationalist theme has simply been replaced by an "antinationalist" one. What has become available, almost uniquely to the writer in English, is a *post*nationalist subject, a fertile thematic that can range all the way from Amit Chaudhuri's intensely personalized narratives, which bypass public concerns, to Rushdie's ideological narratives that deal directly with the dangerous subnationalist and substitute-nationalist growths that sprout from the ruins of secular nationalism. What unites all these diverse writers and writings is the sense of a traumatic sundering from the stable, ordered, progressive, optimistic world of the decades immediately after 1947—the world of the fathers. The moment of that sundering may be located at different points by different people—Naxalbari, or the Emergency, or the destruction of the Babri Masjid in 1996—but there is a sense, at each of these points, of thresholds being crossed, of doors closing behind one.

The politics that flows from the breakup of the Nehruvian consensus is indeed troubled and uncertain, even dangerous. But the development is unquestionably a liberating one for literature. A concern with marginal voices, with giving speech to the silenced, has always been in some sense the eminent domain of literature. The first beneficiary of this historical opportunity is the Indian writer in English—not quite silenced hitherto, but certainly disregarded, relegated to the wings. We shall return to the ironies of this privileged marginality a little later.

The preceding represents an attempt to understand the emergence of this new literature in the context of a domestic, national conjuncture, an epochal moment of political transition, when power shifted away from the metropolitan center. However, in seeking to understand the surprising international currency of this literature—its appearance on the world stage, no less—one would need to identify predisposing elements and tendencies in the international conjuncture as well.

The International Climate

The proximate cause of the surge of international interest in India in the period just around the appearance of *Midnight's Children* is, in retrospect, a little embarrassing. Britain was in the grip of a wave of Raj nostalgia, which was both fueled and exploited by the books that went into the making of two of the most widely watched television series of the time, M.M. Kaye's *The Far Pavilions* and Paul Scott's *The Raj Quartet*.[9] David Lean's execrable movie version of E.M. Forster's *A Passage to India* is a worthy third in that deadly triad. Before these, there was the 1960s discovery of Ravi Shankar by the Beatles, closely followed by the advent of Maharishi Mahesh Yogi and his Transcendental Meditation, and perhaps even the dancing dervishes of Krishna Consciousness. The stage was almost too well set for a bout of energetic, revisionist, subversive narration. The fact that the "subversion" encompassed much more than the tawdry myths of the Raj in no way vitiates the claim that there was an ongoing cultural argument in the West that *Midnight's Children* engaged with and then, quite simply, annexed. Other than the legendary gouty colonel from the Home Counties, the Raj could have had but few defenders, and it was an almost predictable development from the success of *Midnight's Children* to the burgeoning literature that was identified, in a well-known academic publication of the time, as *The Empire Writes Back*.[10]

This time appeared, broadly speaking, to be one of the end of empires. At a crude political level, there was the Portuguese withdrawal from its colonies, Ian Smith's Rhodesia mutated into Zimbabwe, and apartheid South Africa, improbable at the best of times, began to appear unsustainable to all but the pathologically racist. But perhaps more important than all of these was the American defeat in Vietnam. The historical shift that was virtually inaugurated by the achievement of Indian independence in 1947 had worked its way throughout the world. In the

9. M.M. Kaye, *The Far Pavilions* (New York: St. Martin's Press, 1978); Paul Scott, *The Raj Quartet*, 4 vols.: *The Jewel in the Crown* (1966), *The Day of the Scorpion* (1968), *The Towers of Silence* (1971), and *A Division of Spoils* (1975) (London: Heinemann).

10. Bill Ashcroft, Gareth Griffiths, and Helen Tiffin, eds., *The Empire Writes Back: Theory and Practice in Post-Colonial Literatures* (London: Routledge, 1989).

East, too, the Soviet empire was slowly, and then not so slowly, unravel-
ing—until its eventual collapse at the hands of Solidarity and the Velvet
Revolution. It was a hopeful moment, the start of what many believed
was going to be a postimperialist world. The stable structures that had
organized the world for so long appeared to be dissolving with laugh-
able ease. Worlds, people, and ideas that had been securely held apart,
locked within the walls and hierarchies of different imperial structures,
were intermingling across suddenly opened borders. The quondam certainties of the stable mundane world could hardly survive such a powerful tide of dissolution. One notices the rise of various "constructivist"
intellectual tendencies, which, for all the robust practicality of their build-
ing-site metaphors, share a commitment to the notion that all meanings
are arbitrary, contingent, provisional, held together by the scaffolding
of particular purposes and particular conjunctures, true—but for the time
being only.

It is not surprising, then, that there was a marked "post-" tendency in
the intellectual trends and currents of the time, as if something were
over and done with and it was time to make it anew. It was, let us remember, the time when poststructuralism and postmodernism and
postcolonialism all appeared and deposed with almost farcical ease the
effete liberalism that could hardly survive the revelation of its complic-
ity with empire. The intermingling of worlds that could no longer be
held securely apart, locked in the hierarchies of imperialism; the shat-
tering of the certainties of the mundane world, rendered suddenly aswim
and afloat in seas of arbitrarily constructed meanings—all these, expressed through a host of intellectual tendencies and developments, prepared the ground for the emergence and recognition of the apparently
nonmetropolitan, the hitherto peripheral. Thus one notes the prominent
part that notions of marginality and hybridity, revaluing that which had
hitherto been excluded, rethinking the alleged validity of the principles
of exclusion and the sanctity of borders, play in the aforementioned
intellectual trends.

The question of the how and why of these far-reaching international developments will no doubt be answered differently by different people. I have suggested the winding down of empires old and
new as a proximate cause. Others may adduce the migrations, voluntary and involuntary, of large numbers not merely of slaves and other
progress fodder but also of highly educated, articulate professionals
able to comprehend and transcend the perceptions and attributions

of hard cultural difference. Thus, cheap airfares too may be a part of the story—or even, more locally, the achievement of critical mass in terms of both numbers and affluence by Anglophone Indians in the United States.

But perhaps the most significant factor underlying and enabling these developments has been the increase in the reach and power of the global media. The immediate impact of the growing tide of images from distant places was to bring home to decent people throughout the world the realization that distant people—people with flatter noses and darker skins, to borrow Conrad's pithy formulation—are people too. Deserving of attention because they are similar, but also, and quite as crucially, people whose very differences are worthy of attention because they are, at one level, like people everywhere else, adequate subjects of literary attention. This is the moment of liberal multiculturalism, and Indian writers writing in English were, in one way and another, almost uniquely positioned to take advantage of it.

This discovery of India was overdetermined to a degree: many lines of causation and tendency converged here. Under the stresses of its own political processes, mutating from a famously heterogeneous ancient culture into a modern one riven by identity politics, India became a kind of laboratory demonstration of a universal experience: no person is ever and only one person, people are always a multitude of possibilities and potentialities, and outcomes are a complex function of historical chance and circumstance. But an India conceived in this fashion, thus *imagined*, was capable of becoming a metaphor for the world. This was the India that the new literature·sought, with conspicuous success, to present on the world stage.

The Progeny

Before we proceed any further in our discussion of this "Indian literature on the world stage"—or of the nature of the "world stage" itself, and the problematic being of this "Indian literature" on the "world stage" and in India itself—it might be best to put down a few names and titles out of the hundreds that have been published since 1981. This is not a thesis-driven list, adduced here in support of my argument, but one intended to serve only as a context of reference for the remainder of this essay.

Writing in January 1990 about the "remembered" books of the recent past, Shashi Tharoor, author of *The Great Indian Novel,* listed five.[11] The first of these is I. Allan Sealy's *The Trotter-nama* (1988). Tharoor describes it as "a witty, superbly confident saga of Anglo-India." Many people feel that Sealy has not received his rightful attention. However, his rather somber *Everest Hotel* (1998), a stylish meditation on mortality centering on the lives of a disparate group of people in Dehra Dun, a small town in the foothills of the Himalayas, did win one of the top Indian literary awards. Also noted are Amitav Ghosh's *Shadow Lines,* perhaps Ghosh's finest novel to date, and Upamanyu Chatterjee's *English, August,* discussed earlier in this essay. The other two books Tharoor mentions are somewhat incongruous: Gita Mehta's *Raj* (1989), which is really, as he describes it, "a touristy catalogue of princely exotica"—yon novel hath an ancient and fish-like smell—and Shobha De's *Socialite Evenings* (1989). De is a middle-aged mother who has, with the assistance of her publisher, invented a highly salable, sexy, sultry—and, for some, soporific—persona. Her very successful "novels" purport to reveal the shocking truth about the (mainly sexual) antics of the bored and the beautiful. Her *oeuvre* is reminiscent of Clive James's quip about *Dallas:* that it had perfected the technique of putting gloss on pulp.

More deserving of note is Rohinton Mistry, who lives in Canada. Mistry is originally from Mumbai, and his novel *Such a Long Journey* (1992) and collection of short stories *Tales from Firozsha Baag* (1993) are notable for a sensitive depiction of the Parsi community of Mumbai, once socially prominent and now apparently locked in a long process of secular decline. In *A Fine Balance* (1996), Mistry seeks to get beyond the social limits within which he works so finely and encompass rather more of this monstrous thing called India. Another Parsi writer, Firdaus Kanga, attracted a certain amount of attention with his quasi-autobiographical *Trying to Grow* (1990), which tells with wit and panache of his predicament as someone suffering from a condition that renders his bones brittle and liable to fracture. An Indian commentator, somewhat cruelly, described it as "an inadvertent metaphor for a fledgling but burgeoning Indian fiction in English."[12] Well, I suppose it must fledge before it burgeons.

------

11. Shashi Tharoor, "Books Read and Remembered," *Book Review* (New Delhi) (January–February 1990).

12. Partho Dutta, *Book Review* (New Delhi) (March–April 1990).

It is unclear whether Pakistani novels should be considered as part of "Indian literature" for our present purposes. Certainly, Rushdie followed up his India novel, *Midnight's Children*, with a savage Pakistan novel, *Shame*, and a cynic might well argue that sectarian bitterness is a theme common to both societies. However, some recent Pakistani novels, such as Mohsin Hamid's *Moth Smoke* (2000), suggest that Pakistan is sufficiently different to deserve separate attention. Still, there is a potentially fruitful field of comparative literature of the Indian subcontinent waiting to be developed—this side of the "world stage," so to speak.

One writer who is sometimes credited with sparking the current American interest in India is Bharati Mukherjee. Her novel *Jasmine* (1990) has a rural Punjabi lass translated, via an arranged marriage, to a violent America. It should perhaps not be judged too harshly on account of its pioneering status. Everyone in the novel—translated lass, good red-blooded Americans—speaks in one homogeneous dialect. The only exceptions are the Indians in India, who are, naturally, pure Peter Sellers. The theme of persons making difficult transitions, indeed, inhabiting twilight zones for entire, ambiguous lifetimes, has been explored with shocking competence by Jhumpa Lahiri in *Interpreter of Maladies* (2000), which was awarded the Pulitzer Prize.

Oddly, Indian women writing in English came late to feminist consciousness, compared with their "vernacular" sisters. However, the advent of Western feminism in India has had a profound impact. There is a veritable flood of writing—and, indeed, a continent of injustice to be written about. The well-known institution of the "arranged marriage" is only one instance of that denial of full individuality that is so much a part of Indian society. Many writers have written of these matters with feeling and insight: Githa Hariharan's *The Thousand Faces of Night* (1992) attracted a certain amount of international attention, as did Meena Alexander's *Nampally Road* (1991) and Suniti Namjoshi's *Feminist Fables* (1995). Hariharan's *When Dreams Travel* (1999) tackles these somber matters with a deft, comic touch.

It is a little difficult to fit Vikram Seth's obvious talent into any critical narrative. The first novel by Seth, a fine if somewhat overcrafted poet, was a sonnet sequence set in San Francisco, *The Golden Gate* (1986). He followed that up with his voluminous opus, *A Suitable Boy* (1993), which attracted rather more attention for its huge advance than for itself. A baggy realistic epic revolving around the matrimonial intentions of bossy mothers—the arranged marriage again!—it was compared, in the West, to sundry writers, including Dickens, George Eliot, and Tolstoy. In India, interestingly, its Hindi translation was welcomed, by Seth as well as others, as the prodigal's return to its phantom original. The work's alleged affinities with the greats of European realism were of less consequence than its generic similarity to the domestic epics that are standard in other Indian languages and, indeed, on television. Seth's next novel, *An Equal Music* (1999), was woven around the life and work of a London-based string quartet and contained not a single reference to India or things Indian.

One observer remarked in 1994 that "a new spirit of relaxation has invaded the Indian English novel." Writers were more willing to write about their "private lives and angsts . . . their own personal slice of the Indian experience rather than the whole multilayered cake of Indian metaphysics, Maharajas, politics and poverty. . . ."[13] Perhaps the writer who emblematizes this turning inward is Amit Chaudhuri. His first novel, *A Strange and Sublime Address* (1991), was such a fine, delicate evocation of the textures and sounds, the ebb and flow of relationships, in a large middle-class Calcutta family that many people forgot or forgave its lack of narrative drive. This lack appears rather more stark in his later books, which purportedly touch on relatively public themes: *Freedom Song* (1998) and *A New World* (2000). But there is a marked and perhaps significant divergence between the Indian response to Chaudhuri and the "international" one. Chaudhuri was awarded a fiction prize by the *Los Angeles Times*. Another writer who has a similarly split constituency is Vikram Chandra, whose *Red Earth and Pouring Rain* (1995) was awarded the Commonwealth Prize.

One notes the emergence of a pleasant variety of voices, venturing away from the generic clichés, though "pleasant" isn't the obvious epithet that anyone would apply to Raj Kamal Jha's *The Blue Bedspread* (1999). This is an artful narrative about a seriously dysfunctional family. The Indian family—large, noisy, and harmonious—is such a stereotype, endlessly reiterated in social discourse, celebrated high and low in popular culture, that Jha's novel was not received kindly in India. Similarly, Pankaj Mishra's beautifully modulated account of postcolonial cultural anxiety and the inevitably unfulfilled (and unfulfillable) yearning for wholeness and existential form, *The Romantics* (2000), has re-

---

13. Laila Tyabji, "Splintered Loyalties/Cultural Divides," review of three novels, *Book Review* (New Delhi) (September 1994): 25–26.

ceived very favorable attention abroad—the *L.A. Times* award again! But it is, alas, a mirror that Indian readers are not yet ready for.

The publishing sensation of the 1990s was undoubtedly Arundhati Roy's *The God of Small Things* (1997). This is a stylish, classy work that brooks no adjectival limitation: it's not women's writing, or Indian writing, or whatever. It is quite simply literature of a high order and has been received as such on the "world stage," and, as it happens, in India. By what appears to be a miracle—that is, it might well be both inexplicable and unreplicable—Roy seems to have floated clear of all the problems that beset Indians writing in English: the problems of limited social range and access, of being Indian without taking recourse to the familiar theatrical properties, of using a fully literate English, heir to the whole tradition, and not some exoticized Indian subset thereof.

The Politics of Location

Although its significance is a matter of considerable argument, there is no disputing that the newly visible Indian literature is, to a large extent, a diasporic phenomenon. There was a time not so long ago when the mere fact that a writer was located somewhere outside India—diasporic in the West, so to speak, in particular—was enough to rule him or her out of serious cultural contention. Being diasporic was only a more extreme case of the malady that writing in English signified. India was a fate that had to be undergone before one could presume to write about it. Only a daily exposure to its difficulties, suffering alongside, qualified one to talk about the country. And emigrating to the West had a whiff of moral weakness about it, of both chickening out and selling out. All this changed sometime during the 1980s, probably as an effect of the processes of liberalizing and globalizing the economy. Thus, there was an accretion of glamour to the label NRI—the Non-resident Indian. But traces of the old attitude of moral disdain are still around—and, naturally, of its reciprocal, correspondent emotions on the part of the migrants, a certain attitude of guilt and apology or, alternatively, a prickly defensiveness. It is this whole complex of attitudes that is indicated by that oft-repeated phrase "an anxiety about Indianness."[14] Rushdie has asserted, airily, "Literature

---

14. For a full discussion of the "anxiety about Indianness," see chapter 9 of Meenakshi Mukherjee, *The Perishable Empire* (Delhi: Oxford University Press, 2000).

has little or nothing to do with a writer's home address."[15] But the tart comment of an Indian critic helps to identify the rocky terrain that this literature perforce has to negotiate: ". . . in this cruel era of cross-cultural misunderstandings, Rushdie was speaking from an Unknown Location, and, I fear, through an unspecified orifice."[16]

Like it or not, the politics of location is an important element affecting how this literature is regarded, both in India and on the world stage. Indeed, there is another wrinkle to this business: there is a whole ideology of "exile" that frames the manner in which this literature presents itself. The writer's postal address, far from being irrelevant, becomes the guarantee of a different kind of authenticity. The mere distance from the mother country and its raucous, urgent demands endows the writer with a clarifying perspective. And, indeed, many notable modern writers have been exiles—and émigrés, to echo the title of Terry Eagleton's study of some of them. The names come easily enough and are invoked from time to time in the heat of controversy: Henry James and T.S. Eliot, making those significant transatlantic crossings, deriving strength from their double belonging, both to Old Europe and to the New World; Yeats and Joyce, leaving an Ireland from which they derived all their imaginative sustenance; Vladimir Nabokov, a Russian aristocrat set adrift by the Revolution, washing up in America by way of Paris, France; Samuel Beckett, Irishman, Frenchman, nowhere-man. After all, the terrible twentieth century has forced large numbers of people into the state of exile, and the writer, whether exile or voluntary migrant, becomes a kind of living embodiment of the ambivalences and the complexity of the multiple belongings that are inseparable from the condition of exile, endowed with a special kind of inwardness.

This is the kind of claim embodied in Pico Iyer's essay, and Rushdie himself has made it with his characteristic eloquence: "To be a migrant is, perhaps, to be the only species of human being free of the shackles of nationalism. . . . The effect of mass migrations has been the creation of radically new types of human being: people who root themselves in ideas rather than in places, in memories as much as in material things. . . . To see things plainly, you have to cross a frontier."[17] Needless to say, not everyone is entirely in agreement with this (self-serving) descrip-

---

15. Salman Rushdie, introduction to *The Vintage Book of Indian Writing 1947–1997*, ed. Salman Rushdie and Elizabeth West (London: Vintage, 1997).

16. Kai Friese, "We're So Sari," *Village Voice Literary Supplement* (February 2001).

17. Salman Rushdie, "The Location of Brazil," in *Imaginary Homelands*.

tion of exile. (India, for instance, is much beset with NRI nationalism.) Further, it is argued with respect to these contemporary Indian writers that their badges of exile are unearned: these are voluntary migrants, privileged individuals who have moved to the West because of the lure of its material prosperity and are now claiming a dubious moral authority. But, true or false, this is merely *ad hominem*, and it takes us no closer to understanding the politics of location that is inseparable from the larger cultural phenomenon.

There are at least two aspects to this politics. On the one hand, there is the fact of the writers' location in the English-speaking metropoles. But what they—and perhaps their African and Latin American confreres —tell of is a distant Third World. This is the essence of their claim to attention. After all, it is said, they do not write about Manchester or Westchester, they write about Calcutta and Mumbai and other steamy, exotic places. Their location is not merely physical. Much more crucially, it is a location in a modern, international sensibility that gives them the ability to recognize (or crystallize) a new subject, new ranges of experience. This applies as much to Bharati Mukherjee and Jhumpa Lahiri, exploring the comedy and the tragedy that transpire at the cultural interface, as it does to Arundhati Roy, essaying traditional territory in some sense but endowed with linguistic skills and a quality of moral outrage that not only signal her location in the modern Anglophone world but also make her accessible to it. The "new subject," a product of multiple belonging, is not only *outside*—in the sense of historically unprecedented experiences, the Indian immigrant in Southall, the "arranged" bride, fresh from India, marooned in American suburbia—but also *within,* in the sense of a new subjectivity, a new way of perceiving and so imagining the hitherto-solid world.

The other aspect of this politics of location is the one that becomes particularly visible when seen from, say, India. Then, the fact that the writers partake of the glamour of the West, the fact that their voices are amplified by the power and global reach of the media, is what becomes crucial. The fact that the Indian (or near-Indian) writer who writes in English still writes (or appears to write) about India and Indians makes him or her a rival and a competitor of the writer who stayed at home and who also writes about India and Indians but in languages other than English. The writer who writes in an internationally accessible English is, very obviously, endowed with an enormous locational advantage. It would be easy, once again, to dismiss this perception as envy—but that too would be merely *ad hominem*, and serious inquiry into the cultural consequence of this kind of imbalance must go further.

And the Politics of Language

The fact that this "new" literature is written originally in English is, as it happens, of central importance. From the point of view of the international, largely Anglophone reader, the existence of a class of people who have an adequate mastery of English *and* have access to a distant, complex, and intriguing society, exotic but not entirely alien, is tremendously fortunate. Unlike, say, China, India does not have to be mediated by translators and so suffer the inevitable transmission losses, the suspicion of cosmetic adaptation. The only surprising thing is that this phenomenon should have had to wait for so long before it could crystallize. But that, as suggested earlier, might have to do with changes in the international conjuncture that made *an* India, suitably rediscovered and reconfigured, an area of more than specialist "area studies" interest. A kind of Indian being could, in skillful hands, be made to seem emblematic of something both wider and deeper, speaking to the human condition at the end of the twentieth century.

Against this net gain, however, there is a host of complications having to do with the fact that English-in-India is an ineluctable but also ineluctably poisoned legacy. And no matter how sincerely or vehemently Indian writers in English may wish to shed this legacy or (physically) distance themselves from it, turn their backs upon it even, they cannot.

The dialectic of marginality and privilege that underlies this whole development bears particularly poignantly on this matter. English was introduced in India, obviously, under colonial aegis, way back in the early nineteenth century. It was enthusiastically embraced by progressive, advanced sections of the population as the language of modernity, of access to the modern world. During the course of the nationalist struggle, however, the fact of the colonial provenance of its presence in India cast a shadow on its legitimacy. This is despite the fact that an overwhelming number of the leaders of the nationalist movement were not only proficient in English but also owed important elements of their intellectual development to texts and ideas first encountered in English. But the reviled Macaulay had spelled out the intention of colonial education thus: "We must at present do our best to form a class who would be the interpreters between us and the millions whom we govern; a class of persons,

Indian in blood and colour, but English in taste, in opinions, morals and in intellect."[18] The Anglophone Indian is saddled with an impossible burden.

There is uncertainty regarding the prevalence of English in India. On the one hand, there is the endlessly recycled figure of 2 percent of the population, which derives from some census. On the other hand, figures of up to 10 percent or 15 percent have been suggested—on the basis of some shaky extrapolations. What we do know is that the rates of overall literacy are very low—between 30 percent and 40 percent—but that in the literate part of the population the proportion of the (nominally) English-knowing must be considerably higher. Correspondingly, there is a disproportionate number of the English-knowing among the affluent sections of the population, thereby reinforcing the identification of English with privilege, though it must be the case that causation runs both ways: affluence translates into English-competence, and English-competence translates into upward social mobility and (relative) affluence. It is also the case that the upper levels of the intelligentsia, both in the state and the nonstate sectors, are overwhelmingly dominated by the English-knowing. Sales of quality books in English are considerably higher than in any (other) Indian language—but newspaper sales, at least in Hindi, have outstripped those of the English papers. The latter fact would suggest that there is a potential readership for quality books in Hindi, at any rate. But the Hindi belt of the country is also the poorest, so that the people who buy newspapers often do not, and perhaps cannot afford to, buy books. These trends have now been powerfully reinforced by the international linkages of the English-knowing and by the growing international domination of English in the era of globalization. People who were already (perceived to be) privileged have received a further international boost. Thus, it has been credibly suggested that the royalties received by one book—Arundhati Roy's *The God of Small Things*— come to more than the total worth of the Hindi book trade.

This is ironic, because for a considerable period after 1947 Indians writing in English went through a severe crisis of legitimacy. The mere fact of writing in English rendered these writers inauthentic, closed off from access to vast areas of existence, confined to an effete and privileged sphere that did not have enough living substance, "raw life" as it used to be called, to sustain a real literature. Of course, there were stub-

---

18. Thomas Babington Macaulay, "Minute on Education," in *Sources of Indian Tradition*, vol. 2, ed. William Theodore de Bary (New York: Columbia University Press, 1958), 44–49.

born and elegant demonstrations all along that, despite the narrow social range and the aura of privilege, it was possible to create, in English,
in India, those moments of insight and epiphany that are the heart of
literature. But the politics of culture trundled on regardless, and the writer
in English continued to labor under the sign of inauthenticity, until the
recent and remarkable change in that writer's fortunes.

It is often said that the trouble with Indian writing in English is that
English is not originally an Indian language. However, after 200 years of
intense (if involuntary) association, and in view of the facts on the ground,
this is a fatuous assertion to make. After all, the legitimacy of a language
can hardly be decided on demographic grounds. And while the argument
from origins has an obvious appeal in a conservative society, it can hardly
be taken seriously. No, the problem—*and there is a problem*—has to do
with the fact that English *is* an Indian language. It is already there, endowed with a legacy, associations with class and privilege, a particular
social profile that the current bearers of the legacy may well wish were
different. But there—*here*—it is. There is a powerful and numerous class
of people for whom it is, virtually, a first language. There are many others
for whom it will always remain entirely foreign. And there is everything
that lies between those two extremes, rich with possibilities of parody and
caricature, but also, let us not forget, a domain of shame and irredeemable
exclusion. The branded tongue is only a more intimate form of the brand
of economic disadvantage. The only way one can, to some limited extent,
redeem oneself from the intrinsic guilt of this situation is through an insis-
tent awareness of it. Here, innocence *is* guilt.

On Representation

In at least one of the senses of that troublesome word, it must be said
that writers do not "represent" countries, diplomats do. However, on the
"world stage" of our time, some writers who "represent" (certain aspects of) India in a literary sense—in howsoever fragmentary or oblique
a fashion—are also, inevitably, taken to "represent" India in a quasi-
diplomatic sense. And much of the problematic being of this new Indian
literature, internationally, and reflexively within India itself, derives from
the slippage between these two senses of "representation." Writers represent themselves and their world of experience. Anglophone Indian
writers represent, with ever increasing confidence, the perceptions of an
important and, crucially, *intrinsic* element of Indian life. The illusion

that they "represent" India and the totality of Indian life—as if anyone could—is just that, an illusion, even though it may be convenient for the managers of "world culture," and even when it is abetted by some writers. But before we can investigate the working of this "slippage" in any form, it is perhaps necessary to look briefly at the emergence of the "world stage" itself.

In the premodern world, it might be suggested, India was itself something of a world stage. It was a place where people from all parts of the "known" world came to see what they could see, and show what they could show. What was produced in the process, over the millennia, was a wonderfully hybrid culture, enriched by influences whose provenance is lost in antiquity. But the historical antecedents of the world stage of our time lie, it would appear, in the European nineteenth century, coterminous with the age of imperialism. The Great Exhibitions—in London (1851), Paris (1889), and so forth—made the produce of the world available for display under one roof. These, in turn, were translated into the more permanent institutions of the museum and the great metropolitan emporium. What emerged as a consequence of these developments was a distinctly modern form of consumption, ranging all the way from possession to window-shopping—that is, to consuming the world not as product but as spectacle. The crystallization of modern nationalism happened more or less concurrently with these developments, in the metropole, with the sense of imperial mastery over other people and nations.

In the colonies, too, national consciousness developed in response to the experience of colonialism. As the gouty colonels had it, there was no India before the British Raj—which might well have an element of truth in it. The taint of that initial moment of inspiration penetrated deep into the fabric of Indian nationalism. But it is also the case that the nationalism of subject peoples must be a struggle for *self*-representation, for cultural autonomy. It must go beyond committees and legislatures to encompass culture, too.

This struggle for a culturally autonomous modernity is, as it happens, particularly difficult, not least because it remains unclear what constitutes success in this domain. The claim of an *equal* modernity—English education, Western dress, "modern" ideas of democracy, and so forth—inevitably invites the charge of colonial imitation, of "mimicry." The "brown sahib" was a figure of mockery for the colonizers as well as for the "natives." But the quest for something authentically indigenous, autochthonous, and therefore truly "traditional" is also marked, inversely, by the power differentials of the given colonial context. The guarantee of authenticity still lies in the hands of others. Thus, for instance, there is the remarkable coincidence between the "Orientalist" construct of a mystic, spiritual India and the matching one of the conservative "traditionalists."

The world stage of our own time differs in several important respects. The most remarkable and deeply consequential of these is the exponential growth of the media. In becoming predominantly visual, the media have to a considerable extent overcome the barriers of literacy and linguistic difference and are therefore able to broadcast their version of the world worldwide. The other significant development, at least partially attributable to the media, is the attenuation of the arrogant, exclusivist, racist ideas of the past and the corresponding spread of a broadly liberal consciousness. The humanity of *different* others no longer has to be strenuously argued over, except in zones of social pathology. It is equally true that the resultant cacophony, produced once again by the contemporary media, may well result in the putting out of mind, if not quite denial, of the lately recognized humanity of those numerous others. But there is a net gain in liberal sensitivity that is an important element in this story.

The last and crucial difference between the world stage of the nineteenth century and our own has to do with the fact that, in the age of satellite television and the Internet, the world stage is no longer confined to London, Paris, New York. Whereas the world stage of an earlier time *concentrated* the diversity of the world in metropolitan locations, the world stage of our own time, existing in and through the global media, is at least as importantly in the business of framing and *disseminating* that diversity. While in the nineteenth century it became possible for "the world" to be paraded and put on display in the great metropolitan centers of the West, today "the world" is also the spectator: the Grammy Awards happen also in Gorakhpur, and the vociferous Tamil gentleman is also participating in the Florida electoral process, and the Booker Prize is no longer simply a minor British event.

This is indeed a kind of democracy, and the process is exactly mirrored by the erosion of national boundaries, the diminution of sovereignty under the influence of globalization. However, there is a crucial flaw in this apparent democracy, this democracy of appearances. The power differentials of the "bad" colonial past have not disappeared. But power in today's world is not, by and large, a few million tons of bombs here and there apart, mediated by the force of arms. Today's power is, to a large extent, discursive power, the power to set the terms of debate and the rules of engagement, the power to represent oneself and others. And this has everything to do with Indian literature, with the struggle continually to evolve adequate forms of self-representation, to carry on an internal dialogue, within the family so to speak, without being intruded upon by the world, with its spotlights and its boom mikes.

This is because, of course, the Indian literature that is attracting a measure of global attention today is not happening on the world stage alone, even when it is published outside India. One point of entry into this hierarchization of the world of, in this case Indian, literature is provided by the fact, remarkable and remarked, that the "world"—or its impresarios, Western publishers and Western literary agents—is not very interested in publishing translations of Indian works written in languages other than English. In part, this may be due to the fact that the translations are not of very good quality. But this may in turn be only an effect of the lack of interest: unregarded, translation does not attract the best talent. There is a further difficulty that derives from the possibility of translation itself. Thoughtful people are aware of the ultimate impossibility of perfect translation, aware that a translation can ever only be an imperfect substitute for the original. But in today's neon-lit world, in which there are no hiding places, there emerges the illusion, abetted by machines, of perfect translatability and the necessary implication that that which won't translate or doesn't get translated can't be worth much anyway. This creates a kind of easy "universality," but when it is produced within the context of profound inequalities of power and what one Indian historian has termed "asymmetric ignorance," this universality easily becomes oppressive.[19] It becomes the foundation for a global hierarchy, a contemporary version of the great chain of being. Here, the fact of "difference" is denied even as it is superficially affirmed, by being assimilated into the hierarchy as a lesser, *merely local*, form of something else that is present at a higher level. Close on the heels of what started out as cultural generosity, there appears a powerful rhetoric of globality. "Export quality" has long been a coded way of claiming excellence for all kinds of products, such as perfectly formed tomatoes that travel well over continental distances but lack the tang and savor of their ill-formed country cousins, which spoil easily and must be consumed locally. In the era of globalization there emerges, in consumer durables as in cultural products, the notion of "world class," of

19. See Dipesh Chakrabarty, *Provincialising Europe: Post-Colonial Thought and Historical Difference* (Princeton: Princeton University Press, 2000), 28.

"world players." Implicit, and not only implicit, in this rhetoric, there is a hierarchy in which what is "global" is automatically assumed to be better than what is merely "local."

Then there is also a sense that India, unlike, say, Latin America, is *already available* in English originals—and *an* India is. But when that subset is, with or without the collusion of the writers themselves, taken as representative of the whole, then the writers in other Indian languages have genuine grounds for their widespread feeling that their English-language colleagues, lately derided for being comprador and inauthentic, are indeed blocking their sunshine. On the one hand, there results the huge and demeaning desire of substantial and worthy writers to get translated into English. And then, the poor quality of most translations often merely reinforces the prejudice that whatever else there is, other than in-English originals, is perhaps not really deserving of great interest. This is the prejudice that Rushdie's scandalous remark, a mere echo of Macaulay, both expresses and reinforces: ". . . the prose writing—both fiction and non-fiction—created in this period by Indian writers *working in English*, is proving to be a stronger and more important body of work than most of what has been produced in the 16 'official languages' of India, the so-called 'vernacular languages' during the same time. . . . This new, and still burgeoning, 'Indo-Anglian' literature represents perhaps the most valuable contribution India has yet made to the world of books."[20] That "stronger and more important," of course, begs all the relevant questions: Stronger than what? More important for whom?

But it might be best to hear none other than A.K. Ramanujan on the relative significance of "Indo-Anglian" writing as compared with work in the other Indian languages, the so-called regional languages, the so-called vernaculars: "If you take the higher ranges, i.e. the better writers, I think the language writers have greater density, greater range. There is nobody like Tagore or Bose or Karanth or Masti or Adiga or LaSaRa or Karnad writing in English, whether in intensity, output, variety, creative use of our past and present, or power of influence. But on the other hand, if you look at the middle standard—a kind of general competence in writing—I think there are proportionately more competent second-rate writers in English than in the languages."[21]

The deep irony here is that this Indian literature that has attracted

20. Rushdie, introduction to *The Vintage Book of Indian Writing*.
21. A.K. Ramanujan, *Uncollected Poems and Prose* (Delhi: Oxford University Press, 2001).

global attention has made its way precisely by presenting itself as the voice of the disempowered, the silenced, the unheard from. This kind of framing enabled it to seize the opportunity that a certain kind of liberal opening up toward nondominant, nonmainstream cultures created. This little shoot has now ramified into a whole forest of ideology, into postcolonialism and multiculturalism—and the original impulse is in danger of being choked and overwhelmed. Thus, the generous recognition of difference might already be mutating into a corporate ideology of *in*difference, in which that original difference is absolutized and the common humanity of those distant others drops out of view altogether.

The domestic cultural repercussion of the global attention to a particular strand of Indian literature flows from the fact that its self-styled "marginal" voices are heard, here, as the overwhelmingly loud voices of an elite. Amplified by the global media, these voices from the margins of the Western cultural world can sound both loud and arrogant. The glamour and the clamor accompanying this literature is harmless enough in itself, even interesting, in a mindless cross-dressing sort of fashion: writers as pop stars. But there is also, alas, the tidal wave of envy that it produces, and it is hardly surprising that so many fail to find high ground. One sees many worthy, serious writers yearning to be translated into English simply to be able to try their luck on the world stage. It is almost as if their own carefully accumulated literary currency has been devalued because of the activities of distant others—like fumbling "tribals," as we call them, who find that their treasured hoard of herbs and berries has lost all value because a commodities market somewhere has suddenly discovered them, and found them wanting.

But the cultural impact of this phenomenon goes deeper than the envy that afflicts individual writers. What is endangered is the necessary autonomy of non-"world" literary discourses. The very existence of a class of English-wielding writers who can plausibly be seen as "representing" India for a world audience creates a pressure to draw those others also into the world market, if not quite onto the world stage. It changes the possible context of readership, so that even would-be local writers must position themselves to confront "global" readers.

Franco Moretti recently published an essay called "Conjectures on World Literature."[22] It is a tentative, exploratory essay in which Moretti

---

22. Franco Moretti, "Conjectures on World Literature," *New Left Review* 1 (January–February 2000): 54–68.

explicitly disavows the idea that "world literature" is in any manner of speaking an object, a thing. It is, he suggests, a mode of attention, a particular perspective for looking at the literatures of the world. In brief, he argues that the progressive integration of the world into one world-system creates the possibility of reading the world's resistant diversity for patterns and recurrences. What he proposes is a special kind of *distant* reading—as against the *close* reading that has been the staple of literary criticism for most of one century. In such a distant reading, the local particularity of the text becomes less significant than the features that it may have in common with other texts. Moretti has interesting things to say about the process of cultural interaction, in which influences are reciprocal and hegemony is never total, so that the cultural text is produced through the dialectic, operative at several levels, of subordination and resistance. This kind of "world" reading, Moretti acknowledges, is parasitic not only upon native cultural interpreters—critics, mediators—who make the alien texts available but also, crucially, upon those distant but "somewhere local" texts.

The emergence of the world stage, however, raises the prospect of the production, not merely the recognition/refocusing, of something that is "world literature," *ab initio*. The metaphor of the world stage itself suggests that there might well be a *performative* aspect to this literature, playing at this and that, cowboys and Indians. This connects, obviously, with earlier forms of exoticism—peacocks and princesses—but the critical difference is the self-conscious framing of the literature, both by its practitioners and its impresarios, in terms of an ongoing international—"world"—discourse. Exotic it may be, but it must also be theoretically *au fait* if it is to appear on this world stage.

It is possible, of course, that what *appears* as "world literature"—as opposed to what may only be *read* as such, à la Moretti—is also part of a process of collective introspection. Thus, the world stage itself might be a symptom of the emergence of a special kind of global community: geographically dispersed, diasporic, composed of migrants and exiles, this is *not* the global village of technoromantic fantasy. This is the neon-lit ghetto of the globalized, much beset by the lightness of their postmodern being. Relentlessly cosmopolitan, albeit with occasional exotic flavors wafting through, this is the world of the airport lounge, the five-star hotel lobby.

1998–2000: A Chronology

Bandita Sijapati

1998

January 1

The Election Commission announces that polling for the twelfth Lok Sabha elections and state assemblies will be held in four phases: February 16, 22, and 28 and March 7. For the first time, when general elections are being held in winter months, polling in Jammu and Kashmir will take place at the same time as in the rest of the country.

January 3

Finance Minister P. Chidambaram announces that the Voluntary Disclosure of Income Scheme of 1997 has resulted in the unprecedented disclosure of over Rs. 330 million in unreported and illegal income, 30 percent of which was taken as tax.

January 5

Laloo Prasad Yadav of the Rashtriya Janata Dal (RJD) and Kanshi Ram of the Bahujan Samaj Party (BSP) launch a seven-party alternative secular front called the Jan Morcha. The Morcha hopes to make state-level seat adjustments with the Congress Party to defeat the Bharatiya Janata Party (BJP) in the Lok Sabha elections. The next day Yadav directs his party's ministers to resign from the United Front government.

January 12

The BJP announces that the party's prime ministerial candidate, Atal Bihari Vajpayee, will contest from Lucknow (Uttar Pradesh), and the party president, L.K. Advani, from Gandhinagar (Gujarat). The announcement is made via the Internet.

January 21

The Election Commission bans the publication and broadcasting of the results of opinion poll surveys between February 14 and 28 and puts similar restrictions on making public the results of exit poll surveys from February 16 to 28.

January 24

The Congress Party releases its manifesto, in which it claims to be the party of development, participatory democracy, pluralism, a better deal for the poor, and economic sovereignty. It refuses to support the candidacy of former prime minister P.V. Narasimha Rao because he failed to prevent the demolition of the Babri Masjid in Ayodhya.

French president Jacques Chirac arrives for a three-day state visit to India. The next day, he says that India has the "aptitude" to become a permanent member of the United Nations Security Council.

February 3

BJP president Advani releases the party's manifesto, which keeps *hindutva* intact while promising to move toward making India a declared nuclear state.

February 7

The Congress returns to power in Nagaland with a two-thirds majority when forty-eight of its candidates are elected unopposed to the sixty-member assembly.

February 14

About 50 people are killed and more than 200 injured when a dozen bombs explode at short intervals in the textile city of Coimbatore in Tamil Nadu shortly before BJP president Advani is due to speak at an election meeting.

February 16

The first phase of polling for 222 Lok Sabha constituencies in twenty states and union territories is marred by incidents of violence in Bihar. The next day, following reports of large-scale booth capturing in the first phase of polling, the Election Commission orders a repoll in 599 polling stations spread over nine states. On February 18, repolling is ordered in an additional 821 polling stations, including some in Uttar Pradesh.

February 18

C. Subramaniam, elder statesman and former governor of Tamil Nadu, is awarded the nation's highest civilian honor, Bharat Ratna. He is the third prominent figure from Tamil Nadu to be thus honored in recent months.

February 21

Uttar Pradesh governor Romesh Bhandari dismisses the Kalyan Singh government and inducts a new eighteen-member ministry headed by Jagadambika Pal of the Loktantric Congress Party (LCP). The next day, seven LCP members of the legislative assembly return to the BJP fold.

February 22

About 55 percent of the 205 million voters turn out in the second phase of polling for 183 Lok Sabha constituencies in nine states and Pondicherry, with violence reported in Bihar, Orissa, West Bengal, and Andhra Pradesh.

February 23

The Allahabad High Court, in an interim order, defers the dismissal of the Kalyan Singh government in Uttar Pradesh. BJP leader Atal Bihari Vajpayee breaks his two-day-old fast-unto-death. The next day, the Supreme Court directs in an interim order that a "composite floor test" be held in the Uttar Pradesh assembly to determine which of the rival claimants for the chief ministership has a majority in the House. Five days later, Kalyan Singh wins the composite floor test, securing 225 votes against the 196 garnered by his rival. The Supreme Court upholds the interim order of the Allahabad High Court, reinstating Kalyan Singh as chief minister "subject to democratic process."

February 28

The government asks the Jain Commission of Inquiry into the assassination of Rajiv Gandhi to wrap up its operations and conclude its secretariat within a week. The voluminous interim report of the commission, submitted in August 1997, had led to the withdrawal of Congress support from the United Front government, resulting in its collapse and the calling of elections.

About 55 percent of the 145 million voters turn out in the third phase of polling for 131 Lok Sabha constituencies in ten states and one union territory, despite minor incidents of bomb throwing and disruption of polling in West Bengal, Gujarat, Orissa, and Madhya Pradesh.

March 4

Of the 509 seats declared, the BJP front wins 236 of the 543 seats to be filled, the Congress front wins 141, and the United Front 91. The final results, as published later by the Election Commission, are BJP, 182 seats and 25.6 percent of the vote; Congress, 141 (25.8 percent); Communist Party of India, Marxist (CPM), 32 (5.2 percent); Samajwadi Party, 20 (4.9 percent); All India Anna Dravida Munnetra Kazhagam (AIADMK), 18 (1.8 percent); RJD, 17 (2.8 percent); Samata Party, 12 (1.8 percent); Telugu Desam Party (TDP), 12 (2.8 percent); Communist Party of India (CPI), 9 (1.8 percent); Akali Dal, 8 (0.8 percent); Janata Dal, 6 (3.2 percent); Dravida Mummetra Kazhagam (DMK), 6 (1.4 percent); and BSP, 5 (4.7 percent). Only six Independents are elected, with 2.4 percent of the vote.

March 8

The AIADMK general secretary, Jayalalitha, reaffirms the party's decision to stay out of a BJP-led coalition government at the center but says the party will offer "wholehearted support." Three days earlier, the TDP decided to remain neutral in the vote of confidence.

March 10

The chief election commissioner, M.S. Gill, hands over official notification containing the results of the general election (and formally constituting the new Lok Sabha) to the president of India, K.R. Narayanan. The president invites A.B. Vajpayee to demonstrate that he can form a government.

March 12

Vajpayee meets with the president and presents documents showing the support of only 240 members. The BJP's failure to demonstrate the support of the majority compels the president to widen the scope of his discussions for the formation of the new government to include the leaders of other political formations, such as the Congress and the United Front.

March 14

AIADMK leader Jayalalitha submits a letter of "total and unconditional" support of the BJP to the president.

In a quiet coup, Sitaram Kesri is unseated as Congress president by the Congress Working Committee, and in his place Sonia Gandhi is installed. Kesri terms her installation unconstitutional. The All India Congress Committee ratifies the move on April 6.

March 15

President K.R. Narayanan invites BJP leader A.B. Vajpayee to form a government. Vajpayee is reportedly given ten days to prove his majority. The BJP's chances improve decisively after the Congress refuses to stake a claim. The anxieties that have surfaced in the BJP's dealings with the AIADMK are resolved when the AIADMK decides to take part in the government along with two of its allies after the BJP agrees to include all the state-related issues raised by the party in the national agenda.

Sonia Gandhi is elected chairperson of the Congress Parliamentary Party even though she is not a member of Parliament. Within hours of her election, Gandhi names Sharad Pawar as floor leader of the Congress in the Lok Sabha and Manmohan Singh in the Rajya Sabha.

March 17

The "national agenda," described as the "document for governance" by the government-in-waiting, is finalized by the leaders of the BJP and its pre-poll allies. Publicly disclosed the next day, it is completely silent on the BJP core issues of Ayodhya, the scrapping of Article 370 of the Constitution (which ensures special status for Kashmir), and a uniform civil code.

March 19

A.B. Vajpayee takes over as prime minister, heading a thirteen-party coalition government. Leading the list of cabinet ministers is the BJP president L.K. Advani. Of the twenty-one cabinet ministers, ten are from the BJP and nine from its pre-poll allies.

March 22

In an address to the nation, Prime Minister Vajpayee invites his fellow politicians to respond to the polity's requirement of "cooperation and coalition building" and to understand that the "politics of negativism and untouchability has run its course."

March 23

The Telugu Desam Party breaks its twenty-month bond with the United Front and fields G.M.C. Balayogi for the post of Lok Sabha Speaker with the support of the BJP and its allies against the Speaker of the dissolved Lok Sabha, P.A. Sangma, who has filed his papers with the support of the Congress and the United Front. Balayogi is elected Speaker the next day.

March 25

The death toll from the tornado that devastated Midnapore district of West Bengal and the adjoining areas in Orissa rises to 200; 500 persons are still trapped under the debris of collapsed houses, and 3,000 others have been injured.

March 27

The Supreme Court, by an interim order, stays the execution of the death sentence imposed on all twenty-six persons accused in the Rajiv Gandhi assassination case by a "designated court" in Chennai on January 28, 1998.

March 28

The ten-day-old government of Prime Minister Vajpayee wins the vote of confidence in the Lok Sabha. The government's margin of victory is a slim thirteen votes.

March 31

Prime Minister Vajpayee and Home Minister Advani affirm their close links with the Rashtriya Swayamsevak Sangh (RSS) but allay fears that the BJP-led government will be run by "remote control" from RSS headquarters.

April 2

Prime Minister Vajpayee says in the Rajya Sabha that the center has no intention of dismissing the Tamil Nadu government and that his regime will not "misuse" Article 356 of the Constitution. Jayalalitha, leader of the AIADMK, reiterates her demand for the dismissal of the Tamil Nadu government.

April 14

U.S. ambassador to the United Nations and special envoy Bill Richardson meets with Prime Minister Vajpayee in the first formal high-level contact of India's new government with the United States. The meeting proceeds along "positive" lines.

April 15

Finance Minister Yashwant Sinha says in New York that infrastructure development is an item of top priority in India. He invites Americans and nonresident Indians to invest generously in this sector, especially in the development of communications, airports, railways, and power.

April 17

A constitution bench of the Supreme Court, in a significant judgment delivered in the Jharkhand Mukti Morcha bribery case, rules that the Constitution "protects a member of Parliament against proceedings in court that relate, or concern, or have a connection or nexus with anything said, or a vote given, by him in Parliament."

April 20

Prime Minister Vajpayee dismisses Buta Singh from his cabinet following the demand by AIADMK leader Jayalalitha that all ministers indicted or facing criminal investigation be dropped.

April 22

The veteran BJP leader Sunder Singh Bhandari is appointed governor of Bihar and names former Research and Analysis Wing head Girish Chandra Saxena to the position of governor of Jammu and Kashmir.

April 23

The second report of the M. Narasimham Committee on financial sector reforms calls for strengthening the Indian banking system so that it can manage "problems" that will evolve as the country moves toward a more liberal capital account regime.

April 27

India and China begin a new phase of "free and frank" security talks in Delhi. The chief of the Chinese People's Liberation Army, General Fu Quanyou, and Indian defense minister George Fernandes discuss concrete steps to demarcate an interim Sino-Indian boundary and to resolve differences over the suspected Chinese supply of long-range missiles to Pakistan.

May 7

Defense Minister Fernandes says that India needs to strengthen its borders with China and that thus there will be no cut in the strength of the armed forces in those areas. The minister's comments describing China as "India's potential threat number one" evoke a sharp reaction from China. The Congress accuses Fernandes of harboring a "super-agenda" to reverse the foreign policy consensus, built over the years by successive governments, on building bridges with China.

May 11

Prime Minister Vajpayee announces that India has successfully conducted three underground nuclear tests at the Pokhran test site in Rajasthan. Two days later, two more tests are carried out. The United States imposes sanctions on India in accordance with its domestic laws; Germany freezes development aid; Japan suspends $26 million in annual aid; Britain strongly protests; and Canada recalls its envoy from New Delhi. Russia and France, while expressing concern, oppose sanctions. Three days later, British prime minister Tony Blair, as chairman of the meeting of the G8 countries in Birmingham, telephones Prime Minister Vajpayee to convey the summit's "dismay" at the tests and urges India to sign the Comprehensive Test Ban Treaty.

May 16

Reacting sharply to the Chinese Foreign Office's accusatory statement on nuclear tests, India rejects the charges that it seeks hegemony in South Asia and that its action will entail serious consequences to the peace and security of the region and the world at large. The Prime Minister's Office clarifies and modifies an earlier statement by the prime minister and states that "India will not be the first to use nuclear weapons against anyone."

May 28

Pakistan tests five nuclear devices and says that the results are as expected. After an emergency session of the cabinet, Prime Minister Vajpayee says that India is ready to meet any challenge.

The Economic Survey for 1997–98 shows a sharp drop in the growth rate of the economy, from 7.5 percent in 1996–97 to 5 percent in 1997–98.

May 29

Prime Minister Vajpayee assures Pakistan that it faces no threat from India and that New Delhi is open to a comprehensive political dialogue with Islamabad. Vajpayee also reiterates India's offer for a dialogue with Pakistan on the no-first-use of nuclear weapons, adding that New Delhi is prepared for an extensive discussion on confidence-building measures to enhance security in the subcontinent.

June 2

The government announces the 1998–99 budget, which includes plans to raise the defense outlay from Rs. 361 billion to Rs. 412 billion. The Atomic Energy Department budget increases 68 percent and the Department of Space budget grows 62 percent, while the agriculture budget grows 50 percent. Prime Minister Vajpayee claims that the budget is "development and growth oriented" and not "protectionist" and that it will encourage both internal and external investment. The next day, the Vajpayee government, under pressure, reduces the petrol and urea price hikes. On June 12, the entire price increase for urea is withdrawn.

June 6

Pakistani prime minister Nawaz Sharif invites Prime Minister Vajpayee to discuss the arms race in South Asia but also says that India cannot continue its control over Kashmir "any longer." Prime Minister Vajpayee welcomes the suggestion that the two countries resume a dialogue.

June 8

Prime Minister Vajpayee says that if the Supreme Court rules against the construction of a Ram Mandir at the disputed site in Ayodhya, his government will ensure the observance of the rule.

June 12

Beginning what will become a major political dialogue between the United States and India, the deputy chairman of the Planning

Commission, Jaswant Singh, meets with the U.S. deputy secretary of state, Strobe Talbott.

June 17

A special three-member team of the Union Home Ministry arrives in Patna to examine the law-and-order situation in Bihar following the murder of two legislators. While the state government remarks that Bihar is under control, the opposition parties list incidents in order to press for the dismissal of the Rabri Devi government.

June 22

After the Uttar Pradesh assembly speaker bans Pepsi and Coca-Cola in the legislators' canteen within the secretariat in protest against the sanctions imposed by the U.S. government, several other organizations in the state follow suit.

June 24

The Samajwadi Party, led by Mulayam Singh Yadav, breaks its two-year-old ties with the United Front and joins the Rashtriya Janata Dal, led by Laloo Prasad Yadav, to form a new "secular front"—the Rashtriya Loktantrik Morcha.

June 29

The Union cabinet decides to grant full statehood to Delhi and to create three new states—Uttaranchal, Vananchal, and Chattisgarh—thus taking the first step toward fulfilling the commitment made in the BJP-led government's national agenda for governance.

As anticipated by the Indian government, the World Bank clears the next lot of humanitarian assistance to India, totaling $376.4 million.

July 6

Prime Minister Vajpayee informs the Rajya Sabha that the government is committed to introducing a constitutional amendment bill to reserve seats for women in the Lok Sabha and state assemblies during this session even if there is no consensus among political parties.

July 9

Postal service across the country is adversely affected as nearly 5.5 million employees begin an indefinite strike demanding a hike in pay scales, revision of the bonus formula, and permanent status for over 3 million extradepartmental employees. The strike is called off eight days later following a government assurance that it will consider these demands.

July 13

Amid ugly scenes described by Prime Minister Vajpayee as the most shameful in the history of the Indian Parliament, the opponents of the contentious Women's Reservation Bill physically prevent Law Minister Thambi Durai from introducing it in the Lok Sabha.

July 28

The Supreme Court stays the arrest of Laloo Prasad Yadav, former Bihar chief minister, in connection with the "fodder scam" case.

The prime ministers of India and Pakistan meet during a South Asian Association for Regional Cooperation (SAARC) meeting and agree to resume the dialogue process. The meetings of the countries' foreign secretaries in the following days are unfruitful.

August 7

In a major breakthrough in the Cauvery water dispute, the chief ministers of the four riparian states and union territories (Tamil Nadu, Karnataka, Kerala, and Pondicherry) agree on a scheme for implementing the 1991 interim award of the Cauvery water dispute tribunal and for creating a River Valley Authority with the prime minister as its head. Ten days later, the Supreme Court in effect ratifies the agreement by disposing of Tamil Nadu's suit on the matter.

September 3

The twelfth Non-Aligned Movement (NAM) summit endorses an Indian initiative to adopt a broad approach aimed at the total elimination of nuclear weapons. The declaration by the 113-member NAM refrains from condemning the nuclear tests by New Delhi and Islamabad in May of this year, despite a reported strong demand to do so by South Africa, Indonesia, and several other countries.

September 7

Floods continue unabated in Assam, causing devastation in twenty-one districts, claiming 137 lives so far and affecting four million people. This year's floods are described as the worst since 1950.

September 18

Prime Minister Vajpayee outlines a seven-point program to revive the economy despite the increasingly difficult and uncertain international environment. The strategy requires 7 percent GDP growth, a 10 percent rise in industrial production, and a 15–20 percent increase in exports.

September 22

The government recommends that President's Rule be imposed in Bihar and that the state assembly be kept in "suspended animation." The cabinet bases its decision on a report from Bihar governor S.S. Bhandari. The next day, the AIADMK demands that the same standards be applied in Tamil Nadu to dismiss the DMK government. Three days later, the president returns the cabinet recommendation for dismissal and asks the Union cabinet to reconsider it.

September 27

Arriving in Lahore, Pakistani prime minister Sharif speaks of his September 23 agreement with Prime Minister Vajpayee in New York to resume foreign-secretary-level talks, calling it a "major breakthrough." He reveals that India and Pakistan have agreed to resume road traffic across the border at Wagah.

October 11

Union information and broadcasting minister and South Delhi member of Parliament Sushma Swaraj is unanimously elected as leader of the Delhi BJP Legislature Party. She succeeds Sahib Singh

Verma, who was forced to resign as Delhi chief minister hours after the BJP's top leadership decided that his removal would enhance the party's chance of winning the upcoming assembly elections.

October 14

Professor Amartya Sen, the distinguished economist best known for his work on poverty and famine, is awarded the Nobel Prize in economics. He is the sixth person of Indian birth to receive a Nobel Prize.

October 16

Indian foreign secretary K. Raghunath, leading an eight-member Indian delegation to Islamabad, proposes a string of confidence-building measures to his Pakistani counterpart, Shamshad Ahmad, during formal discussions on peace and security.

October 20

The U.S. Congress approves legislation empowering President Bill Clinton to relax the economic sanctions imposed against India and Pakistan imposed in the wake of the May nuclear tests conducted by the two countries.

October 22

China reacts strongly to Prime Minister Vajpayee's meeting with the Dalai Lama, saying it amounts to Indian interference in China's internal affairs and a violation of India's commitment to prohibit Tibetans in India from engaging in political activities. India claims that the meeting was "just a courtesy call."

October 30

The Reserve Bank of India announces stringent provisioning standards for banks following the latest Narasimham Committee report on financial sector reforms.

November 3

Trinamool Congress leader Mamata Banerjee resigns from the Central Coordination Committee of the BJP and its allies to protest the escalating prices of essential commodities. Prime Minister Vajpayee refuses to accept her resignation.

November 11

Reuters wire service runs a story stating that India will need 300–500 percent more bed space in hospitals to deal with the spread of AIDS by the year 2000. The statistics cited indicate that between 12 and 15 percent of the patients in public hospitals are HIV positive and that 30 percent of TB patients and 25 percent of STD patients carry the virus.

November 13

India and Pakistan conclude bilateral talks after making only marginal progress on strengthening friendly exchanges in education, culture, and sports; limited progress is made on the relaxation of visa restrictions.

November 23

Shiv Sena president Bal Thackeray threatens to break his party's alliance with the BJP if the Pakistani cricket team is allowed to visit India and, worse, is allowed to play a match in Maharashtra.

November 26

The Supreme Court declines to stay the trial of corruption cases involving the AIADMK chief, Jayalalitha, and some of her erstwhile cabinet colleagues and senior bureaucrats.

November 29

The Congress defeats the BJP in the assembly elections in Delhi (winning 51 of 70 seats) and Rajasthan (150 of 200 seats), and it retains power in Madhya Pradesh (with 172 of 320 seats). It loses in Mizoram, winning only 6 of 40 seats.

December 5

In a move interpreted as an assertion of power on the part of Prime Minister Vajpayee following the BJP's poor showing in the state assembly elections, Jaswant Singh is appointed as foreign minister, Pramod Mahajan as minister of information and broadcasting, and Jagmohan as minister of communications.

December 11

Trinamool Congress leader Mamata Banerjee creates a sensation in the Lok Sabha when she grabs Samajwadi Party member Daroga Prasad Saroj by the collar and drags him out of the well of the House to prevent him from protesting against the contentious Women's Reservation Bill shortly before its introduction.

December 24

A Russian Foreign Ministry spokesperson announces that the concept of a strategic triangle consisting of China, India, and Russia —part of Russian prime minister Yevgeny Primakov's statement in Delhi—should not be taken as an official proposal.

December 31

Admiral Vishnu Bhagwat is dismissed as chief of naval staff following cautions from Prime Minister Vajpayee and Defense Minister George Fernandes regarding alleged leaks of sensitive information.

1999

January 4

The Gujarat government raids Hindu nationalist activists allegedly involved in recent attacks on Christians. The police arrest the president of the Dangs district Hindu Jagran Manch (Forum to Awaken Hindus), two activists of the local Bajrang Dal (Warriors of the *Hindutva* Revolution), and the defeated BJP candidate for the Dangs-Bansda assembly seat, among others.

January 6

Responding to U.S. ambassador Richard Celeste's remarks the day before that India should specify its requirements for a minimum nuclear deterrence so that it is not seen as an "open-ended threat" to its neighbors, India claims that there can be no "fixity," because the issue is entirely a matter of top secret assessment and perceptions of possible threat, and that nuclear deterrence cannot be fixed as long as the possibility of proliferation remains.

January 9

The cabinet approves the Ninth Five-Year Plan after reducing the public sector outlay and lowering the GDP growth target to 6.5 percent.

January 10

At the end of his daylong visit to the strife-torn Dangs district to assess the situation, Prime Minister Vajpayee rejects the demand for dismissal of the Keshubhai Patel ministry in Gujarat, maintaining that the prevailing situation in the south Gujarat districts is not as serious as it is pronounced to be and that demands by opposition leaders are "politically motivated."

January 14

Under the chairmanship of Communist Party of India leader and former home minister Indrajit Gupta, the all-party Committee on State Funding of Elections submits its report to Home Minister Advani. The committee justifies government funding of elections, saying it is legal, constitutional, and in the public interest.

January 15

India and the European Union, meeting for the third time in a joint commission, agree to bolster "high-level economic dialogue" and to establish joint working groups in areas of mutual interest, especially telecommunications, air and marine transport, and the environment.

January 17

Prime Minister Vajpayee rules out a constitutional amendment or a new legal means of banning religious conversions, maintaining that whatever decision the constituent assemblies have already taken has helped the country to maintain national integrity and harmony.

More than 6.8 million children under the age of five years in Tamil Nadu are administered oral polio vaccine drops, achieving the target set for the second phase of the Pulse Polio immunization program.

January 20

Civil Aviation Minister Ananth Kumar announces that the cabinet has decided to make the five major airports in Delhi, Mumbai, Chennai, Calcutta, and Bangalore, along with seven or eight others to be identified soon, into corporations to bring them into line with international standards.

January 23

Australian missionary Graham Staines, along with his two sons, is burned to death by unidentified attackers in Orissa.

January 29

The eighth round of the India-U.S. dialogue between Indian external affairs minister Jaswant Singh and U.S. deputy secretary of state Strobe Talbott begins.

February 2

After what is officially described as a "no-holds-barred discussion" with the ruling coalition allies, Prime Minister Vajpayee announces that the government will reduce the recent price increase in food grains for those below the poverty line.

February 3

Prime Minister Vajpayee accepts Pakistani prime minister Sharif's suggestion to visit Pakistan by riding on the inaugural Delhi-Lahore bus.

February 4

The first step in the easing of sanctions imposed against India following the nuclear tests is taken when the United States decides not to block the loan for a power project in Andhra Pradesh that is due to be taken up by the World Bank toward the end of the month.

February 5

The BJP defends the government's decision to grant a visa to Salman Rushdie, author of *The Satanic Verses*, saying that it does not think there will be any law-and-order problem if Rushdie visits India.

February 11

National Lok Dal president and former Haryana chief minister Om Prakash Chautala serves notice on the Vajpayee government to either roll back the increase in the prices of rice, wheat, sugar, and urea or be prepared for a withdrawal of support by four of his party's Lok Sabha members. Chautala makes good on this threat on February 16.

February 12

The central government dismisses the Rabri Devi government in Bihar, having reiterated its decision of September 22, 1998, to put the state under President's Rule and place the state assembly in "suspended animation."

February 13

RJD leader Laloo Prasad Yadav and ministers of the dismissed Rabri Devi government are arrested for defying orders prohibiting demonstrations as Governor S.S. Bhandari takes over the reins of government in Bihar.

AIADMK leader Jayalalitha demands the immediate dismissal of the DMK ministry, saying that the law-and-order situation in Tamil Nadu is far worse than that in Bihar. Reacting to this statement, the BJP claims that the situation in Tamil Nadu does not call for the imposition of President's Rule.

February 15

The RJD-sponsored strike in protest against the imposition of President's Rule in Bihar affects normal life throughout the state. Laloo Prasad Yadav and Rabri Devi are arrested and detained on the outskirts of Patna by the police.

February 17

A 56-year-old tribal leader of the Congress Party, Giridhar Gamang, is sworn in as the fifteenth chief minister of Orissa. The previous chief minister, J.B. Patnaik, resigned on February 12 under pressure from the Congress high command, ending his forty-seven-month rule.

February 18

The government moves to crush the eighteen-day-old agitation by air traffic controllers by dismissing six controllers in Mumbai and Delhi who are said to have disrupted flights during their "work-to-rule" protest. It also files criminal complaints against them, seeking their arrest. Air traffic controllers return to providing normal service the next day, having assured the Delhi High Court that there will be no further disruptions of service.

February 20

Prime Minister Vajpayee arrives in Pakistan on the inaugural run of the bus service between Delhi and Lahore. The next day, the two prime ministers sign the Lahore Declaration, which seeks to redefine the relationship between the two countries in the postnuclear situation.

February 25

Chinese ambassador to India Zhou Gang declares that China's differences with India are "temporary" and indicates greater flexibility in accommodating New Delhi's security concerns in South Asia.

February 26

With the Telugu Desam Party eventually giving the Vajpayee government the support needed to override a joint opposition challenge, the Lok Sabha approves President's Rule in Bihar with 279 votes for it and 250 against. All its allies support the BJP, with the exception of the National Conference (which abstains) and the Haryana Lok Dal (which votes against it).

February 27

Finance Minister Sinha presents the budget for 1999–2000, which proposes to collect additional tax revenue mainly through the mechanism of surcharges on income tax and customs and a Rs. 1 excise tax on diesel. Three days earlier, he released the Economic Survey, which pointed to a recovery in economic growth to 5.8 percent in 1998–99 as against 5.0 percent in 1997–98.

March 7

A meeting between Prime Minister Vajpayee and Sonia Gandhi fails to break the deadlock over Bihar. The next day, with the Congress support necessary to ratify the imposition of President's Rule in the Rajya Sabha not forthcoming, the government decides to have President's Rule revoked. On March 9, Rabri Devi is again sworn in as chief minister.

March 13

The controversial patents amendment bill of 1999 receives parliamentary approval, with the Rajya Sabha adopting the bill by a voice vote. India was required to amend its Patents Act in conformity with its commitment to the World Trade Organization.

March 16

The first regularly scheduled bus to Lahore begins its journey from Delhi with twenty-nine passengers aboard.

March 17

The government agrees to the opposition demand that the dismissal of former naval chief Admiral Vishnu Bhagwat and other related defense matters be debated in Parliament.

March 19

External Affairs Minister Jaswant Singh and his Pakistani counterpart, Sartaj Aziz, outline a time-bound "road map" for taking the Lahore process forward during an informal bilateral meeting held at the sidelines of the two-day SAARC Council of Ministers meeting.

On March 25, India announces a relaxation of visa and travel restrictions for eight categories of Pakistani nationals. These include judges of the Supreme and High Courts and senior journalists.

March 29

A massive earthquake in the Garhwal region of Uttar Pradesh leaves at least 85 people dead and more than 130 injured in and around the towns of Chamoli and Rudra Prayag.

April 4

Prime Minister Vajpayee says that his government is ready to face a no-confidence motion in the Lok Sabha and rejects the AIADMK demand for reinstatement of Admiral Vishnu Bhagwat as the navy chief. The next day, Jayalalitha announces that she is withdrawing her two ministers from the central government.

April 17

The Vajpayee government resigns after losing a vote of confidence in the Lok Sabha by one vote.

April 19

Efforts to put together an alternative government are marked by consultations of Congress leader Sonia Gandhi with AIADMK leader Jayalalitha and with CPM leader and West Bengal chief minister Jyoti Basu.

April 21

Remarking on the president's invitation to explore the possibility of forming an alternative government, Congress leader Sonia Gandhi asserts that she will be able to furnish proof of the support of 272 members of the Lok Sabha within two days. However, two days later, she is able to present only 233 names.

April 22

As it becomes clear that no one will be able to coordinate a new ruling coalition, the Lok Sabha approves, by voice vote, the 1999–2000 general budget, the railway budget, and the authorization of funds for the various ministries.

April 26

The president dissolves the Lok Sabha and orders fresh elections conforming to the recommendation of the cabinet and based on his own assessment that an alternative government will be unable to command a majority in Parliament.

May 9

Infiltrators from Pakistan begin shelling army positions and other targets on the Srinagar-Leh road in the Kargil sector of Kashmir. This information is not revealed in press reports until a few days later.

May 11

The Supreme Court confirms the death sentences of four of the twenty-six accused in the Rajiv Gandhi assassination case, reduces to life imprisonment the sentences of three others, and acquits the remaining nineteen.

The Supreme Court dismisses AIADMK leader Jayalalitha's petition against the appointment of special judges by the Tamil Nadu government to try corruption cases against her and also invalidates a central notification transferring the cases from the special judges.

May 14

Defense Ministry officials reluctantly confess that Pakistani infiltrators have occupied "unheld" areas near Kargil in Kashmir. Although reports of shelling and some casualties have surfaced, Defense Minister Fernandes claims in Leh that "reports are created by vested interests to destabilize the country."

The BJP and at least thirteen of its allies formally rename themselves the National Democratic Alliance (NDA) after a meeting of all the parties and groups that voted in favor of the confidence motion.

May 17

Sonia Gandhi resigns as Congress president over the issue of her foreign origins raised by Congress Working Committee members Sharad Pawar, P.A. Sangma, and Tariq Anwar. The committee rejects the resignation.

May 19

As the estimate of the number of infiltrators in the Kargil region continues to increase, sector commander Lieutenant General Krishan Pal claims that "this is a local situation and will be dealt with locally. There is no possibility of its escalation into a war."

May 20

The Congress Working Committee expels Sharad Pawar, P.A. Sangma, and Tariq Anwar. A week later, they launch the National Congress Party.

May 25

The large scale of the Kargil infiltration becomes evident, and it becomes the major news story of the day after fifteen days of fighting. The next day, India launches air strikes against the Pakistan-aided militants, and on May 27 one fighter jet is shot down by a Pakistani missile, marking the beginning of an intense crisis period. The crisis ends on July 5.

May 29

Prime Minister Vajpayee rejects the proposition from Pakistan's prime minister, Nawaz Sharif, that air strikes in the Kargil sector be stopped as a precondition for sending the Pakistani foreign minister, Sartaj Aziz, to New Delhi.

May 31

The Pakistani foreign secretary, Shamshad Ahmad, warns that Islamabad will use "any weapon" in its arsenal to defend the country's territorial integrity.

June 12

The meeting between External Affairs Minister Jaswant Singh and his Pakistani counterpart, Sartaj Aziz, fails to produce a way out of the Kargil crisis.

June 27

The Indian Air Force intensifies operations in the Kargil region by beginning round-the-clock bombardments of enemy positions in Batalik and Dras. Fighting a mounting battle, with considerable casualties, Indian forces have recaptured almost all of the territory occupied by the infiltrators from Pakistan.

Star TV, Doordarshan, CNN, and others send correspondents to the front lines of Kargil. It becomes India's first televised conflict.

July 5

Following an extraordinary meeting of Prime Minister Nawaz Sharif of Pakistan with President Bill Clinton in Washington, D.C., on July 4 (in the course of which the president consulted with Prime Minister Vajpayee by telephone), Pakistan agrees to withdraw its forces from the Indian side of the line of control. President Clinton says that he will take a personal interest in encouraging bilateral dialogue between India and Pakistan after the line of control is fully restored. On July 11, the withdrawal of Pakistan-backed forces begins.

July 11

The Election Commission announces that elections to the thirteenth Lok Sabha will be held in five phases from September 4 to October 1.

The inflation rate drops sharply to a two-decade low of 2.03 percent for the week ending June 26 as prices of food items and primary commodities continue to decline.

July 12

The Bansi Lal regime in Haryana is once again reduced to minority status, less than a month after the Congress high command decided on June 25 to withdraw the support it had extended to Bansi Lal at the time of the crucial vote of confidence. On July 21, Bansi Lal resigns just before a vote of confidence mandated by the governor of Haryana. On July 24, a new government is sworn in, headed by Om Prakash Chautala.

July 13

During the day, the Sensex (Bombay Stock Exchange sensitive index) records an all-time high of 4,678, although it closes lower. The previous high was recorded almost five years earlier.

August 2

In one of the worst train accidents ever in India, more than 250 people are killed and 300 injured when the Delhi-bound Brahmaputra Mail and the Guwahati-bound Avadh-Assam Express collide on the West Bengal–Bihar border.

August 4

In the course of the "Rally for the Valley," Booker Prize–winning author Arundhati Roy and Narmada Bachao Andolan leader Medha Patkar join participants in pledging to protect the Narmada River against a proposed dam that threatens to displace residents from the lower-lying riverbanks.

August 7

The Lok Shakti, the Samata Party, and the Sharad Yadav faction of the Janata Dal formally merge.

August 10

The Indian Air Force shoots down a Pakistani naval antisubmarine and surveillance aircraft, claiming that it intruded ten kilometers into Indian territory in the Kori Creek area in Gujarat. The plane's wreckage is found in Pakistani territory.

August 18

Congress president Sonia Gandhi files nomination papers in the Bellary constituency in Karnataka and is soon followed by BJP leader Sushma Swaraj. On September 10, Gandhi files nomination papers to contest in Amethi, her late husband's constituency in Uttar Pradesh.

September 5

The first phase of polling in the thirteenth general election is held, with 166 million voters casting their ballots in 145 constituencies in ten major states and elsewhere. The turnout is 58 percent, and the chief election commissioner, M.S. Gill, characterizes the polling, in which five persons are killed, as "largely peaceful and satisfactory." On September 11, the second phase of the election is completed, with 152 million voters casting ballots in 123 constituencies. Polling is peaceful, with few irregularities. A week later, the third phase of polling, for 76 constituencies, is marred by the killing of forty persons (many of them policemen), mainly in Bihar in land-mine explosions for which Naxalites are presumed to be responsible. On September 21, the revoting in 399 polling stations is conducted peacefully. The final phase of polling occurs on October 3, when 133 million voters in eleven states cast their votes in 118 constituencies. At least eighteen persons are killed. Nonetheless, the chief election commissioner says, "On the whole, the day went off well."

September 21

Pakistan announces that it has formally filed a case before the International Court of Justice at The Hague to make India pay for the August 10 loss of the reconnaissance aircraft and pay compensation to the families of those killed.

October 6

Counting of election ballots begins. Early results suggest a victory for the BJP-led National Democratic Alliance. Prime Minister Vajpayee and NDA leaders L.K. Advani, George Fernandes, and Mamata Banerjee win, while former Congress finance minister Manmohan Singh loses in South Delhi. The next day, the defeat of Bihar's Laloo Prasad Yadav is announced. Sonia Gandhi wins handily in both constituencies she contested.

October 7

With the results available for almost all the Lok Sabha constituencies, the BJP and its allies in the National Democratic Alliance achieve a substantial majority of over 300 seats. In the final results published by the Election Commission, the seats won and vote shares of the major parties are BJP, 182 (23.8 percent); Congress, 114 (28.3 percent); CPM, 33 (5.4 percent); TDP, 29 (3.7 percent); Samajwadi Party, 26 (3.8 percent); JD (U) (with which the Lok Shakti and Samata Party had merged), 21 (3.1 percent); Shiv Sena, 15 (1.6 percent); BSP, 14 (4.2 percent); DMK, 12 (1.7 percent); and AIADMK, 10 (1.9 percent). The Akali Dal in the Punjab suffers a major loss, winning only two seats.

October 8

Prime Minister Vajpayee initiates the formal process of government formation. By this time, the National Democratic Alliance has been joined by the National Conference Party of Kashmir. The Telugu Desam informs the president that it will support the NDA government but will not join the ministry. On October 12, the DMK decides to join the government. Two days later, the Election Commission formally constitutes the thirteenth Lok Sabha by issuing a notification containing the names of the winners of all 538 of the 543 Lok Sabha constituencies that went to polls.

October 12

The government of Nawaz Sharif in Pakistan is overturned by a coup led by the chief of the army staff, Pervez Musharraf. The Government of India's reaction is muted, with Prime Minister Vajpayee saying the next day that India is committed to "developing friendly and cooperative ties with Pakistan" and External Affairs Minister Jaswant Singh saying that "there is no cause for alarm or anxiety."

October 13

A.B. Vajpayee takes the oath of office as prime minister for the third time. The seventy-member ministry includes L.K. Advani as home minister, Jaswant Singh as external affairs minister, and Yashwant Sinha as finance minister.

October 17

Pakistan's new military ruler, General Pervez Musharraf, announces a unilateral military de-escalation along the India-Pakistan border and a pullback of troops that have moved to the border areas "in recent past."

October 19

The Congress announces that Sonia Gandhi will be the leader of the opposition in the Lok Sabha. She also decides to give up the Bellary seat in Karnataka and retain Amethi in Uttar Pradesh. A week earlier, Gandhi acknowledged that the "prime responsibility" for the party's poor electoral performance rested with her.

October 31

A powerful cyclone hits Orissa. Communication with villages in twelve districts is slowly restored in the next weeks. Twelve days later, the Orissa government reports that the death toll from the cyclone has reached 7,447.

November 9

The BJP central leadership directs Uttar Pradesh chief minister Kalyan Singh to step down and announces the appointment of the former deputy chief minister and senior most state party leader, Ram Prakash Gupta, as his successor. The new government is sworn in three days later.

November 24

Prime Minister Vajpayee claims that the military takeover in Pakistan could escalate the "proxy war" in Jammu and Kashmir and calls upon the armed forces to maintain constant vigil.

November 29

Parliament begins its winter session on a confrontational note, with the Congress staging a walkout from both the houses over the issue of the indictment of Rajiv Gandhi in the Bofors case. Other opposition parties stage a walkout over the move to open the insurance sector to private domestic and foreign companies.

December 2

The Insurance Regulatory and Development Authority Bill passes in the Lok Sabha with Congress support. The bill ends the monopoly of public sector insurance companies.

December 5

Orissa Congress Committee chief Hemananda Biswal is elected leader of the Congress Legislature Party after Chief Minister Giridhar Gamang agrees to step down following the demand by a majority of his party's members of the legislative assembly that he be replaced on the grounds that he failed to handle the situation effectively in the wake of the cyclone.

December 9

Kalyan Singh, the former Uttar Pradesh chief minister and one of the most prominent Scheduled Caste leaders of the BJP, is expelled from the party.

December 14

Samajwadi Party leader Mulayam Singh Yadav aggravates the gender row by contending that if a large number of "inexperienced" women were elected to the Lok Sabha and the state assemblies on the strength of special reservations, they could pose a threat to the national interest in difficult situations.

December 24

An Indian Airlines aircraft with over 170 persons aboard is hijacked by militants shortly after takeoff from Kathmandu and lands in Kandahar after briefly touching down in Amritsar, Lahore, and Dubai. One of the passengers is killed en route, and twenty-six are released in Dubai. The hijackers at first demand the release of thirty-six militants detained in connection with the Kashmir conflict belonging to several militant organizations including the Harkat-ul-Mujahideen, Lashkar-e-Taiba, and Hizb-ul-Mujahideen. On December 31, the Indian government agrees to release Maulana Masood Azhar, a resident of Bhawalpur, Pakistan; Mushtaq Ahmad Zargar, a resident of Srinagar; and Ahmad Umar Sayed Shaikh, a Pakistani-born British citizen and London School of Economics graduate. They are escorted to Kandahar by Foreign Minister Jaswant Singh, and the hijacked passengers return to Delhi. On January 3, 2000, Prime Minister Vajpayee accuses Pakistan of being responsible for the hijacking.

2000

January 3

The Sensex gains 369 points, reaching an all-time high of 5,375 in the wake of frenzied buying support by speculators and heavy purchases by foreign institutional investors.

January 7

The K. Subrahmanyam Committee on the "intelligence failure" with respect to the Pakistani incursions in the Kargil area of Kashmir in 1999 submits its report to the prime minister.

January 14

The seventeenth Karmapa Lama, a young monk whose position gives him a large following among Buddhists and who came secretly to India on January 5 from his monastery in Lhasa, conveys his desire to the Dalai Lama to remain in India and seek political asylum. On January 11, the Government of India decided not to grant him asylum.

January 19

The Uttar Pradesh government claims further improvement in the power generation and transmission situation in the state as a strike by more than 90,000 employees of the state electricity board enters its fifth day.

January 24

The president gives assent to the Constitution (Seventy-Ninth Amendment) Act of 1999, extending reservations for Scheduled Castes and Scheduled Tribes in the Lok Sabha and state assemblies for a period of ten more years, up to January 25, 2010.

January 25

The Uttar Pradesh electricity board employees' union calls off a strike begun on January 14 to protest the planned privatization of the power sector and the radical restructuring of the state electricity board after being defeated.

February 1

The Vajpayee government decides to go ahead with its proposal to set up a national commission to review the working of the Constitution.

February 2

Former Tamil Nadu chief minister Jayalalitha is convicted by a special court in the "Pleasant Stay Hotel" case on the charge of falsification of records. She is sentenced to rigorous imprisonment for one year and fined Rs. 1,000 for each count against her. Violent protests by AIADMK supporters follow.

February 20

The list of Indian Administrative Service and Indian Police Service officials against whom the Central Vigilance Commission recommends action on charges of corruption swells to 107 with the addition of 16 names to the commission's website.

February 24

Sonia Gandhi leads Congress Party members of Parliament in a protest against the lifting of the ban on government employees' participation in Rashtriya Swayamsevak Sangh activities by the BJP government of Gujarat.

February 29

Finance Minister Yashwant Sinha presents the 2000–2001 budget in Parliament. The budget contains no major proposals for additional reforms, although there are measures that push reforms forward.

March 1

The National Democratic Alliance government takes the first step toward sliding the middle class out of the public distribution system by withdrawing subsidized sugar allocations for the above-poverty-line population and by raising the prices of rationed rice and wheat to levels higher than those on the open market.

March 3

Samata Party leader Nitish Kumar is sworn in as chief minister of Bihar in a move that evokes much criticism. After widespread protests in the streets, Kumar resigns on March 10, and Rabri Devi is returned to office three days later.

March 5

In Orissa, a Biju Janata Dal (BJD)–BJP coalition ministry headed by the BJD president, Naveen Patnaik, takes power.

March 7

China asks India to renounce its nuclear weapons program as the two countries conclude their first-ever security dialogue in Beijing.

March 8

The Gujarat government withdraws its controversial notification of January 3, thereby reimposing the ban on its employees' participation in the activities of the RSS.

March 17

One day after the Rabri Devi government wins a vote of confidence with Congress support, the Bihar governor allows the Central Bureau of Intelligence to initiate prosecution proceedings on corruption charges against the chief minister and her husband, former chief minister Laloo Prasad Yadav. Formal indictments are handed down on April 4.

March 19

U.S. president Bill Clinton arrives in New Delhi en route to Bangladesh. His five-day official visit begins on March 21. The visit proves to be a resounding success. In addition to substantial talks with the prime minister, the president, and others, President

Clinton addresses Parliament, visits Jaipur, and addresses industrialists in Hyderabad.

March 20

Unidentified assailants kill thirty-five Sikhs in Chattisinghpura village in Jammu and Kashmir in one of the worst incidents of violence in the state in the last decade. Later, two state ministers are attacked by villagers when they visit the area. This incident draws U.S. and international attention since it takes place on the eve of U.S. president Bill Clinton's official visit to India.

March 29

Biennial elections to the Rajya Sabha in Uttar Pradesh, Rajasthan, Karnataka, Himachal Pradesh, West Bengal, Jammu and Kashmir, and Orissa are held.

April 5

Bihar chief minister Rabri Devi and her husband, Laloo Prasad Yadav, appear in court in the "disproportionate assets" case. The court rejects Laloo Prasad Yadav's bail petition but grants bail to Rabri Devi.

April 12

The World Bank announces the approval of $111 million credit to Andhra Pradesh for undertaking the District Poverty Initiative project, which is designed to reach and empower families in the state's six poorest districts. On April 26, the World Bank approves nearly $750 million in loans for several other projects in India, including more than $500 million allocated to development schemes in Uttar Pradesh.

May 11

The one-billionth Indian, a newborn girl named Aastha, is officially recognized in Delhi. Addressing the nation on the occasion, Prime Minister Vajpayee describes the situation on the population front as serious.

June 3

Tamil Nadu chief minister M. Karunanidhi makes the provocative remark that Sri Lanka should either agree to a "territorial separation" on the lines of the Czech Republic and Slovakia or grant more rights to its Tamils to enable a "permanent solution" to the ethnic strife there.

June 18

In the aftermath of the killing of thirty-four *dalits* and others on June 16, the Bihar government announces fresh administrative measures to cope with the growing incidents of violence in the state.

June 19

Anticipating the vote on the report of the State Autonomy Committee, the BJP announces its opposition to any autonomy package for Jammu and Kashmir that would return the state to its pre-1953 status. A week later, the Jammu and Kashmir legislative assembly adopts a resolution accepting the report.

June 21

The International Court of Justice declares that it has no jurisdiction to adjudicate the dispute brought before it by Pakistan against India in the case of the shooting down of a Pakistani aircraft on August 10, 1999.

July 4

The Union cabinet rejects the June 26 resolution (the so-called autonomy resolution) of the Jammu and Kashmir assembly, though at the same time it commits itself to a greater "devolution of powers" to all states.

July 6

India and Nepal sign an agreement to establish a specialized joint unit to counter terrorism and share information about criminals operating along their common border.

July 15

The Maharashtra government permits the city police to prosecute Shiv Sena chief Bal Thackeray for his "inflammatory" writings of 1993. After much public protest, Thackeray surrenders to arrest on July 25, but the case is immediately dismissed by a magistrate because of the six-year delay.

July 23

Union minister for law, justice, and company affairs Ram Jethmalani is forced to resign from the cabinet after a public quarrel with the chief justice of India.

July 24

The Hizb-ul-Mujahideen issues a unilateral cease-fire offer in Srinagar. The following day, the Muttahida (United) Jihad Council—a consortium of *jihad* groups based in the Azad Kashmir territory of Pakistan—disavows the cease-fire offer and suspends the Hizb-ul-Mujahideen's membership in the council.

August 1

Thirty-one pilgrims and porters are massacred in Pahalgam as they walk on a pilgrimage to the Vaishnodevi Temple in Jammu.

August 8

Bangaru Laxman is unanimously elected as the new BJP president. Laxman will be the first *dalit* president of the party and also the first from a southern state.

August 21

The daylong deliberations by seven chief ministers and representatives of two state governments over the "discriminatory" recommendations of the Eleventh Finance Commission end with an assurance from Prime Minister Vajpayee that the points raised will be considered in the second report of the commission, expected by the end of the month.

August 23

Union power minister P.R. Kumaramangalam, one of the most promising young leaders of the BJP, dies unexpectedly.

August 25

The death toll due to heavy rain and floods in the city of Hyderabad rises to 105.

September 14

Prime Minister Vajpayee, in an address to a joint session of the U.S. Congress, claims that India is a robust economy undergoing substantive reforms. He also strongly criticizes Pakistan. The next day, the prime minister meets with President Bill Clinton and calls for a "regular, sustained partnership" between the two countries. On September 18, President Clinton hosts a state dinner with 700-some guests for the prime minister, saying that he and the Indian leader have built "the strongest and most mature partnership" the two countries have known.

September 29

A special court in New Delhi convicts former prime minister P.V. Narasimha Rao in the Jharkhand Mukti Morcha case on charges of bribing members of Parliament to buy votes in order to save the minority Congress government in a no-confidence motion in 1993. On October 12, he is sentenced to three years in prison and a fine of Rs. 200,000. On November 7, the Delhi High Court suspends the sentence and grants Rao bail.

October 3

On the occasion of the visit of Russian president Vladimir Putin, India and Russia agree to develop a common approach toward Afghanistan and to coordinate political, diplomatic, and military steps regarding the unfolding crisis there.

October 9

Former Tamil Nadu chief minister Jayalalitha and her associate,

Ms. Sasikala, are convicted and sentenced by a special court to three years and two years of rigorous imprisonment, respectively, in two corruption cases.

October 14

The Rashtriya Swayamsevak Sangh issues an indirect threat to the BJP-led NDA coalition, saying that any government opposing the construction of a Ram temple at the disputed site in Ayodhya will have to face "consequences."

October 18

The Supreme Court approves the resumption of limited construction of the controversial Sardar Sarovar dam on the Narmada River. The decision sparks major protests by the Narmada Bachao Andolan, led by Medha Patkar.

October 28

The CPM-led Left Front accepts Jyoti Basu's offer to retire from the office of chief minister of West Bengal on health grounds. Buddhadev Bhattacharya takes over as chief minister on November 6.

Rajnath Singh is sworn in as chief minister of Uttar Pradesh along with eighty-five ministerial colleagues.

November 1

Chattisgarh, carved out of the state of Madhya Pradesh, becomes the twenty-sixth state. On November 8 it is followed by Uttaranchal, formed from the Himalayan hill region of Uttar Pradesh, and on November 15 by Jharkhand, formed from the southern districts of Bihar.

November 5

The Jharkhand Mukti Morcha (JMM) decides to break its ties with the National Democratic Alliance at the state level after the latter rejects its demand to install JMM leader Shibu Soren as the first chief minister of the new state of Jharkhand.

November 15

The Kannada cinema idol Rajkumar is released by his kidnapper, the notorious gang leader Veerappan, after being detained for 108 days.

November 16

The Union cabinet clears the proposal to reduce the government's equity holding in nationalized banks from 51 percent to 33 percent, disregarding the one-day strike on November 15 by bank employees against the "privatization" of the public sector.

November 18

The marriage of the children of Pakistan-based Jammu and Kashmir Liberation Front chairman Amanullah Khan and India-based Hurriyat Conference leader Abdul Ghani Lone is celebrated in Islamabad.

November 19

Prime Minister Vajpayee announces a unilateral cease-fire in Kashmir during the holy month of Ramzan (Ramadan).

November 24

In a major step, India and China exchange maps of the "line of actual control" in the middle sector of their common border.

November 27

Security forces suspend all combat operations in Kashmir in line with the Ramzan cease-fire. The next day, the rejection of the cease-fire by the Hizb-ul-Mujahideen is made evident by a land-mine explosion that kills three soldiers. On December 4, despite continuing attacks by militants, Prime Minister Vajpayee indicates that the government is not averse to extending the current cease-fire beyond Ramzan provided that Pakistan responds in a "substantive" manner. On December 20, the cease-fire is extended by a month.

December 10

The National Democratic Alliance adopts a unanimous resolution reiterating the secular agenda of the government. A controversy was provoked by Prime Minister Vajpayee's December 7 statement, regarding Ayodhya, that the "Ram temple can be built at the disputed site where a temple already exists, and the Masjid can come up at an alternate site."

India carries out possibly the largest public health effort in the world by immunizing 130 million children against polio as part of India's Pulse Polio program.

December 27

The city of Kathmandu continues to remain tense for the third day as the Nepali government insists that Indian film star Hrithik Roshan publicly apologize for his alleged derogatory remarks about the country and its people. The film star denies having made any such remarks.

Abbreviations and Glossary

Some Common Abbreviations
AIADMK: All India Anna Dravida Munnetra Kazhagam
BJP: Bharatiya Janata Party
BSP: Bahujan Samaj Party
DMK: Dravida Munnetra Kazhagam
IAS: Indian Administrative Service
MLA: Member of the Legislative Assembly
NDA: National Democratic Alliance
NRI: Nonresident Indian
OBCs: Other Backward Classes
RBI: Reserve Bank of India
RSS: Rashtriya Swayamsevak Sangh
SAARC: South Asian Association for Regional Cooperation
SCs: Scheduled Castes
STs: Scheduled Tribes
SP: Samajwadi Party
TDP: Telugu Desam Party
VHP: Vishwa Hindu Parishad

All India Anna Dravida Munnetra Kazhagam (AIADMK). Tamil
nationalist party in the state of Tamil Nadu led by Jayalalitha, one of
the most powerful women in Indian politics. Although enmeshed in a
series of corruption cases, she led the party to a landslide victory in
the 2001 elections in Tamil Nadu and has now become, once again,
chief minister of the state.

Arya Samaj. Literally, "society of the Aryans"; a movement of "protes-
tant" Hinduism founded by Dayanand Saraswati in 1875. Rejecting,
among other things, the "accretions" to the Vedas of caste, idol wor-
ship, and ritual, it campaigned also for the "reconversion" of Muslims and others to Hinduism. Its greatest strength has been in the
Punjab.

Ayodhya. A small city in east-central Uttar Pradesh believed to be the birthplace of Ram (or Rama, the god-king who is the hero of the *Ramayana*). Site of the disputed Babri mosque/Ram temple shrine. The mosque was demolished on December 6, 1992, provoking widespread rioting and a major political crisis. *See also* Babri mosque.

Babri mosque/Ram temple (Babri Masjid/Ramjanmabhoomi). Literally, "mosque of Babur/birthground of Ram." Ram (or Rama), an avatar of the god Vishnu and the hero of the *Ramayana*, is believed to have been born in Ayodhya on a particular spot of ground on which a mosque was believed to have been built by the Mughal emperor Babur (r. 1526–30). The mosque was demolished on December 6, 1992, and a shrine to Ram was installed on the site. *See also* Ayodhya.

Bahujan Samaj Party (BSP). Led by Kanshi Ram and Mayawati, the party of the *dalits* and other "underclass" social groups. It is mainly an Uttar Pradesh party, but it does have significant support in Punjab and Madhya Pradesh.

Bharatiya Janata Party (BJP). Party formed from the Janata Party by elements of Jana Sangh, with support mainly in northern India. It favors a Hindu nationalist ideology, but its appeal also derives from the reputation for discipline and integrity of its core leaders. At present the single largest party in Parliament, and the core party of the governing NDA coalition, it received 24 percent of the vote in the 1999 election. Its strength is greatest in the western and northern states of Delhi, Gujarat, Himachal Pradesh, Madhya Pradesh, Maharashtra, Rajasthan, and Uttar Pradesh.

Congress Party. The dominant Indian nationalist party since independence, it formed the government after the 1991 elections. In the parliamentary elections of 1996 and 1998, it lost strength in terms of both seats and vote share, ending its fifty-year reign as India's only national party. In the 1999 parliamentary elections, it gained marginally more vote share than the BJP but lost a significant number of seats. Also known as the Congress (I), the name of the faction created by a party split in 1977 and initially led by Indira Gandhi (the "I" stands for Indira).

Dalit. Literally, "oppressed" or "ground down," the term for people of the Scheduled Castes preferred by militant and educated ex-untouchables and by many others who sympathize with their aspirations.

Dravida Munnetra Kazhagam (DMK). Tamil nationalist party led by M. Karunanidhi, who served as chief minister of Tamil Nadu from 1969 to 1976, 1989 to 1990, and 1996 to 2001.

Election Commission. The constitutionally established autonomous body that is responsible for conducting national elections, including the declaration of polling dates, preparation of voters' lists, certification of parties and candidates, establishment of rules for the election campaign, and management of the polling and counting of ballots. The chief election commissioner is joined by two additional election commissioners who serve fixed terms.

Emergency. Declared by the Indira Gandhi government in June 1975, it lasted twenty-one months. Opposition leaders were jailed, press censorship was imposed, and the Constitution was amended to restrict the judiciary. It ended with the defeat of Indira Gandhi in the 1977 election.

Finance Commission. Established under Article 280 of the Constitution, finance commissions—the most recent one being the eleventh—make recommendations (which are typically accepted unchanged) to the national government on the allocation to the states of taxes collected by the central government and grants-in-aid.

Gandhi, Indira. Daughter of Jawaharlal Nehru and prime minister from 1966 to 1977 and 1980 to 1984, when she was assassinated by her own Sikh bodyguards.

Gandhi, Mohandas K. The preeminent leader of India's fight against British colonial rule from 1919 until independence. He was assassinated in January 1948 by a Hindu nationalist fanatic. Also known as Mahatma Gandhi and Gandhiji.

Harijan. Literally, "people of God," the name Mohandas K. Gandhi used for the Scheduled Castes. *See also dalit.*

Hindutva. Literally, "Hindu-ness," the term was used as the title of a book written in 1922 by Hindu nationalist leader V.D. Savarkar to argue that Hindus were a nation. It is now used as the equivalent of "Hindu nationalism."

Indian National Congress. *See* Congress Party.

Jana Sangh. Properly, the "Bharatiya Jana Sangh" (Indian People's Party), founded in 1951 with an ideology of Hindu nationalism, it developed strength in western and northern India. It reemerged as the present-day Bharatiya Janata Party after merging with other parties to form the Janata Party in the crucible of the 1977 elections that ended the Emergency rule of Indira Gandhi.

Janata Dal. A party formed from the Jan Morcha, the Janata Party, factions of the Lok Dal, and a Congress Party splinter known as the Congress (S). In 1989, it had 141 of the 144 seats held by the National Front in the Lok Sabha that formed the government led by V.P. Singh. After several splits and mergers, it survives at present only in the state of Karnataka.

Jati. Caste or subcaste that defines acceptable interactions in marriage, dining, and other caste-related practices.

Kargil. A town in the Ladakh region of the state of Jammu and Kashmir. It gave its name to the crisis of a miniwar between India and Pakistan in May–July 1999 that erupted when insurgents and Pakistani troops crossed the line of control on the icy mountain heights overlooking it and other territory along the Srinagar-Leh road.

Lok Sabha. Lower house of India's bicameral Parliament, equivalent to the British House of Commons. All but 3 of its 545 members are directly elected from district constituencies for a five-year-maximum term.

Mahabharata. One of the two major epics of India, it describes the internecine warfare that resulted from the feud of succession involving descendants of the legendary king Bharata.

Mandal Commission. The common name—from its chairman, B.P. Mandal—of the Backward Classes Commission. The Mandal Commission report, published in 1980, proposed far-reaching government regulations to increase the employment of "backward" classes.

Member of the Legislative Assembly (MLA). The equivalent of a member of Parliament at the state level.

Mujahid (pl. mujahideen). A person who physically fights in a *jihad* ("holy war" in the Islamic tradition). In India, including Jammu and Kashmir, this means fighting against the Indian state and other institutions and people considered to be non-Muslim.

National Democratic Alliance (NDA). Formed just before the 1999 election, a coalition whose leader and major constituent is the Bharatiya Janata Party. The present national government, elected in 1999, is formally that of the NDA. There were twelve other parties in the alliance at election time; some have departed and others have joined since.

Nehru, Jawaharlal. Nationalist leader who served as prime minister from 1947 until his death in 1964.

Nonresident Indian (NRI). A formal government designation for persons of Indian birth residing outside of India, including those who have become citizens of another country. Among other special privileges, NRIs have the right to own certain kinds of property that other foreigners cannot own.

Other Backward Classes (OBCs). "Backward" classes other than the Scheduled Castes and Scheduled Tribes. Typically defined in caste terms to mean the nonelite, nonuntouchable *jatis*.

Panchayat. Literally, a "council of five." A village or *jati* council. The *panchayati raj* system of rural local self-government introduced in 1959 was entrenched in the Constitution as the Seventy-Third Amendment in 1993, with institutions at village, block, and district levels now exercising significantly enhanced political and financial powers.

A major feature of the new system is the reservation for women of not less than one-third of the seats of the village council and of chairpersons of the *panchayati raj* body at each level.

Planning Commission. Government body that prepares five-year plans, which provide a broad framework for public and private economic goals.

President. In India, the equivalent of a constitutional monarch who gives formal assent to bills but whose powers are severely restricted. Elected by members of Parliament and the state legislatures for a five-year term in 1997, the present incumbent, K.R. Narayanan, is the first *dalit* to hold this office.

President's Rule. Suspension of a state's assembly and direct rule of the state by the central government through the centrally appointed governor, typically when the state government loses its majority or is deemed unable to govern due to a "disturbed" political situation. It has sometimes been used by the central government to topple opposition-controlled state governments.

Rajya Sabha. Upper house of India's bicameral Parliament. All but 6 of its 256 members are elected by the state legislatures for staggered six-year terms. Roughly equivalent in power to Britain's House of Lords.

Rashtriya Swayamsevak Sangh (RSS). Literally, "National Volunteer Association"; militant Hindu organization founded in 1925 and associated with the Bharatiya Janata Party, the Vishwa Hindu Parishad, and the Bajrang Dal—the members of the "Sangh parivar" (RSS family). The RSS draws its membership mainly from urban and lower-middle-class voters and seeks the consolidation of a Hindu nation.

Reservation. The provision for quotas in legislative bodies, civil services, educational institutions, and other public institutions, typically in proportion to the percentage in the population, for qualified members of Scheduled Castes and Scheduled Tribes, and, in some places, Other Backward Classes.

Samajwadi (Socialist) Party (SP). Led by Mulayam Singh Yadav, a former defense minister of India (1996–98) and chief minister of Uttar Pradesh (1989–91), this party is mainly confined to that state and draws support largely from the OBCs.

Samata Party. Confined largely to Bihar, this party is led by George Fernandes, defense minister in the BJP-led 1998 and 1999 governments until his resignation in 2001, following charges of corruption.

Sanskritization. A term coined by the eminent social anthropologist M.N. Srinivas to describe the process of upward social mobility in which a *jati* gives up certain practices considered to be polluting and adopts other practices usually associated with upper castes, such as vegetarianism.

Scheduled Castes and Scheduled Tribes (SCs/STs). The "schedule" refers to a list of untouchables, or Harijan, castes and tribes drawn up under the 1935 Government of India Act and subsequently revised. Legislative seats as well as government posts and places in educational institutions are reserved for members of these castes and tribes.

Shiv Sena. Militant nativist communal organization founded in Bombay in 1966 to agitate against South Indian immigrants to the state of Maharashtra. Alleged to have played a major part in the riots of December 1992 and January 1993 in Bombay, following the demolition of the Babri mosque. In alliance with the BJP, the Shiv Sena won the March 1995 elections in Maharashtra. Its founder and all-powerful leader is Bal Thackeray.

Shudras. The fourth and lowest caste in Hinduism. *See also varnas.*

Sikh, Sikhism. The religion of Sikhism was founded in the sixteenth century by the first guru, Nanak, drawing on Hindu devotionalism and Islam. Persecuted by the later Mughal emperors, Sikhs developed into a martial community, led by the tenth and last guru, Gobind Singh. A Sikh kingdom in central Punjab was defeated by the British in the mid-nineteenth century.

Singh, Jaswant. Minister of external affairs in the BJP government since late 1999, he has also held charge of the Defense Ministry since mid-2001. He has served as finance minister and deputy chairman of the Planning Commission. One of Prime Minister Vajpayee's closest advisors.

South Asian Association for Regional Cooperation (SAARC). Organization formed in 1985 to enhance cooperation in social, economic, and cultural development. The SAARC members are Bangladesh, Bhutan, India, the Maldives, Nepal, Pakistan, and Sri Lanka.

Swadeshi. Literally, "(one's) own country." A nationalist slogan from the early twentieth century that asked Indians to boycott foreign goods, especially cloth, in favor of Indian manufactures. More recently used to indicate an ideology of economic self-reliance.

Telugu Desam Party (TDP). Confined entirely to the state of Andhra Pradesh, where it has ruled for most of the years since its formation in 1982, this party is led by Chandrababu Naidu, the present chief minister, now in his second five-year term. A major supporter "from outside" of the National Democratic Alliance.

Trinamool Congress. Confined to the state of West Bengal, this party split from the Congress Party in 1998. It is led by the charismatic woman leader Mamata Banerjee and has supported the BJP-led National Democratic Alliance, withdrawing from and then rejoining the government.

Varnas. The four castes of textual Hinduism: brahmins (priests), kshatriyas (warriors), vaishyas (merchants and farmers), and shudras (workers serving the families of the other *varnas*). At present, a categorization into which various *jatis* are placed; thus, "caste clusters."

Vishwa Hindu Parishad (VHP). A movement seeking to reinvigorate Hinduism. Leader of Hindu sentiment and organizer of actions in connection with the Babri mosque/Ram temple controversy. Its precise responsibility for the demolition of the mosque is not clear.

Yadav. An agrarian (cowherd) caste of the Gangetic Plain, it forms a substantial bloc within the "backward" castes; leaders of the community have governed as chief ministers of Uttar Pradesh and Bihar.

Yadav, Laloo Prasad. Leader of a segment of the OBCs of Bihar, he served as chief minister until forced to resign when charged in a major corruption scandal.

About the Contributors

Alyssa Ayres is Assistant Director for South and Central Asia Policy Programs at the Asia Society, where she has worked since 1998. In this capacity, she is responsible for the research, design, fund-raising, implementation, and outreach of programs concerning the foreign policy and politics of South Asia and for the development of a new program area focused on Central Asia. Ayres has helped establish the Society's presence as a neutral forum for discussion and exchange on U.S.-Iran relations—one of the only such fora in the United States. She is Project Director of the joint Asia Society–Council on Foreign Relations Independent Task Force on India and South Asia.

Sadanand Dhume is a foreign correspondent in Jakarta for the *Far Eastern Economic Review* (*FEER*), where he writes about business, politics, security, and society. He was *FEER*'s New Delhi Bureau Chief from June 1999 to October 2000. Dhume has worked as an associate producer at msnbc.com, as an on-air reporter in New Delhi, and at Chile's only English-language newspaper. His pieces have appeared in *Foreign Policy*, the *Wall Street Journal*, *Harvard International Review*, and the *Earth Times*.

John Echeverri-Gent is Associate Chair of the Woodrow Wilson Department of Government and Foreign Affairs at the University of Virginia, where he also teaches. He is the author of *The State and the Poor: Public Policy and Political Development in India and the United States* and is currently working on two manuscripts, entitled *Where's the Party: Political Parties and Economic Reform in Argentina, Brazil, China, and India* and *Reforming India's Stock Exchanges in a Globalizing World*. Echeverri-Gent has been a trustee of the American Institute of Indian Studies since 1996.

Christophe Jaffrelot is Director of the Centre d'Etudes et de Recherches Internationales (CERI) and the editor of *Critique Internationale*. He holds degrees from the Paris Institut d'Etudes Politiques (IEP),

Université Paris 1–Sorbonne, and the Institut National des Langues et Civilisations Orientales (INALCO). Jaffrelot received his Ph.D. in political science from the IEP in Paris. He lectures in South Asian politics at the IEP, Université Paris 1–Sorbonne, and INALCO.

Joydeep Mukherji is Director of the Sovereign Ratings Group at Standard and Poor's, which he joined in 1996. He works with credit ratings in Asia and the Western Hemisphere. His current responsibilities include undertaking credit analysis on India, China, Hong Kong, Canada, and the Philippines. In addition to country credit reports, Mukherji has published occasional papers comparing the ratings of China and India, discussing fiscal issues and the information technology sector in India, and examining economic trends in the Philippines.

Mark Nichter is Professor of Anthropology at the University of Arizona, with a joint appointment to the Department of Family and Community Medicine. In addition to anthropology, Nichter received postgraduate training in international health and cross-cultural psychiatry. He is currently the coordinator of the graduate medical anthropology training program at the University of Arizona.

Philip Oldenburg is Associate Director of the Southern Asian Institute at Columbia University, where he also teaches in the political science department. He has edited or coedited eight previous volumes in the *India Briefing* series and is the author of the Asia Society's *Asian Update* "The Thirteenth Election of India's Lok Sabha (House of the People)." His current research is on the grassroots foundations of state legitimacy in India.

Alok Rai was appointed Professor of Literature in the Humanities Department of the Indian Institute of Technology, New Delhi, in 1991. He was Senior Fellow at the Nehru Memorial Library in New Delhi from 1985 to 1987. Rai holds graduate degrees from the University of Oxford and University College, London. He is a frequent reviewer for many mainstream Indian journals. He has also published numerous articles and books, among which *Hindi Nationalism* (2000) looks at the politics of language in India through a study of the history of one language—Hindi—to show how the transformation of language in this case was tied up with the politics of communalism and regionalism.

Bandita Sijapati has been working as a research analyst with Harris Interactive, New York, since August 1999. Her responsibilities include performing statistical analysis of survey results for various projects ranging from public policy, election polls, financial matters, and e-commerce to health care. She graduated from the School of International and Public Affairs, Columbia University, with a master's of international affairs degree in economic and political development and international economic policy in May 2000.

David Van Sickle is a doctoral candidate in medical anthropology at the University of Arizona, where he works closely with Professor Mark Nichter. He has done field studies in remote jungles of Mexico and was involved with the Glacier/Bob Marshal Ecosystem Project, a Wildlands Study program through San Francisco State University. Van Sickle recently received a grant from the Rockefeller Foundation and the World Health Organization to conduct an extensive research program in India.

Index